Ultimate Guide for
Professional Organizers

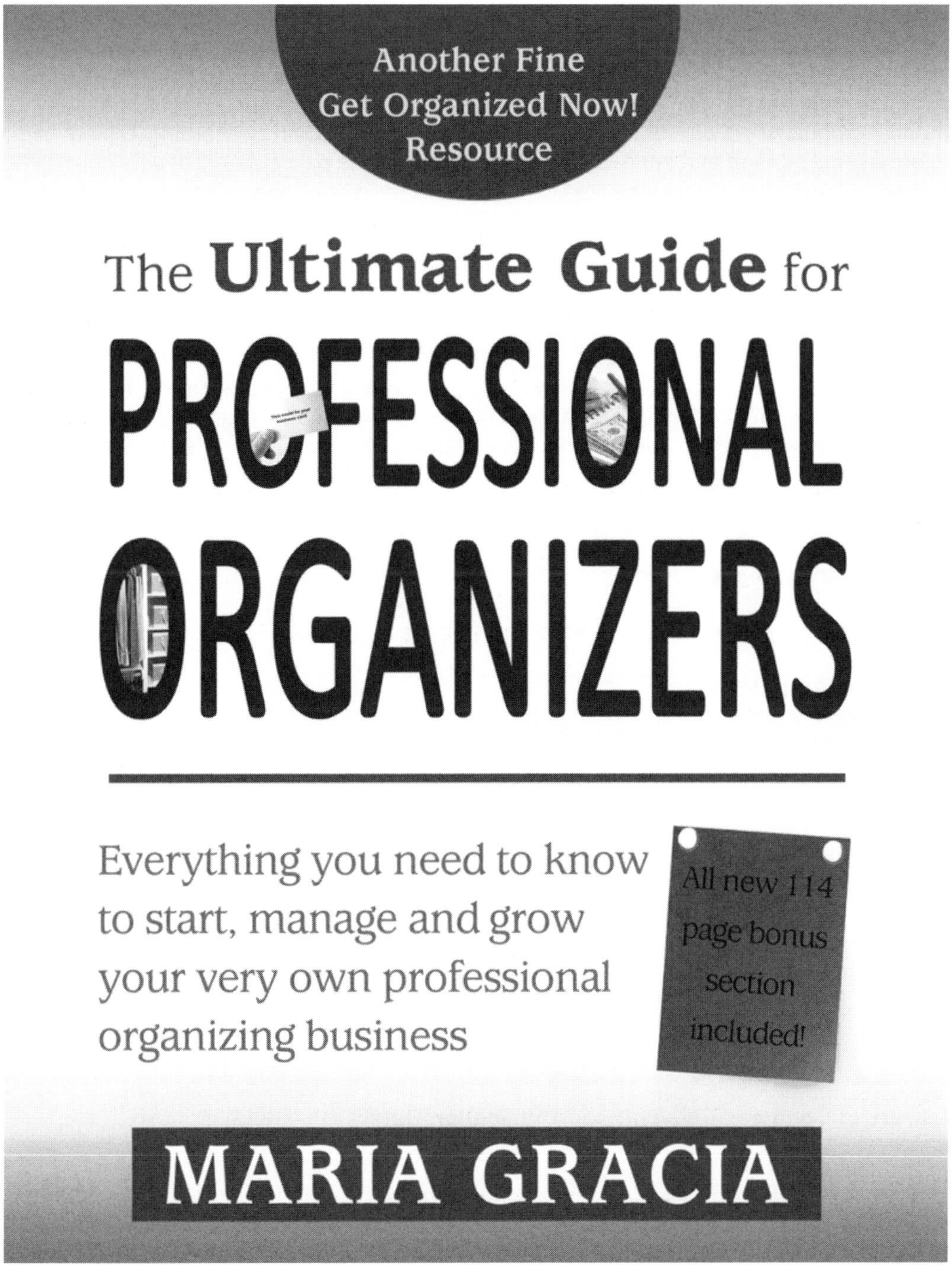

Another Fine
Get Organized Now!
Resource
The Ultimate Guide for
PROFESSIONAL
ORGANIZERS
Everything you need to know
to start, manage and grow
your very own professional
organizing business
All new 114
page bonus
section
included!
MARIA GRACIA

Published by BlueMoon Publishing.

This publication is designed to provide accurate and authoritative information in regard to the subject matter covered. It is sold with the understanding that the publisher and the copyright owner are not engaged in rendering legal, accounting or other professional service. If legal advice or other expert assistance is required, the services of a competent professional person who specializes in that particular field should be sought.

While due care has been exercised in the compilation of this guide, we are not responsible for errors or omissions. This reference is intended to assist in providing information to the public, and the information is delivered as accurately as possible.

Senior Executive Editors: Joseph Gracia, Sandy Drifka

Cover Design: Cathi Stevenson of Book Cover Express

Cover Graphics: BigStockPhoto.com

Please direct any comments, questions or suggestions regarding this book to:

BlueMoon Publishing
611 Arlington Way
Watertown WI 53094
USA

Library of Congress Cataloging-in-Publication Data

Gracia, Maria
    Ultimate Guide for Professional Organizers/by Maria Gracia
    ISBN # 978-0-615-24353-5 $34.95

    Library of Congress Control Number 2008933144

    Reference: Business, Marketing.

ISBN # 978-0-615-24353-5

Printed in the United States of America.

Special Acknowledgement

The marketing information and marketing pieces in this book

are based on marketing concepts developed over the past 30 years

by my husband and best friend, Joe Gracia.

Joe is an expert in both traditional offline marketing

as well as marketing on the Web.

Over the past 15 years, he has made his clients

millions of dollars in increased sales and profits with his unique

approach to small business marketing and management techniques.

When we founded Get Organized Now! together,

Joe worked side by side with me

developing and refining our business systems and Web site.

I can't imagine a better person with whom to be in business

and to share my life.

Table of Contents

Introduction

Congratulations on starting your own professional organizing business! Over the years, I've found that by helping people become better organized, I've been helping people live better lives. You can do the same and I'm sure you'll find this business to be fun, rewarding and very profitable. In fact, the reason I wrote *The Ultimate Guide for Professional Organizers* is because I've been so excited about this business—so excited, that I just had to share it with you!

This guide will help you start your business, manage your business, develop an effective marketing strategy to begin building and growing your customer list, help your customers and give you the information you need to expand your business. The possibilities are endless. They're limited only by your imagination. Its principles are based on the Give to Get Marketing approach, created and developed by my husband, marketing expert Joe Gracia. This approach has resulted in thousands of increased sales for businesses around the world.

In addition to all of the information you're about to discover, you'll also find ready-to-use forms and logs. These are all available so you don't have to waste time coming up with your own. The work is done and you're free to copy these forms or to take the information and duplicate the forms on your computer. You'll also find examples of an ad, a press release, a direct mail letter, a door hanger and other marketing vehicles that are proven to work when applied correctly. You, your designer or your printing company can use them as a guide for creating your own marketing vehicles. It's a snap!

After reading this guide, spend some time in my online Discussion Forum for Professional Organizers. Ask any questions or share ideas that come to mind. By doing so, you'll have the opportunity to brainstorm with other professional organizers around the world! Here is the link:
www.getorganizednow.com/forum/ubbthreads.php
Once you're there, just click on "Help for Professional Organizers." I hope you enjoy this journey and I wish you the greatest success in your professional organizing business!

Maria Gracia
www.getorganizednow.com/po.html

Chapter 1
The Basics

What is a professional organizer?

A professional organizer is an individual who provides personal assistance, consulting, coaching, ideas, publications, seminars and/or products to help others get organized. Professional Organizers can specialize in a number of different areas including, but not limited to:

- ✓ behavior modification
- ✓ billing systems
- ✓ closet design/organizing
- ✓ computer consulting
- ✓ ergonomics
- ✓ errands/personal shopping
- ✓ events/meeting planning
- ✓ filing systems
- ✓ financial/bookkeeping
- ✓ goals/achievement/motivation
- ✓ health insurance claims
- ✓ home organizing
- ✓ home staging
- ✓ memorabilia
- ✓ office organizing
- ✓ packing/moving/relocation
- ✓ paper management
- ✓ project management
- ✓ records management
- ✓ space planning
- ✓ systems/workflow
- ✓ time management

But it goes beyond this. As a professional organizer, you'll be helping to improve lives and make the world a better place. You'll be helping to decrease stress, increase productivity and improve environments. You'll be helping people to find time to reach their goals, spend with their families and improve their health.

By being a professional organizer, you'll be helping people live healthier, more balanced, happier lives.

What does a professional organizer provide?

Professional organizers can provide a wide array of services and/or products, including, but not limited to:

- ✓ hands-on organizing assistance
- ✓ books, video/audio cassettes, newsletters and other publications
- ✓ one-on-one consulting
- ✓ group seminars and workshops
- ✓ other consulting (email, telephone, Web, teleclasses, etc.)
- ✓ organizing products (filing systems, greeting card organizers, etc.)
- ✓ training courses for other professional organizers

What you choose to provide should be based on your skills, your experience and what you love to do. If you love what you're doing—if you can't wait to wake up every morning to do your thing—you'll then have the greatest potential to succeed in anything you do. Find your passion. You need to have a passion and drive for what you're doing.

What is a day in the life of a professional organizer like?

The nice thing about this profession is that you can design and customize your business based on your specific preferences and goals. You might wake up at 6:00AM and handle your administrative work, meet with a client at 8:00AM for an organizing project and do your marketing later in the afternoon.

Alternately, you may prefer waking up at 10:00AM on weekdays and handle only organizing projects throughout your work day, and then save up your administrative and marketing work for evenings or weekends.

Some professional organizers just handle their marketing, while other Professional Organizers do the jobs for them.

Maybe you won't have hands on organizing jobs at all, but you'll opt to do organizing workshops or time management seminars.

Perhaps you may instead write books or create products, and sell them at tradeshows or on the Internet.

You can even run your business just selling someone else's products and books.

There are so many different ways to be a Professional Organizer and you call the shots. Design your business the way you see fit and make it something you absolutely can't wait to do each day when you wake up.

Define yourself as a "teacher," a "doer" or both

Some professional organizers see an organizing problem and immediately jump in and start fixing it. These people are seen as "doers." They get the job done and they get it done well.

Others know that if you just "do," once you leave your client, the mess will quickly return. These people realize they must be "teachers." Throughout the organizing job, and perhaps in follow-up sessions, you would be teaching your client the concepts of organization, telling them the "why's" and how's" of what they're doing and having them do all the work. You would be correcting them along the way when you see them doing something that's likely not going to turn out well in the end.

Yet others, are both "doers" and "teachers." They actually do the job, but teach their clients along the way.

If you're a "doer" alone, you may get follow up organizing jobs from the same customers, which could be good for you financially. Negatively, if the client ends up in a big mess again shortly after your session, he or she may feel you didn't do such a great job to begin with. In other words, in being just a "doer," you're taking chances on not getting referrals, or even getting some poor exposure.

In being a "teacher" alone, you likely won't get organizing jobs from the same customers, because you'll be focusing on giving your clients your knowledge— enough so they could keep up and maintain themselves. This will give you a sense of satisfaction of a job well done. Of course, this is not always the case, and not everyone who you teach will learn. This could be frustrating.

I think one of the best things to do, is be both a "doer" and a "teacher." You go in and do the organizing job, with the help of your customer so they can see exactly what has to be done to get the job done right. You teach along the way, giving handouts for your customers to refer to. You offer follow-up sessions to help maintain the organizing job and to coach your clients. You genuinely care about getting your client on the road to proper organizing habits and you win financially and emotionally along the way.

Do I need special certification?

NAPO, the National Association of Professional Organizers, does provide information regarding organizing courses and the ability to receive certification, although neither is required for you to be a professional organizer. If you're interested in obtaining certification, you should contact NAPO for details.

However, whether you want formal training and/or certification, it is entirely up to you. You don't need it to make it in this business.

In addition, you should be aware that while NAPO could be a very helpful association to belong to, membership is not required for you to be a professional organizer.

Do I have to be organized to be a Professional Organizer?

Technically, no. Morally, probably.

There is no written rule that you have to be organized to be a professional organizer. In my opinion, if you're talking the talk, you should walk the walk. I can't imagine giving advice to someone and not listening to my own advice myself.

My house is organized. My office is organized. My schedule is organized. I have well thought out goals and deadlines. I have plenty of time to do the things I love to do in life—because I'm organized.

Does this mean you can never have anything out of place or never over-schedule something on your calendar? No, everyone experiences some periods of chaos in their lives here and there. However, if you can't organize yourself, how can you feel good about giving someone else advice to do so? And what would you do, for example, if you get a surprise visit from a client or a reporter, and your house is a mess? That would not be good for your business.

I do know some professional organizers who are not-so-organized. Although they are in business and are making money, I would not feel good recommending their services to anyone I know.

If you're not organized and your friends and family don't see you as a very organized person, I suggest you either turn the tables and begin applying the organizing concepts you teach or rethink professional organizing as a career.

Is this field primarily for women?

There's no doubt that the majority of professional organizers are women. This, in no way, means that a man can't be a professional organizer. In fact, a number of men have been extremely successful in this industry. The bottom line is, if you love what you do and you're good at it, you should continue doing it regardless of your gender.

What qualifications do I need?

An extensive education is not required in this field. A college degree is not a requirement.

However, in order to gain the credibility you need to excel as a professional organizer, you will need to provide clients with proof of your qualifications. This includes past experience, education, certifications, organizing hours, special accomplishments, customer testimonials, workshops you've conducted and/or media you've been involved with.

You have to know exactly how to help your customers. Know your business inside and out. Customers are going to expect you to be the expert and to help them solve their organizing dilemmas.

On occasion, prospective clients will ask you for your credentials. Be prepared to tell them what they need to know and to provide them with a written explanation if requested.

Clients might ask, "What qualifies you to be a professional organizer?" When meeting with a prospective customer, it is imperative to have a concrete and confident answer to the "what makes you qualified" question.

Make it a project of yours to come up with a list of everything that qualifies you to be a professional organizer. Then organize that list into an answer that you can provide to people, in oral or written form.

Your qualification work list

Here are some questions to think about. Use the space below each point to jot down the answers to each of the questions you can answer.

The basic idea is for you to determine what your current qualifications are and to think about what you would like to add, or improve, on your qualification list. You should return to this area again and again as you gain more experience and expertise.

- ♦ Are you an organized person?

- ♦ Have you organized your home or your office?

- ♦ Do you have a family that you've had to keep organized?

- ♦ Have you organized others?

- ♦ How many hours of organizing jobs have you completed?

- ♦ What successes have you had? Do you have client testimonials?

- ♦ What organizing books have you read?

- ♦ What organizing seminars have you attended?

- ♦ What kind of past experience do you have from companies you used to work for before you became a professional organizer?

- ♦ What types of projects have you organized?

- Did you manage people?

- Did you work on special events?

- Are you a member of NAPO?

- Do you attend local, or national, NAPO meetings?

- Are you aware of industry trends?

- Do you serve on any organizing committees?

- Have you written any organizing publications? Books? Booklets? Articles? Newsletters?

- Have you created any organizing products?

- Do you have a Web site? If so, how many unique visitors do you get on a daily basis? On a monthly basis?

- Do you have a newsletter, ezine or blog? How many subscribers read it?

- Have you been interviewed by the media? Or have any of your articles appeared in publications?

♦ Do you have a degree in a certain area that enhances your career as a professional organizer?

Now that you've answered these questions, take a few moments to summarize your qualifications. Then, revisit this summarization every year and determine what needs to be adjusted according to qualifications you've added or improved during that time.

I am qualified to be a professional organizer because:

_____

_____

_____

_____

_____

What skills do I need?

Many professional organizers are already organized people. However, it is important that you have expertise in the area of organizing that you are going to be selling.

For instance, if you're planning on specializing in creating filing systems, you must know the ins and outs of effective filing systems. Perhaps you're planning on conducting time management workshops. If so, you must know the essentials of effective time management.

Visit your local bookstores and local libraries. Read every book you can about the organizing subject you're planning to assist people with. Read industry publications. Attend organizing seminars. Seek mentors—people who have successful businesses. Continuous learning is the name of the game and you can never learn enough about your field.

The next key is practice. You can read as many books about golf as you like, but you'll never learn how to play golf until you begin to swing the club.

You should not practice, however, on a paying customer. Your first few jobs can be complimentary, volunteer jobs. Perform a bunch of organizing jobs gratis until you feel you have the skills necessary to begin charging for your expertise.

One more very important note is to "practice what you preach." If you're a professional organizer, you must be organized. This means you must have a clutter-free, organized home or office. This means you are able to manage your time well. This means you know how to set and achieve goals.

How do I choose my specialty?

It's certainly fine to be able to perform lots of different organizing jobs. However, very often, being a "jack-of-all-trades," can be a detriment.

If someone is specifically looking for help in managing his time, coining yourself a "Time Management Expert" is much stronger than saying "you help to organize basements, kitchens, home offices and time."

The specialty you choose really depends on you, your skills, what you feel comfortable doing and a number of other criteria. Of course, just because you choose a particular area to focus on now, doesn't mean you can't change your mind later.

When I first started out as a professional organizer, I focused on helping people organize their offices and I specialized in paper management, paper flow and filing systems.

Later, when I started my Web site, I changed my focus to home residents instead. I found that there were so many women on the Web who needed help organizing their homes. I decided to focus more heavily on these folks. I also felt I gained a greater personal satisfaction helping people organize their homes and their family life.

You have to test the waters for yourself to determine in which direction you want to steer your boat and find the area that you get the greatest satisfaction—personal satisfaction and financial satisfaction— that you want out of your professional organizing business.

Keep your past experiences in mind as you work to develop your focus. Are you familiar with filing systems or would you prefer organizing closets? Are you more comfortable with individual time management consulting or are you confident enough that you're willing to teach large groups?

This is not something that you have to "put in stone" today. It's just something to keep in mind as your business grows.

Very often, the area you end up focusing on is one that gradually evolves. For instance, perhaps you thought you wanted to help people organize their collections, photographs and other memorabilia. But as it turns out, the majority of your jobs are photo organizing projects alone.

Learn from your experiences and each job you get. Keep asking yourself exactly where you would like your business to be now, 5 years from now, 10 years from now and 20 years from now.

How do I gain that "expert" status?

As long as you know "how" to organize, you can gain your expert status fairly quick. First, adopt the attitude "I can organize virtually anything I put my mind to", whether it's clutter, someone's schedule or a storage situation. Once you have that positive attitude, you'll simply begin building your credentials.

Do some complimentary jobs and get yourself customer testimonials. The more you have, the more experience you'll gain and the more valuable comments you'll be able to add to your portfolio.

Offer your knowledge to the media, in terms of submitting organizing articles or offering your time to do interviews.

Create a Web site and begin getting known on the Internet. You can submit articles, tips and ideas to various Web sites or start a discussion forum and/or an organizing clinic on your own site. Become a moderator on a high traffic, popular

discussion forum. Become an expert contributor on other related Web sites.

Although it's not necessary, you may wish to be certified as a Professional Organizer through NAPO or another professional organizing organization. In doing so, you'll gain more knowledge about the profession. Plus, you'll get your "letters." As you already know with PhD's, having those letters after your name immediately puts you on a higher level with people.

Speak. Talking in front of people will help you gain that expert status quickly. Give a talk at your local Chamber of Commerce, a church or educational group, or a business.

If you can do something for someone in high status, like for the president of a company, a known actor/actress or a public organization like the library, that increases your expert status.

You'll gain even higher expert status if you write a book or create a product. The possibilities are many.

Benefits of initially offering complimentary jobs

If you're a new organizer just starting out, it will be beneficial for you to offer your first few organizing jobs for free. These can be offered to a variety of people and organizations, such as friends, relatives, a church, an associate, a business office or a charity organization.

Offer it to anyone you come across that could use a little—or a lot—of organizing help. Don't offer it to someone who is already very organized.

The benefits of offering these free sessions are:

♦ You can determine if this is the type of business you're truly interested in starting and running.

♦ You can test your skills, expertise, the time it takes you to complete certain jobs and your interaction with other people.

♦ You can build organizing hours for your credentials.

♦ You can get some client testimonials for your portfolio.

Chapter 2
National Association of Professional Organizers (NAPO)

What is it?

NAPO, also known as the National Association of Professional Organizers, is a non-profit, professional association whose members include organizing consultants, speakers, trainers, authors and manufacturers of organizing products.

Founded in 1985 by Beverly Clower, Stephanie Culp, Ann Gambrell, Maxine Ordesky, and Jeanie Shorr, it is the only national association of and for organizers with members located all over the world.

There are also local chapters throughout the United States which you can find out about if you join NAPO. These local chapters include groups of professional organizers located within a specific city or state. Local chapters, which hold regular meetings, are helpful because in addition to NAPO's annual conference, you have the opportunity to network face-to-face with other organizers throughout the rest of the year.

What is NAPO's purpose?

In a nutshell, NAPO's purpose is to:

1) promote the field of professional organizing.

2) help to make the public aware of professional organizing.

3) provide support, training, education and a networking forum for members.

According to NAPO, the mission of the National Association of Professional Organizers is to develop, lead, and promote professional organizers and the organizing industry.

A professional organizer enhances the lives of clients by designing systems and processes using organizing principles and by transferring organizing skills. A professional organizer also educates the public on organizing solutions and the resulting benefits. NAPO (pronounced NAY-poh) currently has approximately 4,000 members throughout the U.S. and in 8 other countries.

How do I join and what do I get?

It's very easy to join NAPO. You visit their Web site (www.napo.net), fill out a membership application and pay your annual fee. For individuals, this is about $200 per year. A NAPO representative will get back to you and let you know whether or not your membership has been accepted.

From that point on, you will begin receiving the NAPO newsletter, be listed in the NAPO member directory, have the opportunity to receive referrals and receive information on the industry and the annual organizing conference.

Basically, NAPO gives you the opportunity to network with other people in your field and to keep abreast of events, products, services and trends within the organizing industry.

What does the NAPO newsletter include?

NAPO's bi-monthly newsletter provides valuable information and news about the field of organizing including industry trends, articles from members, and information relevant to running a successful organizing business.

It also includes sponsor ads from other professional organizers on products and services they provide, and sponsor ads from large organizing-related companies that offer products and services to NAPO members, often at discounted prices.

Will NAPO market my business for me?

Please be aware that NAPO cannot and will not market your business for you. The only person that can market your business is you.

While NAPO does provide referrals to you when the opportunity arises, they do not proactively market for you individually. If a prospect happens to call NAPO, NAPO will then refer that person to an organizer in the prospect's area.

NAPO's referral service is basically a perk of belonging to the group. You might get occasional referrals from NAPO, but you should not in any way depend on NAPO's referral program alone to grow your business.

What are the benefits of joining NAPO?

Here are the top 5 benefits that I've come up with:

1) If you plan on using the media or organizations to help you grow your business, it gives you credibility when you can say that you belong to a national association.

2) Letting your customers know that you're a member of a national association gives you added prestige and trust.

3) You can learn something from every single person you meet. NAPO gives you the opportunity to speak with or write to experts, fellow professional organizers and other people in your field.

4) You will receive the NAPO newsletter, plus catalogs and information, on a regular basis so you're always aware of the new events, technology, products, services and information in your field.

5) You will be able to market your books, services and products to other organizers, which can increase your bottom line.

What is NAPO's Code of Ethics?

NAPO's Code of Ethics is a set of principles to provide guidelines in our professional conduct with our clients, colleagues, and community. If you join NAPO, you'll be asked to accept and adhere to their Code of Ethics, which for most people is not very difficult to abide by. *(Source: http://www.napo.net)* Here is what NAPO expects, ethically, out of its members:

As a member of the National Association of Professional Organizers, I pledge to exercise judgment, self-restraint, and conscience in my conduct in order to establish and maintain public confidence in the integrity of NAPO members and to preserve and encourage fair and equitable practices among all who are engaged in the profession of organizing.

Clients: Working Relationships

- I will serve my clients with integrity, competence, and objectivity, and will treat them with respect and courtesy.

- I will offer services in those areas in which I am qualified and will accurately represent those qualifications in both verbal and written communications.

- When unable or unqualified to fulfill requests for services, I will make every effort to recommend the services of other qualified organizers and/or other qualified professionals.

- I will advertise my services in an honest manner and will represent the organizing profession accurately.

Confidentiality

- I will keep confidential all client information, both business and personal, including that which may be revealed by other organizers.

- I will use proprietary client information only with the client's permission.

- I will keep client information confidential and not use it to benefit myself or my firm, or reveal this information to others.

Fees

- I will decide independently and communicate to my client in advance my fees and expenses, and will charge fees and expenses which I deem reasonable, legitimate, and commensurate with my experience, the services I deliver, and the responsibility I accept.

- I will make recommendations for products and services with my client's best interests in mind.

Colleagues

- I will seek and maintain an equitable, honorable, and cooperative association with other NAPO members and will treat them with respect and courtesy.

- I will respect the intellectual property rights (materials, titles, and thematic creations) of my colleagues, and other firms and individuals, and will not use proprietary information or methodologies without permission.

- I will act and speak on a high professional level so as not to bring discredit to the organizing profession.

What is GO Week?

Founded by NAPO, GO Week, also known as Get Organized Week was created in 1992 to focus on the benefits of getting organized and the tools and techniques necessary to achieve that goal.

GO Week occurs annually, usually the first full week in October. NAPO members voluntarily sponsor and participate in hundreds of events and programs around the country. These include workshops, community service organizing projects, contests, media appearances and more. GO Week offers excellent opportunities for your business. The media is always interested in national events.

For instance, I teamed up with a fellow organizer colleague of mine to do three-minute news segments every morning on a local television station during a past GO Week. The main theme of the segments was "Get Organized Week." Each day we came up with a sub-theme. One day was organizing your paper. Another day was organizing your closet and so on.

This was extremely successful. Each segment resulted in a minimum of 1,000 people visiting my Web site. Plus, we both received dozens of sales and leads for our businesses. In fact, it gets even better. By doing segments such as these, you'll be getting your foot in the door for other media opportunities.

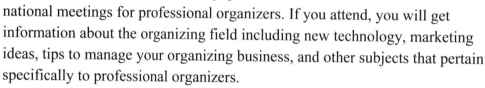

NAPO'S annual convention

NAPO holds an organizing convention every year. This is one of the few popular national meetings for professional organizers. If you attend, you will get information about the organizing field including new technology, marketing ideas, tips to manage your organizing business, and other subjects that pertain specifically to professional organizers.

The convention is not included in your NAPO membership dues; it is an additional cost. You're responsible for all costs and arrangements associated with travel, accommodations and meals.

The convention location changes every year and once you're a member, you'll be notified of the specific location for that year.

If you're comfortable speaking in public and you have a specific area of expertise that will benefit other organizers, you might be interested in holding presentations at the annual events. If you're a NAPO member, you will receive information about holding your own presentations at the conference.

This could be a good opportunity for you to gain credibility among your organizing colleagues, to practice your speaking skills and to sell your services, books and/or products on site.

How can I get more involved with NAPO?

Your best bet is to join a local NAPO chapter. There are chapters in many areas, and it's likely you'll find one not far from where you live. Once you're involved with a chapter, you can get involved in various committees and run for various positions. Being on a NAPO committee, or even the Board of Directors, will give you yet more knowledge in the profession and higher expert status with your clients and the media.

Are there other organizing associations besides NAPO?

Certainly. A few that immediately come to mind are the Professional Organizers of Canada (www.organizersincanada.com), which I've heard very good things about. They are a Web-based organization.

There is also the International Association of Professional Organizers. Their web site is: www.organizingtheworld.org I believe they also have a certification program.

I'm a member of NAPO and therefore most familiar with what they provide. I don't get anything for promoting NAPO. I just think they've been good for me and the organizing industry in general.

You'll need to do your homework on the other available organizations. A simple search on the Web will help you get more educated on what is available and the organization(s) that will help you and your business benefit the most.

Chapter 3
Getting Started

How do I choose a business name?

When choosing a business name, the best place to start is to come up with a list of possibilities. Try to come up with 25 to 50 to choose from. It's generally a good idea to choose a business name that reflects what you do and one that, when people see it or hear it, they'll know pretty much what you're about immediately.

Be careful of choosing something that, once you grow or expand, will no longer be appropriate. For instance, if you choose Sally's Home Organizing Services, but you decide to organize offices later, your business name is going to be outdated.

You also have to be sure your name isn't being used by someone else. Look in your phone book, search extensively on the Internet, check with your Secretary of State's office and more. In other words, really do your homework. Your business name should be unique.

It's also important that you really love your business name, so choose something you can live with for many years to come.

How should I structure my business?

In general, you have four options to choose from. Here is what they mean in a very simplified manner, but speak with your accountant to get more information and to determine the best set up for your business based on your needs:

- Sole Proprietorship: You're the sole owner of your business and you're personally responsible for all business liability. This is the structure most professional organizers choose.

- Partnership: You share legal and financial responsibilities of your business with one or more partners.

- Corporation: Not directly connected to your personal finances. In a lawsuit, the corporation is sued—not the individual.

- Limited Liability Company: A combination of partnership and corporation.

How much money do I have to invest to get started?

Good news! The start-up costs for starting your own professional organizing business are extremely low.

In fact, the one thing you should not do when starting your organizing business, or most businesses for that matter, is to invest a lot of money into it upfront. While you eventually may have to invest in your business from time to time for it to be very successful, initially it's best to be conservative.

Do I need office space?

You do not have to rent office space. In fact, most professional organizers work right out of their homes or apartments. You'll even be able to get a tax savings by working out of your residence—an extra bonus!

Renting office space shouldn't be a consideration until you're bringing in plenty of money and you wish to expand your business to include employees.

What do I need to set up shop?

You don't need to run out and buy file folders, organizing accessories, a label maker, or anything else.

Once you get your first client, you can then look into picking up the tools you need to make your job easier. As long as you have the essentials—a calendar, some business cards, a telephone, a pen and some paper—you're all set to begin.

What about business cards, brochures and stationery?

Don't spend your life savings on expensive business cards, brochures and stationery. Think conservative—simple, inexpensive, black and white. Impress with your expertise and skill, not with your stationery. Later on, when you're bringing in some money, you can always upgrade your stationery if you'd like.

Do get yourself inexpensive business cards. I get 500 cards printed for less than $30 from my local printer.

If you can, you may consider creating your own business cards on your computer and printing them out a few at a time. You can get blank business card stationery—generally 10 business cards to a sheet—from an office supplies store. These work well with most home printers and are perforated.

Do I need a logo?

Too many professional organizers spend countless hours trying to come up with a logo—or they spend hundreds of dollars having someone design their logo. For small businesses, logos don't do a thing to increase sales. If you want to make money, you should not spend a ton of time on things that will not help to increase your bottom line. Your company name alone could be your logo—just like Sears or JCPenney. In fact, the more simple it is, the more professional it is.

Should I begin to invest money to promote my business?

Don't spend hundreds of dollars on Yellow Pages ads, newspaper ads and other expensive marketing vehicles initially to promote your business. There are other free and less expensive ways to get your feet wet. We'll be discussing these later in this guide.

Do learn everything you possibly can about marketing, before you spend a dime on marketing promotion. In addition to this guide, I strongly suggest you get yourself a copy of the Give to Get Marketing Solution, which is available from the Give to Get Marketing Web site: www.givetogetmarketing.com

Should I quit my current job?

If you're already working in another job and your sole income is coming from that job, don't quit your current career until you have enough money coming in to support yourself. It's going to take a little while to get your business off the ground.

If your spouse is bringing in enough money to support both of you, you might discuss the possibility of you focusing solely on your professional organizing business, rather than working at it part-time.

However, I still recommend that you make sure this is the type of business you'd like to work at before quitting your current job. You can always phase into a full-time business when your paid projects increase.

Do I need a computer?

While you can certainly start off in this business without a computer, a bit down the line I recommend you get a good computer with online capabilities (preferably a cable or DSL Internet connection as opposed to a phone line connection) and a laser or inkjet printer. If you're serious about doing well in this field, you will eventually need a computer to keep track of your contacts and your marketing numbers. While pencil and paper work, an automated system is the best way to do this.

It will also be necessary to write letters and press releases—much easier to do on a computer. In addition, with computer capabilities, you can use the Internet to find information to manage and market, review organizing products, research what your competitors are up to, and other information associated with your business.

What is the SBA and can they help me with my business?

The SBA, or Small Business Administration, is a government organization dedicated to helping small business owners. They have many online courses, free of charge, that you can take advantage of such as Starting a Business, Finances and Employee Management. You can find them online at www.sba.gov

You'll also find a wealth of information in their free web library. It's a wonderful resource and one worthy of checking out.

If you live in Canada, the Canadian government offers an Online Small Business Workshop. You can find out more on this link: www.cbsc.org/osbw

What is SCORE and can they help me with my business?

SCORE is an organization of retired business executives who act as business coaches—free of charge! There is likely a local SCORE office near where you live. You basically call and make an appointment. Discuss the possibility of matching an executive to you that has worked in a similar type business.

SCORE also offers classes and materials you can purchase. Visit their web site at www.score.org for more information and/or to find the nearest SCORE location.

What are the government requirements?

Once you determine that you have a viable business—you've already secured a few jobs—it's important that you find out what licenses you need.

There are many types of licenses and you need one to operate legally almost everywhere. Getting a business license may be required by your bank to open a business checking account and may also help in the event of an IRS audit as evidence that your business tax deductions are legitimate.

If your business is located within an incorporated city limit, the city will issue the license. If you're outside the city limit, the county will do it.

Licenses cost between $5 and $300, depending on locality and take anywhere from an hour to 90 days to obtain.

Depending on the type of organizing projects you're conducting, state and city governments may require additional licenses.

Most states require that sole proprietorships and partnerships that are conducting business under a name other than the owner(s) must file for a fictitious business name statement, or a DBA (Doing Business As) certificate.

The DBA certificate is generally obtained at the Clerk of Court of the county in which business will be conducted. Fees are typically very low and most courthouses have records that may be searched to determine if your suggested name will be unique.

You should also do a thorough Internet search on the company name you're thinking of to ensure it's not one that someone else is already using. Google can be helpful in this aspect.

To obtain a DBA, you will probably be required to advertise your fictitious business name in a legal or daily newspaper in your community for three weeks. You must renew your fictitious business name periodically, usually once every 5 years.

The IRS requires corporations, partnerships and sole proprietorships with employees to receive a Federal Employer Identification Number (EIN). This is used to report your personal and business taxes, as well as taxes you withhold from employees.

If you're a self-employed sole proprietor without employees, you can use your Social Security Number, unless you have a Keogh account—a retirement savings plan that's available only to self-employed people.

Check with the Small Business Administration for more information: www.sba.gov

Do I need business insurance?

Having business insurance is not a requirement in this field in the United States. However, you should use your best judgment when deciding whether or not it is a necessity for you. (It may be a requirement in other countries, so be sure to do your homework if you live outside of the US.)

If you concentrate on seminars or coaching, insurance may not be necessary. However, if you do a more physical job, it may be appropriate.

For instance, if you're a closet organizer and part of your expertise is installing closet systems, insurance is something you probably want to look into. With insurance, you can cover yourself if you accidentally break or damage something in your client's home.

When and if you do decide to take out a business insurance policy, speak with your current insurance provider. He or she will help you determine the best type of policy based on your specific needs.

Do I need a special bank account?

As with any business, you should not mix your personal expenses and income, with your business expenses and income. Keeping your personal finances and your business finances separated is a must.

To do this properly, you should open a business checking account.

Go to your bank and speak to them about opening your business checking account. They will go over the details with you and you'll be all set in no time at all.

Once you have a business checking account, use it to make all of your business related purchases. Also, use it to collect any business income.

Should I start my business on my own, or should I team up with someone else?

That's entirely up to you. When you're independent, you're in control of exactly where you want to go, how much money you want to make, what clients you wish to work with and so on.

When you're working with a partner, you have to make "committee" decisions. This basically means you won't be able to always "get your way." If you feel you would be content and happy with this type of partnership arrangement, then you should do what you're most comfortable with.

My husband and I share our main business together. However, we have two separate web sites that we each run fairly independently. Although this is the case, we do collaborate often and we work very well with each other.

In the end, the important thing is that you're happy with what you're doing both in your heart and in your wallet.

How should I structure my business day?

When you're running your own business—especially running one out of your home—you must be careful not to allow home related events and tasks to take priority over business related events and tasks.

Set your business hours and stick to them. I usually work from 9:30 in the morning, until 5:00 at night, Monday-Friday—with an hour in between for lunch. Prior to our daughter's school days, we hired a babysitter to come in for a few hours each day to entertain her. In doing so, we were able to give 100% of our attention to the business.

Of course, your hours will fluctuate some days due to early client appointments, late organizing projects, etc.

However, realize that when you're running a business, your business hours should be separated from your home and family hours as much as possible. This will help to ensure you're spending enough time on your business, and giving your family the attention they deserve when you're not working.

A typical business day might be structured something like this:

8:30 - 9:00	business reading
9:00 - 1:00	organizing projects
1:00 - 2:00	lunch
2:00 - 3:00	administrative (proposals, thank you letters, calls, updates)
3:00 - 5:00	marketing
5:00 - 5:30	make tomorrow's To Do list, set goals, tidy your desk

What attire do I need?

This depends on the type of organizing you're doing. First, no matter what type of organizing you're conducting, you should always have a nice business outfit for your meetings with potential customers. A business suit if you're meeting in a corporate setting, or casual business attire if you're helping home residents would be appropriate. Here are some other practical guidelines:

♦ **Residential organizing:** If you're going to be organizing people's homes—filing systems, closets, basements—appropriate attire is a pair of casual pants, a casual shirt and comfortable shoes (not sneakers). Jeans may be appropriate if it's a job in which you'll be moving boxes or getting dirty. Be sure you discuss with your client what you'll be wearing and what he or she should be wearing—since your client will be helping you in most cases. This way, you won't have to wait at your client's house for her/him to find appropriate clothing.

♦ **Office organizing:** If you're going to be organizing business offices, appropriate attire is casual business dress. Jeans are inappropriate for most office jobs. Wear comfortable shoes (not sneakers).

♦ **Residential consulting/workshops:** If you're not going to be doing any hands-on organizing and will be sticking to coaching and consulting, casual business dress is the most appropriate choice.

♦ **Business consulting/workshops:** If you're not going to be doing any hands-on organizing and will be sticking to coaching and consulting, casual business dress or a business suit are the most appropriate choices. Use your judgment. If you're going to be helping a clerk in an office, casual business dress should be fine. However, if you're going to be helping a president in a big company, a business suit—with a tie for men—would be most appropriate. The rule of thumb when you do business workshops is you should be dressed one-notch better than your audience.

Can I run this business, while staff members do the work?

If you'd prefer marketing your business, while others are doing the work, you can certainly do so. For instance, you can be the person handling all the marketing, while other professional organizers do the organizing jobs for you. Another possibility is to have someone handle all your administrative work while you do the marketing work and organizing jobs. I actually use a fulfillment service to box up all of my book orders—about a thousand boxes a month. Doing so alleviates me of this work so I can spend my time growing my business.

Whenever you're working with others, of course, you'll also have to manage those people to be sure they're running things as you see fit. You also have to have the money coming in to pay employees or outsourcing firms. If you hire employees early on, for example, you probably won't be able to pay your staff members a steady salary initially. You may have to hire people and pay them on a per-project basis. There are not too many people willing to accept sporadic jobs like this. They won't always have work, which means they won't always have a paycheck.

With employees, you will also have to handle management issues, such as staff members not showing up for work on certain days or employees using organizing systems with your customers that you may not totally agree with.

In addition, it will be necessary for you to speak to your accountant to determine whether your staff members are to be considered contractors or employees. This is based on various criteria. If they're considered employees, you'll have to pay necessary wage taxes.

This is just one of the many reasons that we outsource to printing firms, virtual assistants, fulfillment services, etc. and not hire employees.

I am not, in any way, telling you not to hire others. If you have intentions of growing very big, you will not be able to do all the work yourself. You'll have to determine how far you'd like to climb up the ladder and who you'd like to take on your journey.

Should I take on a partner so I don't have to go solo?

Think long and hard before you start a business with someone else. Partnerships are usually started with the idea of splitting up the workload, but sometimes end in problems and frustration.

The goals of one person are not always the goals of someone else. This means that your business would be constantly pulled in two different directions.

One person may work harder than the other partner. This can cause ill feelings and can even break friendships.

One person may come across as "the leader," rather than an equal partner. How do both of you feel about this happening?

Who is going to do the less desirable organizing jobs? Cleaning out and organizing a garage is very hard, physical work, while organizing and maintaining computer files is a cleaner job, but can take more knowledge and skill.

If you decide to partner up with someone, at minimum be sure both of your roles are well-defined. Work out the various scenarios and come up with ways you'll both be able to compromise so both of you are content.

Some partnerships do work out, but it takes commitment and sacrifice. Before you put yourself into a partnership situation, especially with a family member or friend, work out a plan in case one of you wants to jump ship, so the other person isn't left high and dry—and so you don't lose your relationship at the same time.

What if I like the organizing aspect, but don't like the business aspect?

There's just no getting around it. If you have your own organizing business, you have to run an all-encompassing business. You can't just organize, and not pay attention to all the other aspects of your company.

If you only want to organize, but don't want to think about any other aspect of your business, you might consider just working for someone else. You'll still get money for organizing projects, but you won't have to do anything else.

A true business owner is able to handle all aspects of his or her business. This certainly doesn't mean you have to "do" everything, but you do have to be willing to run your business, and that means being on top of the various parts of your business that keep it running smoothly.

Ways to conquer fear

I felt the following article, *written by Melanie Unger*, was perfect for inclusion in this guide. Fear is something many professional organizers fear in many aspects of their business. This article addresses those fears and helps one move past those obstacles.

———

The title above is a bit of a misnomer, as I don't think we ever quite find the one true way to actually "conquer" our fears. Fear is the biggest immobilizer we have facing us in our quest to become more, do more, and take risks for our future. This article addresses aspects of fear, recognizing those aspects, and how to use practical strategies to address this fear to move on and achieve your goals.

When I started my own professional organizing career, I had read, re-read, researched and read some more, then pondered, and pondered some more. Some of this pondering and waiting was most certainly due to fear! I had been "reading, researching, and essentially waiting" to begin my career as a professional organizer for nearly 5 years! Why so long?

Part of my personality includes some streaks of perfectionism. When you combine fear and perfectionistic tendencies, the two characteristics can cause near paralysis in terms of making a move toward a new, exciting, and scary opportunity!

Hopefully, you don't share these personality qualities to the same degree, but if  you do, you're not alone (many professional organizers are definitely "Type A," perfectionistic types of people—that is actually partly what makes us good at what we do).

Fear is deceptive. For instance, during the years of my "preparation" to become a professional organizer, I knew that I had the skills to do hands-on organizing, since I had been helping people organize for years. I also had the "PR" experience since I had been in the teaching profession for over 15 years. What I initially thought I was doing was right on the mark; after all, who wouldn't take the time to research to the best of one's ability in order to be prepared to take a new step in one's future?

This sounds fundamentally "correct," inherently, but I think I was missing the point. You see, I was preparing so much for so long, that I was in effect avoiding the next step I needed to take. I needed to move forward and begin! Now, I'm not saying that you shouldn't prepare, read, and research in order to become more educated and to make proper decisions regarding any new change in your life. I knew that I needed to research such things as how to set up my business legally, how to go about setting my rates, how to handle paperwork, and many other aspects of starting a new business. But from there, I just needed to move forward.

I've been working my professional organizing business for a short time now, and as each day goes by, I know I have much to learn and many things to experience. Certainly, I am far from being any kind of expert. But what I do know is that taking the step to do something that is a life dream, something that I've wanted to do for so long, is so worth it.

I knew that no matter how many days went by, that the next day, I'd still want to help others become more organized.

I knew that I was not going to be perfect (a hard lesson to learn), and that I would need to grow from making mistakes (another hard lesson to learn). But not taking that first step in beginning my professional organizing business in the face of fear would have been the biggest mistake of all.

You see, we cannot conquer fear, really. We can face it daily, work with it, work through it, and learn to deal with it. But it never really goes away. I still feel fear in most new situations (my first contact with a new client during a phone consultation, an assessment session with a brand new client, my first organizing session with that client, etc.).

Working through that fear is key. We become professional organizers in order to truly touch lives. In order to do that, we must work through our fears. When we do, we can feel so proud that we are working well within our calling.

I hung an encouraging quote about fear by Mark Twain in my office. It reads, *"Courage is resistance to fear, not absence of fear."*

Practical Steps in Dealing with Fear

❖ Recognize the signs of fear. Do you frequently question an idea, a step, or a decision—many times before taking any action? Do you feel symptoms of panic? Do you find yourself backing away from doing something?

❖ Acknowledge fear. Don't hide from it. Realizing it for what it is can be a healthy first step.

❖ Decide what can be done in stages to get you one step closer. Read a book, talk to a mentor, write down your ideas, do a practice session for free, etc.

❖ Reflect on small steps and act on more decisions. Make a working list of things to do. It helps you become more accountable to the tasks at hand, and helps them to be more real when you read them more than once on an active "to do" type of list—no matter how scary or overwhelming the tasks seem.

❖ Continue this process and evaluate how things turn out. The key is activity – be actively doing something to progress toward your goal(s).

❖ Share your small successes with close friends and family members. This makes your actions more real and will prompt you to do more!

by Melanie Unger, Copyright 2008, Organized Inspirations, LLC

Melanie Unger founded Organized Inspirations, LLC, a residential organizing company, out of her dream to provide personalized organizing solutions to individuals and families, as well as special populations, such as teachers and students. Melanie desires to guide others to become their most organized in order that they become more productive, and lead happier, more inspired lives. She is a member of the National Association of Professional Organizers (NAPO) and Faithful Organizers. For more information, please visit: www.organizedinspirations.com or send an e-mail to: melanie@organizedinspirations.com

How do I find a mentor or coach?

Want to prepare yourself and be coached along the way? What better way to do so than by finding yourself a mentor or coach? You would probably be surprised with how much some people will share about their business for a small fee or even free. Some people would be willing to meet with you for one or two sessions. Others may set up a long-term relationship and get together with you once a week or every month for a year or two.

There are many professional organizers who will do this and market themselves as doing so. You can find them through a search if you join NAPO. You can also seek out successful professional organizers that you know about and ask them if they'd be willing to mentor or coach you.

Another possibility is not using someone who is a professional organizer as a coach, but rather a general business coach or a marketing coach.

Whoever you decide to use, it should be someone you feel good about—someone who guides you in the direction you wish to go, and someone who makes you feel good about yourself.

Mentoring or coaching can be done in person, on the phone or via email. Many mentors and coaches also have time limits and question limits. Be sure you work this out prior to your first session.

Before your sessions, prepare your questions ahead of time and bring them. This way, you're not wasting your time or their time. Take notes so you don't have to ask the same questions more then once. If they tell you something that you don't quite understand, don't be afraid to ask them to explain it again.

Whether someone is mentoring or coaching you for free or for a fee, if you feel they've gone above and beyond to truly help you in your business, consider giving them a gift to show your appreciation—from time to time and at the end of your last session.

Chapter 4
The Bottom Line

How much money can I make?

That's entirely up to you. It will be based on your goals, knowledge, skill, creativity and dedication. If you're a go-getter, the professional organizing field can certainly be a very lucrative one for you!

You may choose to do as little as 1-2 personal organizing projects each month and make $200 to $1000 each month. Or, if you're really ambitious, you might expand your services, write a book, hold seminars and/or invent an organizing product—and bring in thousands each month!

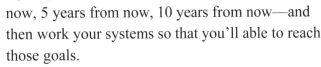

> ### Say what?!
>
> Thomas Watson, the chairman of IBM in 1943, once said, "I think there is a world market for maybe 5 computers."
>
> Even the most successful and influential business people, make false assumptions.
>
> Before you say, "I don't think there's a big enough marketplace for my services," make sure you do enough market testing to know if that statement is true or false. Don't guess.

So, the question isn't really: "How much money can I make?" The true question is, "How much money do I *want* to make?"

You should come up with the figure you'd like to make now, 5 years from now, 10 years from now—and then work your systems so that you'll able to reach those goals.

Of course, you do have to be realistic. For instance, if you plan to limit your business to personal organizing—actually driving to someone's home or office and, let's say, setting up filing systems, your income will be limited. You can only charge so much for this type of service. You can only be in one place at a time, so you would be limited by how many jobs you could take on each week. Plus, your body can only endure so much work.

On the other hand, if you choose to write a book or create a product once and then sell that product over and over again, you have a much greater chance of ensuring an income level that could be infinitely multiplied. If you diversify and do a few different things—write a book, create a product and teach time management courses, for example—your income potential will be even greater. It all depends

43

on your expertise, motivation, drive, experience, available time, skill and creativity.

Is there a big enough need for my organizing services?

The only person that could determine the answer to this question is you. You might be thinking, "Well, there are 6 other professional organizers in my area. So, there's probably not a need for another organizer." Or maybe a colleague told you she tried to start a business as an organizer in your area, but it didn't work out for her. You may conclude that it probably wouldn't work out for you either.

Beware of coming to conclusions that are based on nothing more than untested assumptions. There are so many variables involved. For instance, perhaps the other organizers in your area aren't filling some of the many needs in your marketplace. Or perhaps they can't get organizing jobs because they don't have the skills and expertise needed to market their businesses. I cannot emphasize enough that you must *always base your conclusions on testing and solid numbers.*

Unless you understand the basics of marketing and you've tested your market, your services/products, your offers, etc., then the question about whether there is a need or not for the particular services or products you want to sell is one that hasn't been answered yet. The magic words are "test, test, test." The numbers will reveal the answers you need.

Is there lots of competition in this business?

There are other professional organizers. There are a few thousand that belong to the National Association of Professional Organizers (NAPO) alone and since you don't have to belong to NAPO to be a professional organizer, there are probably a few thousand more.

However, that doesn't mean that you have lots of competition. After all, you could have five professional organizers who live within a few blocks of you (unlikely), but if none of those five organizers knows how to market his or her services, that means you have no competition at all.

Another example might be the specialty niche you've chosen. For instance, there may be a few organizers in your area who specialize in home organizing, but perhaps you specialize in office organizing. In fact, after attending some local NAPO meetings in Wisconsin, I've discovered that the majority of the attendees all have a different market and all have varied specialties.

Personally, I don't consider other professional organizers to be my "competition." Instead, I consider them all to be valuable resources. Often, I'll receive calls or email messages from prospects that need organizing services. Since I now focus on writing and selling books and products from my site, I refer them to other organizers in my area. You can do the same thing and you can benefit from it:

Small Business Administration

The U.S. Small Business Administration, established in 1953, provides financial, technical and management assistance to help Americans start, run and grow their businesses.

With a portfolio of business loans, loan guarantees and disaster loans worth more than $45 billion, in addition to a venture capital portfolio of $13 billion, SBA is the nation's largest single financial backer of small businesses.

The SBA also plays a major role in the government's disaster relief efforts by making low-interest recovery loans to both homeowners and businesses.

For more information, visit: http://www.sba.gov

♦ Contact other organizers in your area and ask them if they would be willing to pay you a referral fee based on the initial project of any referrals you pass on to them. Most will be happy to accept and reciprocate. A 15%-20% fee on the initial project is generally appropriate. However, you might also charge a flat fee, such as $25 or $50.

♦ You can give the referral away as a good will gesture, with no referral fee required. Let the other organizer know that you would also love any referrals that he/she can pass on to you.

If you focus on continuously improving your skills as an organizer and a marketer, the concept of competition will be meaningless.

Should I get someone to invest in my business?

If you're just starting out, I hesitate to recommend that you ask someone to invest in your business, before you've proven that it can be very profitable for both you and your investors. You'll prove that with concrete numbers. For instance, some new entrepreneurs get people to invest in their product before they even know if the product will sell. The people who invest want their money back within a reasonable timeframe and with interest, of course. It will be a very uncomfortable situation if those products don't take off and the investors lose their money.

Therefore, if you feel you have an incredibly great product or service that you have been profitably selling on your own for a few years, you might then consider getting some investors to help you move ahead. Once you're at this level, you're then into the big leagues.

Should I take out a loan?

As I mentioned, the money needed to start your own professional organizing business is minimal. If you can refrain from taking out a loan, you won't have to worry about paying that loan back later.

If you're on an incredibly tight budget and you really feel you need to purchase a computer or other piece of equipment and you can't do so without a loan, than taking out a loan is probably justifiable. However, don't take out a loan and immediately begin spilling that money into running "untested" ads for your business that haven't been proven to generate prospects.

If, after you're established, you feel you want to take out a loan to buy materials in bulk, for a product that you've been selling on a regular basis, that's also justifiable. You can check with your bank, or the Small Business Administration, for more information on taking out a loan:
www.sba.gov

How many hours per day do I have to work to bring in the bucks?

When thinking about your business, it's imperative to plan your hours and your finances. Let's say someone offered you $1000 to help organize her house, but you end up spending 50 hours to do so. That means you just made $20 per hour— without taking into consideration any expenses you may have incurred. This is a pretty low hourly rate for a business owner.

Your goal from the start is going to be determining how quickly you can get a job completed correctly, and still make at least $35 an hour to start.

If you work 8 hours per day, and you charge $35 an hour, you'll make $280 per day, minus any expenses (8 hours x $35). If you do this three days each week, you'll make $840 per week. ($280 x 3 days). If you do this three days each week for a year, you'll make $43,680 annually ($840 x 52 weeks), minus expenses.

You'll have to do the math to determine how many hours you wish to work and how much money you wish to make. It's going to be different for everyone, depending on your knowledge, energy level, experience and financial goals.

Of course, all of this depends on how well you market your business. The money will only come in when you convert your prospective customers into paying customers, which will generate repeat business and referrals.

How can I determine if I'm making a profit?

Are you taking in more than you're spending? That's the easy question to ask. Let's say you just purchased an ad in the newspaper for $300. The organizing jobs that resulted from that ad came out to $450. That means you made $150 profit—as long as you didn't spend any extra money on office supplies, etc. If, after that organizing job, you get a referral, you just made more profit.

On the other hand, let's say you just mailed out 1000 direct mail letters to generate prospects and let's say it cost you 75 cents per letter between printing and postage. That comes out to $750. In the end, from the direct mailing you make just $600. That comes out to be a $150 loss—not so good.

The above is a very simplified description.

A more advanced way of thinking is gross profit versus net profit. For instance, let's say you recently purchased $2000 worth of office and computer equipment and/or you had to pay an employee to stuff and send out your mailing.

Gross profit is sales minus all costs directly related to those sales, such as manufacturing expenses, raw materials, labor, selling, marketing and other expenses. So, if your sales came out to $600, but your expenses came to $750 for your mailing and $2000 for your furniture/employee expenses, your gross profit is going to be **minus** $2150!

In other words, be careful about your spending. If you're constantly spending money, chances are you're not bringing enough in to support all that spending.

I have lofty financial goals? Can I reach them?

If your financial goals are lofty, you're going to have to work hard to reach them. If your goal is to make $100,000 each year, you're not going to reach that goal by securing a home organizing job every so often.

The question truly is, how hard are you willing to work to reach your $100,000 goal? If the answer is "very hard" you'll be determined to find more avenues to bring more money in. If the answer is "not very hard," you're going to be sorely disappointed looking at your finances at the end of each year. For the most part for most people, money doesn't come easy. You have to work for it.

Chapter 5
Marketing Your Business:
General Overview

The "Give to Get Marketing" Web site

This section is meant to give you a general overview of how to effectively market your business. However, in addition, I strongly recommend you visit the Give to Get Marketing Web site at

www.givetogetmarketing.com

My husband, Joe, who is a world renowned marketing expert, owns and runs this site. It's chock-full of free tips, ideas and systems to help you market your business effectively. This Give to Get approach is what we've used and continue to use, to grow our Get Organized Now! business.

What's the difference between a business plan and a marketing plan?

In general, a business plan is a description of your business and a projection of the sales, expenses and profit you plan to make from your business over the next 3-5 years. On the other hand, a marketing plan describes who you plan to sell to, what you plan to sell to them and how you plan to attract those people to your business and convert them into customers.

Do I need a formal business plan when I'm just starting out?

I've seen so many organizers make the mistake of spending hours and a great deal of money, on a formal business plan during the early stages of their businesses— very often this results in wasted hours and wasted money.

You can't possibly predict what numbers your business is going to be bringing in before you know exactly how to market and before you've had a few solid year's worth of paying customers. Therefore, a formal business plan at this stage of your organizing business would be based on nothing more than guesses—most of which will probably turn out to be way off-base.

A few of the reasons you would take the time to create a formal business plan are if you're applying for a loan, applying for a merchant account or looking for investors. Most organizers do not need these in the early stages of their business development. The last thing you want to do is spend time and money creating a formal business plan, just to file it away and not use it again.

I recommend that you have a good idea of how much money you'd like to make by the end of this year and next year. Break it down into how much you need to bring in each month. You can then use your marketing plan to help you achieve those goals. This is called a "napkin business plan." It shouldn't cost you a thing and it should take less than an hour for you to put together.

If you need a formal business plan to apply for a merchant account or a loan, stop at your local computer software store and pick up business plan software templates, fill in the blanks and print it out. You can also go to the Small Business Administration Web site to find sample business plans: www.sba.gov

Do I need a marketing plan at this early stage?

Absolutely, but it doesn't have to be an expensive, formal plan. Basically it should answer:

♦ who you plan to sell to

♦ what you plan to sell to them

♦ how you plan to attract those people to your business

♦ and how you plan to convert them into customers.

You should be able to write your marketing plan on "one sheet" of paper.

Keep in mind that this early marketing plan is a "living document" that you will constantly revise as the weeks and months go by. Why? Because it's impossible for you to predict in the early stages of your business the answers to these questions.

As you test your marketing strategy and you begin to get results/numbers, you will begin to solidify and discover what works best for your business. You'll adjust your marketing plan according to this knowledge.

The Passive versus the Proactive approach

When it comes to marketing your business, running a few ads that announce your business and services and waiting for the phone to ring is definitely not the way to go. If you choose to take this sort of "passive" approach, you will end up with very few clients, if any. In order to grow your business, you have to take a more "proactive" approach to marketing your business.

Realize that the marketing end of your business is even more important than the actual organizing or consulting services that you sell. If you say things like, "I'm an organizer, not a marketer," then you're going to have an extremely difficult time making it in this business or any small business for that matter. Marketing is essential.

If you understand that marketing is everything you do to attract and keep customers, it should be clear why every small business owner must be an effective marketer.

How much time should I dedicate to marketing my business?

The percentage of time you spend marketing your business depends on your goals and your motivation level. I try to spend anywhere from 50% to 75% of my work day marketing and the remainder of my time creating products, doing seminars, consulting and so on.

Many professional organizers ask how many hours they would have to work to be able to make this a successful business for them. Again, this depends on your goals and your motivation level.

During my first year in business, I worked anywhere from 10-12 hour days. Now, I keep my workday to approximately 5-6 solid hours per day. You should know that my hours are based on my goals. I want a balanced life—time for my business, but also time for my family life and for the other things in life that I enjoy doing—and I want a full-time, successful, profitable business. That's exactly what I have. I achieved my goals by setting them clearly and working towards them every day.

Can I get someone else to market for me?

Please understand, unless you have thousands of dollars to pay for a personal marketer or publicist, "you" are the only person who can market a small to medium size organizing business effectively. Even if you could afford a full-time marketer or publicist, it's very unlikely that you could make enough money to pay for him/her, plus make any kind of a profit—unless you're as big as Martha Stewart.

This also means that you can't call your local newspaper or Yellow Pages representatives and expect them to create an effective ad for you. Yes, they can provide a typical ad layout, but it's unlikely they will be able to provide you with an ad that will pull lots of response for you. This takes a solid understanding of marketing, as well as complete knowledge of your business and your goals. Only "you" can have that knowledge.

The media is in the business of selling space and time. While their intentions are often good, they're not in the business of selling your services or products. This certainly doesn't mean that you can't generate response from ads. It means that you have to apply an effective strategy to your ads and any other marketing vehicles you decide to use for your business if you expect anything substantial from them.

Once you have an effective and profitable strategy, if you feel that you need people to help you implement that strategy, that's fine. However, you must be in control of your marketing at all times.

How will I know if I'm marketing effectively?

Your numbers will tell you. In a nutshell, you want to make sure you're bringing in more money than you're spending. For example, let's say you run an ad that costs $150. You'll have to bring in at least $150 in gross profit—sales minus direct expenses—just to break even. You don't make a profit until you've finished paying for all of your expenses.

It's extremely important to determine what marketing efforts are working for you and which are not. That's why you must track every single one of your marketing efforts. We'll discuss this more in-depth later.

Your strategy

Before you do anything, realize that effective marketing is based on a strategy. It's not something you do once and then wait for the sales to come in. It's also not something you can come up with today and then roll with it.

Your marketing strategy takes time to plan, test and improve.

Having a strategy may sound complicated, but in reality, it's an overall plan of how you accomplish something. Just as you need a strategy for baking a cake or going to the mall or going on vacation, you also need a marketing strategy.

A few of the most basic questions you'll be starting off with will be . . .

The idea is to keep moving people into your next list:

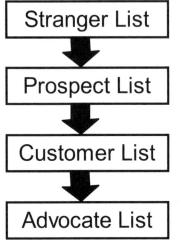

Stranger List
↓
Prospect List
↓
Customer List
↓
Advocate List

♦ Who do you want to sell to? Are there enough of them to make a profit?

♦ How will you generate prospects?

♦ What services or products do your prospects want?

♦ How can you provide a solution that will be a) helpful for the customer and b) profitable for you?

♦ How will you convert those prospects into customers?

♦ How will you be sure your one-time customers become repeat customers? Lifetime customers? Advocates?

You won't be able to answer these questions off the top of your head. For instance, to even be able to start to answer question number one, you'll have to do a few marketing tests first.

As long as you understand that it's going to take a little while to get your business off the ground, you'll be ok.

Don't try to rush. Take it one small step at a time. In the end, if you learn how to effectively market and you do so continuously, you will have a very profitable professional organizing business.

Your lists

In order to build your business, you have to be aware of and understand the importance of lists. There are 4 basic lists that you should be aware of:

♦ **Stranger List:** Your first list will be your Stranger List. An example of a Stranger List might be a list of names/addresses that you purchased from a list company. Another example of a Stranger List might be the people who read a particular newspaper. In this case, you would not have their names or addresses. But, no matter, this list is exactly what the name implies—a group of people who don't know you exist. It's nearly impossible to sell directly to strangers. Your prospects will come from this list.

- **Prospect List:** Every time someone contacts you about your offer, their name/address and any other contact information should immediately be put into a database, or a spreadsheet, or an index card system, etc. This is your Prospect List. You'll need this contact information to follow up with your prospects later. Your customers will come from this list.

- **Customer List:** This is a list of names/addresses of people who have made at least one purchase from you. The only time someone is to be considered a customer is when they've given money to you. Your repeat business and advocates will come from this list.

- **Advocate List:** This is a list of people who absolutely love your products and services. They rave about your business to anyone who will listen. They continuously refer new business to you. This list is very important, because the more you keep in touch with your Advocate List, the more your business will be referred.

The idea is to keep moving people in a sequence. They should start off on your Stranger List. A percentage will then move on to your Prospect List, your Customer List and finally your Advocate List.

One-step marketing (an ineffective approach)

Many business owners use the common one-step marketing approach. This means you run an ad or send a letter and then expect people to buy your services or products directly from that effort.

You'll recognize examples of one-step marketing wherever you look.

Open up any newspaper you have laying around. Ignore the big company ads because these are a horse of a different color. I think it's safe to say that you don't have the money it takes to market like most big businesses do—strictly for image.

While Prudential and Pepsi have millions of dollars to keep their name prominent in the marketplace, unless you're rich you're not going to be able to do this.

Instead, look at the smaller company ads—other organizers, insurance agents, travel agents, therapists, realtors, plumbers—and you'll see that most ads basically contain the business owner's name, the company name, a bulleted list of a few services or products and a phone number. Some may also have additional lines that say "call for more information," or "free consultation," or "in business for 25 years," or "reliable and dependable."

These are all one-step ads and they typically pull little or no response. The bottom line—people rarely buy in one step. For example, if you run an ad for your organizing business, even if it's an effective ad, most people aren't going to call you and say, "Hello. I'm interested in your organizing services. Where do I send the money to get started?"

If getting business were this easy, everyone would be rich. You may ask, "Then why do these businesses continue to run these ads?" Here are a few reasons:

♦ They don't know they're not getting response from these ads. There's a very good chance that they're not tracking where their calls are coming from. They could be getting some calls and just assuming those calls are coming from their ads. Two words of advice to you—*never assume*. These calls could be coming from something else—like referrals—which means those ads might not be pulling anybody.

♦ They think that they have to run an ad 7-12 times to get any response. This is not true. If you don't get at least some response from your ad or sales letter the very first time you run it, something is wrong. Either you're not including all of the necessary criteria in your ad or letter to get people to respond, or maybe your target isn't reading that particular publication. Perhaps your headline isn't captivating. Possibly, your offer isn't strong enough, or you haven't included any offer at all. The list could go on and on, but I strongly recommend you don't continue to run an ad that gets absolutely no response. If you don't get response the first time, you need to make some adjustments.

♦ They think it's good enough to "get their name out." Unless you're a big company like Federal Express, it's going to be extremely difficult and costly, if not impossible, to get a large portion of the general marketplace to begin recognizing your business name. Most professional organizers just don't have the money necessary to run full-page ads and TV/radio spots every single day. The type of marketing that works effectively for professional organizers is called "direct response marketing," which is marketing that produces immediate response to marketing efforts; not marketing that just "gets your name out." That's called Image/Awareness marketing and not only is it likely that you can't you afford it—you don't need it.

♦ They figure that they don't have time for effective marketing and it's quicker to just run a one-step ad. This is ludicrous. If an ad is not generating a positive response, then you're doing nothing more than throwing away your money. If you don't have time to market, you shouldn't be in business for yourself. You can work for somebody else who knows how important it is to market effectively.

Why don't most people respond to one-step marketing?

There are many reasons why most people don't respond to one-step marketing. Here are just a few:

♦ People are overloaded with advertising these days. Between newspapers, magazines, Web sites, radio spots, billboards, signage and more, the average person probably sees over 3,000 or more advertising messages/logos in any given day. Unless you're offering something that people are going to 1) notice and 2) be extremely interested in, then you have little or no chance of getting any response. When you use the one-step approach, people don't have a compelling reason to respond. So, they don't.

♦ People are naturally skeptical when it comes to any form of advertising, especially advertising that makes exaggerated promises. After all, there are a lot of businesses out there running ads, sending letters and so on. How do people know who to trust? How can they be assured that if they call your business, they won't have to listen to a pushy salesperson? How can they be assured that they are inquiring about the right type of service for their needs? What if they're just looking for some initial information, but are not willing to buy right now? What if they don't want to contact you, because they're pretty sure they can't afford you?

♦ People don't know whether to contact you, or to contact one of your competitors. If you're running a one-step ad, just like two or three or ten of your competitors, it's a toss-up for a potential prospect. The person will then just pick one business, which means you have absolutely no control over gaining that person's future business or not. Or, even worse, the person will procrastinate on calling anybody—which happens very often when he/she doesn't have an urgent need. After all, if your water pipes just burst, you would have to call a plumber immediately. But with organizing services or products, the need is hardly ever that much of an emergency.

♦ People don't know what to ask. They're not experts in your business, so there's a good chance they won't know what types of services or products you offer, how you can help them or how they can effectively define their problem. Since most people don't wish to feel dumb when they contact you, many will hesitate or not contact you at all.

♦ Most one-step ads make it difficult to get people to respond, by putting up obstacles. People are not sure what to call for, what to do, when to call, who to speak to and so on.

♦ While you may get a few people responding to one-step marketing, you'll be greatly limiting your response. There may be a few people out there who are "hot prospects"—people who already have a burning desire for your services or products. Those people may respond to your one-step marketing. But unfortunately, there are rarely enough "hot" people for you to make a good living. If you settle on only getting the hot ones, you'll be missing out on all of the business you can get from the warm ones—people who may have an interest in your service or product, but who are not ready to buy right now.

One final important note: people who are warm, rarely, if ever, respond to one-step marketing.

I'm not convinced that one-step marketing won't work.

Some people need to see for themselves that one-step marketing brings in very little, if any, response. If you feel you'd like to give one-step marketing a try, then you should do so. Run a one-step ad or sales letter and track that marketing effort by counting your responses. You'll get your answer within 7 days.

If you get no response, you'll know immediately that something is wrong. If you get one or two responses, you'll never know if you could have gotten 10 or 20 responses instead.

My only advice is not to drain your savings account on testing one-step ads, letters, Web sites, etc. I can personally guarantee you that any one-step marketing effort will shy in comparison to the two-step marketing effort, but I welcome you to come to your own conclusions.

Two-step marketing (an effective approach)

Again, most people will not buy immediately from your ads, or business letters, or Web site. It's too soon. They don't *know, like or trust* you at this point. You will get little, if any, response if you use the one-step approach.

The Two-step marketing approach is very effective for small businesses, especially for professional organizers.

The general strategy is:

1) You run ads, send letters, do press releases or conduct seminars to first generate *prospects*. These are people who have a genuine interest in getting organized. You need to get these prospects' contact information for follow-up.

2) You then follow up repeatedly over time with these prospects and convert a percentage of them into first-time customers, then lifetime customers.

Why do I need prospects?

Not everyone in the world is going to be interested in the services or products you are offering, which means that every person in the world is not a potential customer.

You may say, "Well, any one who has a disorganized home is a prospect." Not true.

Just because someone has a disorganized home, doesn't necessarily mean he or she "wants" to get it organized. Believe it or not, some people are perfectly happy being disorganized.

Until you come in contact with people who have expressed an interest in your product or service, you are marketing to strangers. Strangers are the people reading the newspaper, or reading your letter, or visiting your Web site.

You don't know who they are, because they haven't decided to tell you who they are yet. It is extremely difficult, if not impossible, to get strangers to buy your products or services.

So, rather than trying to market to strangers, it is much more effective to market to prospects. Prospects are people who have responded to your ad, letter, newsletter, or Web site and have requested something from you. You either have their address, phone number, fax number or email address.

It is much easier to get "prospects" to buy your services and/or products.

What will I have to do to convert prospects into customers?

Once you begin to generate prospects and collect their contact information, it will then be necessary for you to follow-up with these prospects. We're going to be reviewing follow-up more deeply later. Keep in mind, however, that in order to get as many customers as you possibly can, it will be necessary for you to follow up with your prospects anywhere from 1 to 12 times depending on your follow-up experience and skill.

This seems like it will be an awful lot of work and time.

Growing a successful business takes a good deal of time and effort. If it were possible to succeed in a day, then everyone you know would be out partying on a

yacht in the Caribbean. It just doesn't work that way.

If you're serious about growing your business, you won't take marketing lightly.

Keep in mind that once you have an effective strategy to attract prospects to your organizing business, and an effective strategy to convert those customers into first-time and then repeat customers, you'll keep using that marketing strategy over and over again. In other words, it will get easier and easier as you grow your business.

If you want a few customers, market your business a little. If you want lots of customers, market your business a lot. It's that simple.

Chapter 6
Generating Prospects

Your target

Choosing a target audience for your service or product can really help you get the largest possible percentage of people responding to your marketing. For instance, if you want to help homeowners, you can specifically target homeowners and exclude businesses.

This will allow you to 1) focus your attention on your target so you have the very best chance of getting their attention and 2) invest your time and money exclusively on your target so you're not wasting it on someone who would not have a desire for the service or product you're offering.

This doesn't mean that you can't have more than one target audience. For instance, you may want to target homeowners for your closet organizing services. Then, later, you might want to target small businesses for your file management services.

However, it is important to focus on one target audience with each individual marketing effort. This is because you can't effectively market the same exact way to everybody. The offers you give to homeowners will be different than the offers you'll give to small businesses.

Determining if there is enough of an interest for what you are offering cannot be answered by a mere guess. It also can't be determined by what someone else has told you.

Just because one organizer tells you that he or she has had a difficult time marketing time management consulting services in his or her area, doesn't necessarily mean there isn't a need or a want for time management services.

It could be that the organizer you spoke to doesn't know how to market effectively. There's a good chance they're trying to market with the ineffective one-step marketing approach.

The only way to tell if there is sufficient interest is to get your offer in front of enough people, see if they respond to that offer and count your responses.

Your offer

Once you know who your target audience is going to be, the first step for generating prospects is to come up with a compelling offer that your target market will immediately respond to.

A compelling offer is something you offer to people that is so inviting that they can't possibly let it pass them by.

If you offer your organizing services initially, that is not going to be very compelling to most people. Most people, even if they're potential prospects, will have a million excuses why they wouldn't immediately call you to take you up on your offer. They might think you charge too much. They might feel uncomfortable inviting you over for a consultation. They don't want to talk to a pushy salesperson. The reasons are endless.

So, by offering your organizing services, or consulting services, or book, or video, etc., expect very low, if any, response to your marketing. You might get one or two hot people—people with an immediate and urgent need—calling you, but you'll be missing out on all of the warm people—people who don't have an immediate need, but who may buy later.

You might offer a free consultation, but this is a weak offer for generating prospects. Think about it. You probably wouldn't put yourself in the position of accepting a free consultation from someone else if you weren't quite ready to buy something.

Offering a free consultation at this stage is like saying, "Come to my sales presentation." Most warm people will not respond to this type of offer. It's too soon. It's too scary.

The best type of offer to use to generate prospects is one that will put people at ease; an offer that will take away any fear; an offer that is enticing, but not threatening.

Your compelling offer might be a free booklet of organizing tips, an audio cassette containing time management ideas or an info-pak containing some simple systems for setting up a filing system.

Now think about it. A person who is disorganized reads your ad offering your free booklet or reads your letter offering your free audio cassette. Let's say that all she has to do is send you an email or a fax asking for it. All of a sudden the fear begins to diminish. This person doesn't have to speak to someone right now. She is happy that you're offering her something that she's interested in. This person has already begun to *know, like and trust you.* As soon as this person responds to your offer and has given you her contact information, she is a prospect and you're ready to begin following-up to build a good relationship.

Now is a good time for you to begin deciding what you can offer to potential prospects to get them to respond. Can you come up with a booklet of 35 clutter-control tips? Can you record some tips on an audio cassette? Can you come up with some organizing articles?

Decide on an offer that is not seasonal. For example, you might not want to make your offer, "101 Tips to Organize for the Holidays" because you'll only be able to make that offer around the holidays. Then, you'll have to come up with an entirely different offer for the rest of the year.

Once you come up with a good offer, you can use that offer forever. You will never have to change it. Who cares if someone who already responded to that offer sees it again in a magazine? He has already responded to that offer. You have his name and contact information in your database. Only be concerned about "new" people seeing your offer. Remember, you are building your Prospect List. Your first-time customers will come from that list.

> **Don't Fear Free**
>
> During coaching sessions I've conducted, organizers have said, "I'm really afraid of offering something for free. What if I get thousands of people asking for it? How will I afford the printing and the postage?" Most people overestimate the response they'll get to any of their marketing— including free offers. There are many reasons why most people don't respond to any offers, including free offers. Here's what you should expect from an offer of a free tips booklet or info-pak:
>
> Direct mail mailed to 100: 1-2 responses or 1-2%
>
> Ad in a small local newspaper with a circulation of 30,000 readers: 1-10 responses.
>
> So, as you can see, you're going to get just a few responses to your free offer. But you'll get a lot more than if you tried to set up an appointment or sell your services/products directly in your ad.

Your vehicles

Once you come up with an effective offer, you're now ready to decide how you're going to *deliver* that offer to your target market. That's where your vehicles come into play.

A vehicle is a means for you to deliver your offer. Common marketing vehicles are ads, direct mail letters, workshops, networking, articles, referrals, publicity, news releases, flyers, media interviews, door knob hangers and so on.

Some vehicles are free and/or very low cost. Other vehicles require more of a financial investment. The vehicles that are going to work best for you depend on a number of factors. For instance, it may initially cost more to do direct mail, but direct mail might pull the highest response for you. Or perhaps you'll determine that advertising your offer in the newspaper ultimately cannot bring in enough response to pay for your expenses. In this case, you might decide to market exclusively on the Web.

In addition, some vehicles require more of a time investment than others. For instance, you might not have the time to spend in networking meetings a few days a week, so perhaps you'll opt to work on a referral system instead.

While different vehicles will pull different numbers of response for you, you have to be very careful not to blame a low response on the vehicle. For instance, many professional organizers have stated, "I used direct mail once. It didn't work." Most likely, it was not the direct mail that didn't work. It was probably the offer that was weak, or it wasn't well targeted, or a number of other things. Blaming the vehicle is like blaming the messenger, because you don't like the message.

In addition, you may determine that you'd like to choose three or four of these vehicles and use those to market your business. This is perfectly fine. Some businesses use one vehicle; some use many. It's up to you to determine which vehicles(s) work best for you.

Here is one thing to keep in mind. If you're using a vehicle that's working well—let's say referrals—and then you choose to use another vehicle—perhaps direct mail, that second vehicle should be *in addition to—not in place of* your first vehicle.

So many people make the mistake of turning off the first faucet and then turning on the second faucet. Instead, keep all of your effective faucets running to generate the highest possible number of prospects and subsequent customers.

Here are just some of your vehicle options to generate prospects. Be sure you avoid the one-step approach. Apply the two-step Give to Get Marketing approach to all of your marketing vehicles. And remember to test small first.

- ✓ ads in newspapers or magazines
- ✓ ads in phone books
- ✓ ads in calendars and other publications
- ✓ ads in electronic publications and Web sites
- ✓ articles (yours)
- ✓ articles (written about you and your business)
- ✓ business cards
- ✓ brochures
- ✓ flyers (inserted in newspapers)
- ✓ flyers (posted or handed out)
- ✓ direct mail letters
- ✓ direct mail flyers
- ✓ direct mail postcards
- ✓ doorknob hangers
- ✓ email
- ✓ fax
- ✓ hand outs or samples
- ✓ in-person visits (business, organizations, residential, etc.)
- ✓ Internet
- ✓ interviews (print, radio, television, Internet, etc.)
- ✓ networking
- ✓ newsletters
- ✓ news releases
- ✓ radio commercials
- ✓ radio programs (your own)
- ✓ referrals
- ✓ signage (billboards, magnetic signs, posters, counter signs, etc.)
- ✓ telephone (telemarketing)
- ✓ television commercials (cable or commercial)
- ✓ television program (your own)
- ✓ trade shows
- ✓ Web site
- ✓ ezine
- ✓ blogs
- ✓ free workshops or seminars

Each vehicle you use should include:
- ✓ a headline or title targeting your specific prospects

✓ a headline stating your offer

✓ a description of your offer

✓ a clear call-to-action telling the person exactly what you want him/her to do to get the offer. Give them a number of ways to respond: write, call, fax, email, visit

✓ a sense of urgency so they don't procrastinate: call today, available for a limited time, visit the Web site before September 30th

✓ a pressure reliever like, "there's absolutely no-obligation"

✓ a tracking code so you can determine which vehicles are working for you and which aren't

In addition, when someone responds to one of your marketing vehicles, get his or her contact information immediately, begin building a relationship and send out your offer—booklet, tips-pak, infopak, etc. within 3 days.

Very important note:

Any numbers listed throughout this section depend on a number of variables including how strong your offer is, if you're targeting well, if you included all of the necessary elements, the amount of effort you put in, your skill level, your experience, the professionalism of your vehicles and so on. These numbers are solely based on "two-step" marketing. Numbers are simply estimations based on my experience in this particular field. Your results may differ due to the above variables.

They are printed here to give you a realistic idea of what you can expect when everything we've described is carried out well.

Also, these estimations are the "number of prospects" you can expect; not the number of paying customers. You must first generate prospects, then follow-up to convert a percentage of them into paying customers.

♦ **Ads in newspapers or magazines:** You can use classifieds, small display ads or full page ads in local or national publications.

✓ **Targeting:** Make sure you choose the newspapers or magazines that best target your prospects. For instance, if your business is geared towards the residential market, don't run your ad in a newspaper that caters to the business market and vice versa.

- ✓ **Proper section:** Newspapers and magazines have many different sections you can run your ads in. Before you choose the section, think about what you're offering first. For instance, if your business focuses on uncluttering homes, you will probably want to run your ad in the Lifestyles or Decorating Section. If your business centers around offering relocation services, you may consider placing your ad in the real estate section.

- ✓ **Size is important:** If your ad is tiny, it can easily be missed. Of course, larger ads cost more money. You would have to determine if running a larger ad would be worth your investment.

- ✓ **Design it well:** Your goal should be an ad that pulls response—this will not necessarily be a cute, humorous or fancy ad. Here are some basics:

  - **The headline:** Just like your head is at the top of your body, your headline belongs at the top of your ad. Your headline should clearly state your offer. If possible, have the headline reversed—white, bold font on a black background. It will stand out more. For the headline, stick with a sans serif font such as Arial Bold, Helvetica Bold or Impact.

  - **The body:** For the body copy, use Arial or Helvetica. Clearly state the particulars about your offer in bulleted format. Never use white body type on a black background. It's extremely difficult to read. Always use black type on a white background for legibility.

  - **Use appropriate graphics:** You should only use graphics that are going to enhance your message. For instance, if your offer is a free booklet, you might want to show a graphic of the booklet. Don't use doo-dads or irrelevant graphics just for the sake of decorating your ad.

  - **Make it clean:** Don't print text over pictures or busy backgrounds. If it's not easy for a person to read, it won't be read.

- ✓ **Positioning is important:** If your ad ends up in the middle of a newspaper surrounded by other ads, there's little chance of it being seen. You only have about 3 seconds to catch someone's attention. Unfortunately, you don't always have control over where the publication decides to position your ad. But you should always ask for good placement. Try to get placement above the newspaper fold, in the upper right hand corner. Second choice would be above the fold, in the upper left hand section.

✓ **Know what numbers to expect:** Just because a newspaper or magazine has a circulation of, let's say, 30,000 readers, that doesn't mean that 30,000 people will read your ad—or even "see" your ad. Only a small percentage will see your ad and even a smaller percentage of those people will respond to your ad. Estimated prospect response for a 4" x 4", two-step ad in a local, community newspaper may be:

Minimum: 1-2 prospect responses
Expected: 3-7 prospect responses
Outstanding: Over 7 prospect responses

✓ **Response time:** Most people respond within 7 days, so expect the majority of your responses to come in 7 days after the ad runs.

♦ **Ads in phone books:** Unfortunately, not everyone is aware that professional organizers even exist. This field is not as well-known as the dental field or the accounting field. Therefore, many people won't even think about looking in the phone book for your business. However, there are a few people who are familiar with the professional organizing field who might use the phone book as a reference.

Plus, if someone refers you, a potential customer may want to look up your contact information in the phone book.

✓ **One-year commitment:** When you run a phone book ad, you usually have to commit for one year—because the phone books are only printed once per year. Just be sure you track any responses you get from your phone book ad(s) so you can decide next year whether or not it's worth running again. This will also give you the opportunity to change the ad copy, size, etc.

✓ **Types of phone book ads and listings:** You can either run a simple in-line listing, a boxed ad, or a display ad. Your listing should probably be under a category such as "Organizing Services," although if you're including a more specific service, such as closet organizing or relocation, you may also consider an additional listing in a more specific section.

✓ **Size matters:** If you're going to place a phone book ad for prospecting, one of the rules of thumb is to "run an ad as big as your competitors' biggest ad." When going through phone books, people look at the bigger ads first. They assume that "the bigger the ad, the better the company." Of course, you'll have to test small first to determine if this is justifiable.

✓ **Design it well:** Follow the same design rules as listed in the "Ads in Newspapers or Magazines" section in this guide.

✓ **Know what numbers to expect:** Again, most people don't look in the phone book for professional organizers. So, you're not going to get a ton of people responding to your phone book ad no matter how strong your offer. If you run an in line-ad, don't expect more than 1-2 calls per month, if that. Estimated prospect response for a small, display ad may be:

Minimum: 1 prospect response
Expected: 2-3 prospect responses
Outstanding: Over 3 prospect responses

By the way, when you're adding up the number of phone book calls you receive, your "current customers" don't count in that calculation—only new prospects.

♦ **Ads in calendars and other publications:** Other publications for displaying your ads are church or community calendars and bulletins, ceremonial or theater programs, even place mats.

✓ **Business card size ads:** Very often, these types of publications accept business card size ads. Many people opt for the lazy option and use their business card layout for their ad layout. Your business card is not an ad and it is unlikely to generate any response unless you have a very strong, noticeable offer on it.

✓ **Know what numbers to expect:** Very few people read ads in these types of publications. In fact, usually the money for these ads goes to a special cause—such as a donation to support the organization. However, if the ad space is inexpensive and you wish to support a particular cause, by all means, do so. Approximate prospect response rates may be:

Minimum: 1 prospect response
Expected: 2-3 prospect responses
Outstanding: Over 3 prospect responses

♦ **Ads in electronic publications and Web sites:**

✓ **Tracking:** Electronic publications such as ezines (also known as email newsletters) and Web sites very often sell advertising space. Just as you must track any form of print advertising, you must also track your electronic advertising.

✓ **Text-only ads:** One of the electronic advertising formats is "text only ads." These ads are exactly what they say—text only. No pictures, graphics, clipart or borders. I use text only ads often and I've pulled tremendous response—sometimes thousands of responses—from publications, sites and newsletters with large readership.

✓ **Banner ads:** Another form of electronic advertising is "banner ads." These are basically display ads that are usually formatted in long, rectangular boxes. You can include graphics, borders, etc. and you have more flexibility with fonts, colors and/or animation. You should know that many large companies are dissatisfied with the results of their banner ads. And if the large companies can't get people clicking on their ads, the smaller companies will have an even more difficult time.

✓ **Know what numbers to expect:** The numbers for text ads differs from the numbers for banner ads. Prospect percentages are based on the number of people who are getting the electronic publication, or who are visiting the Web site:

Text Ads:
Minimum: 1-5%
Expected: 6-10%
Outstanding: Over 10%

Banner Ads:
Minimum: < than 1%
Expected: 1%
Outstanding: Over 1%

♦ **Articles (yours):** How are your writing skills? One of the best and least expensive ways to deliver your message is by writing tips articles related to your products and services and offering them to the media for free. The media gets content that will interest their audience and you get free exposure for you and your company.

> **My resource box**
>
> Always include a resource box with every article you write. Be sure it includes your compelling offer, so that interested people will have a compelling reason to respond to it.
>
> My resource box always says:
>
> By Maria Gracia
> Get Organized Now!
> www.getorganizednow.com
>
> Want to get organized? Get your free Get Organized Now! Idea-Pak, filled with dozens of tips and ideas to help you get organized, at the Get Organized Now! Web site.

✓ **Submit your articles:** Submit your articles to newspapers, magazines, Web sites, ezines, blogs, etc. using a consistent article submission format. You can submit the same article to many publications. These publications are not required to print your articles. If they feel your submitted articles will benefit their readers, there's a good chance they'll print yours.

✓ **Some publications pay for articles:** If you're planning to get paid for your articles, you must come up with a price for which you're willing to sell them. However, generally when articles are

paid for, you lose the rights to sell them to or share them with any other publication. So before you sell an article for, let's say $100, consider the amount of money you could make if you use the next approach.

✓ **Your resource box:** You can submit your articles that tell editors or publishers that they can print your article free of charge—in their print or electronic publication—as long as they include your resource box. This very often is more beneficial than getting paid for articles, because not only will you be exposing your business to dozens, hundreds or thousands of potential customers, you'll also attract dozens—even hundreds—of prospects to your business.

Your resource box might look like this:

by Jane Doe - All About Organizing, Inc.
Want 23 ideas to help you get better organized at the office? Call 555-5555 and ask for our free Office Organizing Tips Booklet #23.

✓ **Your own column:** You may determine that you love to write, in which case you might consider seeking out a specific publication that you can write a regular column for. This would give you lots of credibility, plus you'll be regularly exposing your business and compelling offers to lots of potential customers.

✓ **Know what numbers to expect:** Percentages are based on the number of people who are getting the particular publication and whether the publication is a national publication, local publication or electronic publication. Estimated prospect response may be:

National print media or broadcast publication (circulation per million):
Minimum: 1-199 prospect responses
Expected: 200-499 prospect responses
Outstanding: Over 500 prospect responses

Local print media or broadcast publication (circulation per 10,000):
Minimum: 1-10 prospect responses
Expected: 11-25 prospect responses
Outstanding: Over 25 prospect responses

Electronic publication (Web site or ezine: based on 1,000 visitors or subscribers):
Minimum: 1-10 prospect responses
Expected: 11-25 prospect responses
Outstanding: Over 25 prospect responses

- **Articles (written about you/your business):** If you can get a respected newspaper, magazine or other publication to write an article about you and your business, there's a good chance you'll be able to generate lots of qualified leads.

One article written about my company in the Milwaukee Business Journal brought a few thousand new prospects to my Web site and generated many prospects for organizing consulting sessions and workshops. It also resulted in a few dozen immediate sales for my book and other organizing products.

- ✓ **Your offer:** If you can, try to get the writer to include a free offer that people can call for in the article. For instance, if you have a free tips-pak, that would be an excellent item to have included in the article. Not all writers will do this, but definitely ask. Don't be wishy-washy about it. Tell the writer that you'd really like your free offer included.

- ✓ **At minimum, do this:** If, in the end, the writer refuses to include your offer, at minimum get him or her to mention your Web site—if you have one—or your contact information. You will get some exposure, but believe me, it will be nothing like the exposure you can get if your free offer is included in the copy.

- ✓ **Prepare notes:** Before the reporter visits or calls you, be sure you write down some notes about yourself or your business that the writer will find interesting. Be prepared. If you are nervous, talk about your business to a spouse or a friend first and/or talk into a tape recorder. Be careful— whatever you say has an excellent chance of being printed.

- ✓ **Know what numbers to expect:** Percentages are based on the number of people who are reading the particular publication and whether the publication is a national, local or electronic publication. Estimated prospect response may be:

National print publication (circulation per million):
Minimum: 1-199 prospect responses
Expected: 200-499 prospect responses
Outstanding: Over 500 prospect responses

Local print publication (circulation per 10,000):
Minimum: 1-10 prospect responses

Expected: 11-25 prospect responses

Outstanding: Over 25 prospect responses

Electronic publication

(Web site or Ezine: based on 1,000 visitors or subscribers):

Minimum: 1-10 prospect responses

Expected: 11-25 prospect responses

Outstanding: Over 25 prospect responses

♦ **Business cards:** Have business cards on hand wherever you go—no matter where it is. You never know when a business opportunity will arise.

✓ **Your Offer:** Include a compelling offer on the front of your business card, so that those who receive your card have a good reason to contact you.

✓ **Reverse side:** Don't forget about the reverse side of your card. If you can't fit what you want to say on the front, have your offer printed on the back.

You might also want to use the reverse side for your referral system by including a line that says Referred by _____. When you hand your insurance agent your business cards, for instance, write his name on the reverse side. When he gives out your cards, the person contacting you will remember who they were referred by and you'll have the opportunity to thank the referrer.

✓ **Avoid gimmicks:** Avoid getting very creative with your business card. While you can certainly choose a style and/or color to match your personality, put the greatest emphasis on your offer first. It's the most important element.

The front of your business cards is meant to be printed horizontally. There's a very specific purpose for this. People put business cards in their Rolodex and they're always inserted horizontally. If you print the front of your business cards vertically, when people put you in their Rolodex, your name is going to be sideways—making it difficult to find and to read.

✓ **Cost savings:** To really save on cost, you might consider making your own business cards on your computer and printing them on business card

sheets that can be purchased at most office supplies stores or a company such as Paper Direct:
www.paperdirect.com

✓ **Know what numbers to expect:** The number of responses you'll get depends on how many business cards you give out. Based on you giving out 100 cards to qualified people, prospect response rates may be:

Minimum: 1-4% prospect response
Expected: 5-10% prospect response
Outstanding: Over 10% prospect response

♦ **Brochures:** Brochures that include strong offers may be used to generate prospects. However, a brochure with only your company name, contact information and a few services you offer is a weak prospect generator.

✓ **Replace your brochure with a presentation folder:** Please note that you don't *need* a brochure. In place of a brochure, I include all of the information I like sending to prospects in a nice presentation folder. The cost of getting a brochure printed isn't generally worth it for most professional organizers. However, whether you have a brochure or not is completely up to you.

✓ **Do it yourself first:** If you're just starting your business, you might be better off creating your brochures yourself on your computer and printing them out as you need them. This will be easier on your wallet. Plus, since you may want to change your brochure along the way until you've found one that works well for you, you won't get stuck with 500 brochures that you don't wish to use. You can get lovely, professional brochure paper from a company such as Paper Direct.

✓ **Get it professionally printed later:** Once you're happy with your brochure and you feel that it's helping you to bring in more business, you can then get it printed by a professional printer. I recommend you stick with a simple, stock format that is one or two colors. If you choose something more elaborate, chances are the only thing you'll be increasing is your cost.

✓ **Don't hand them out randomly:** Brochures should rarely be used as prospect generators. They're too expensive to be handed to strangers and are better used as supplements to letters or flyers, or handed out to prospects—people who have asked for your information.

✓ **Know what numbers to expect:** Prospects rarely come from brochures alone. Brochures are meant to "supplement" your letter, flyer, etc. If you use your brochure and nothing more to generate prospects, expect these approximate prospect response rates for every 100 brochures sent out:

Minimum: 1 prospect response
Expected: 2 prospect responses
Outstanding: Over 2 prospect responses

♦ **Flyers (inserted in newspapers):** Create your flyer with a strong benefit-focused message, strong offer and call to action and then have it inserted into newspapers.

  ✓ **Try flyers in community newspapers:** Many small community newspapers will charge from $50 -$100 per thousand flyers that are inserted in their newspapers. In this case, you are also responsible for the printing costs.

  ✓ **Better chance of being seen:** Flyers are a nice alternative to small space ads. Small space ads often get lost among all of the other newspaper ads. But large flyers—8 1/2" x 11" in size—have a much better chance of being seen.

  ✓ **Paper color:** You can try to save some money by having your flyers printed on white paper. However a nice bright color, such as yellow, may be more of an attention-getter.

  ✓ **Design it well:** You have lots of space on a flyer, so you can describe your offer more elaborately and even include a personal letter, testimonials, a bio, etc. Don't include lots of wasted white space.

  ✓ **Know what numbers to expect:** Since you would normally include your insertions in small, community publications—larger publications would usually be cost prohibitive to insert a flyer—you may expect:

Local print publication (circulation per 10,000):
Minimum: 1-5 prospect responses
Expected: 6-10 prospect responses
Outstanding: Over 10 prospect responses

♦ **Flyers (posted or handed out):** Post your flyers in high traffic areas on bulletin and display boards, shop windows, etc. or hand them out.

✓ **Post your flyers:** It won't hurt to post your flyers on bulletin boards, shop windows, restaurants, check out counters or anyplace else where potential prospects will see them. Be sure you check with the store owner or person in charge to determine if you're allowed to do this. Or, you may opt to hand them out. You'll have to determine if this type of marketing is worth the time and effort it takes to do this. Remember, you don't have to do this yourself. A high school kid looking for a few extra bucks may be willing to help you out.

✓ **Design it well:** You have lots of space on a flyer, so you can describe your offer more elaborately and even include a personal letter, testimonials, a bio, etc. Don't include lots of wasted white space.

✓ **Know what numbers to expect:** It is difficult to estimate how many people will actually notice your posted flyer. Posted flyers are everywhere and they're invisible to most of us. However, you may get a few prospects here and there. So, if it's easy to post your flyer, it's worth a try. Some approximate numbers based on 100 flyers posted in high visibility areas:

Minimum: 1 prospect response
Expected: 2-3 prospect responses
Outstanding: Over 3 prospect responses

♦ **Direct mail letters:** It's only "junk mail" to the people who don't want it. Chocolate lovers love getting chocolate catalogs and offers in the mail. My husband and I go to plays by one of our local theater groups because of postcards we receive from them in the mail. By mailing your message, you have the opportunity to provide as little or as much detail as you like.

✓ **Buying a list:** There are a number of list companies available from whom you can purchase a list of names and addresses. You might choose to do this especially if you're going after a particular target, such as homeowners or women 35-49. Very often, the list provider can give you exactly what you're looking for, for as little as 10 cents per name, or as much as $1 per name—this depends on how targeted you want your list to be. Or if you're trying to save money, you can pull contact addresses right from the telephone book. However, your only targeting choice would then be geographical—people who live in a certain area.

✓ **First class or third:** With any direct mailing, you can either mail first class or third class. Third class takes a bit more work and you'll have to check with your post office to determine exactly how this must be done. I've heard nightmare stories about third class mail never making it to the recipients. However, these are rumors and I can't really tell you whether or not they're true or if third class mail is any less reliable than first-class mail. Of course, I've never been brave enough to take a chance on third class mail and I'll probably stick with first class.

✓ **Include a headline:** Just because it's a letter doesn't mean it doesn't deserve a headline. Determine what your offer to your potential prospects is and then include that offer in a headline.

✓ **Include a P.S.:** Don't forget to include a P.S. reminding potential prospects of your compelling offer. Very often, the P.S. is one of the first things they'll read when they open your letter.

✓ **Use computer generated labels:** Many direct mail books will tell you to hand write the addresses on your envelopes or to stick lots of low denomination stamps that equal the first class postage rate on the envelope. After extensive testing, we've come to the conclusion that this is nothing more than a waste of time. Print a sheet of labels, stick them on your envelopes and use one regular first class stamp.

✓ **Increasing response:** There's a good chance you'll increase your response by including a postage-paid post card that the person interested in your offer could mail to you. Always give lots of ways to respond, to make it easy for people to take advantage of your offer.

✓ **Know what numbers to expect.** Remember, not everyone who gets your letter will be interested in your offer, no matter how powerful it is. Not everyone is a prospect. Based on a mailing of 200 letters, expect these approximate prospect response rates:

Minimum: 1-2 prospect responses
Expected: 3-4 prospect responses
Outstanding: Over 4 prospect responses

✓ **Minimum test mailing:** The minimum direct mailing for a test mailing has to be at least 200 letters to give you a usable sample.

♦ **Direct mail flyers:** Flyers can also be mailed to potential prospects to generate some leads for your products and services.

✓ **How to use your flyer:** Use these as stand-alone pieces, stick them in addressed, stamped envelopes and mail. You can fold your flyers in thirds and use the opposite side of the paper for the person's mailing address and a stamp. This will eliminate the need for an envelope.

I usually don't recommend this route because there's a good chance the flyer will get ripped or crushed, either in the postman's bag or in the mail sorter. However, if you're using a very strong cardstock paper, this may be an option. This is called a self-mailer.

For whatever reason, self-mailers rarely get as good a response as flyers or letters mailed in envelopes. But, you may want to test both and use the format that produces the best response for you.

✓ **Know what numbers to expect:** Based on 200 mailed flyers:

Minimum: 1-2 prospect responses
Expected: 3-4 prospect responses
Outstanding: Over 4 prospect responses

♦ **Direct mail postcards:** Direct mail postcards are an alternative to direct mail letters.

✓ **Stay within postal regulations:** Rather than mailing a large 8 1/2" x 11" flyer, you may opt to mail a smaller postcard to potential prospects. Postcards are less expensive to mail than regular, first class envelopes. Check with the post office to be sure your postcard is within the regulatory length and width for first class postage, otherwise you may get your mailed postcards back with a "postage due" stamp.

✓ **Design it well:** Keep in mind that a portion of the postcard must be reserved for the person's address and the stamp. Check with the postal service for all of the design rules and guidelines.

✓ **Know what numbers to expect.** Based on 200 mailed postcards:

Minimum: 1 prospect response
Expected: 2 prospect responses
Outstanding: Over 2 prospect responses

◆ **Doorknob hangers:**

✓ **Hang on residential doorknobs:** Doorknob hangers can be hung on residential doorknobs throughout your community and may be a very inexpensive way of marketing your services or products.

✓ **Do it yourself or delegate it:** It does take time to walk from home to home, so you'll have to determine if the results you achieve are worth the time it will take to do so. Remember, you might be able to find a kid who would like to make some extra money, who is willing to do this for you.

✓ **Attach it to the doorknob:** Please note that doorknob hangers must be attached to doorknobs. It is illegal to put mail inside someone's mailbox unless you're a postal carrier.

✓ **Print it yourself or have it done professionally:** Companies such as Paper Direct sell special doorknob hanger blanks. You create your promotional copy on your computer and then print it up on this special paper. Be sure to also check with your local printer or copy shop to see if they can print doorknob hangers for you. They may be less expensive, especially if you're planning to get a significant number printed.

✓ **Know what numbers to expect:** Based on 200 doorknob hangers:

Minimum: 1 prospect response
Expected: 2 prospect responses
Outstanding: Over 2 prospect responses

- **Email:** Sending unsolicited, bulk email to strangers is taboo on the Internet. It's called spam—and people don't appreciate it. However, that doesn't mean that you can't contact prospects by email—people who have agreed to receive your email. This is also known as "opting-in."

- **Fax:** We wouldn't recommend faxing your message to strangers. It can be an intrusion and in some states, it's illegal. However, just like the notation made about "opt-in" email, the same is true for "opt-in" faxes.

- **Hand-outs or Samples:** In some cases, you might want to hand out a sample of what you're selling, such as a free chapter in your latest book or a mini-version of a product you've created, as long as the sample is being used as a prospect generator—in other words, your free offer of your idea-pak, or booklet, or tips-pak is clearly stated on the sample.

  - ✓ **Types of samples:** If you're selling a book, you might offer a free sample chapter if you can get it printed on a page or two. Be sure you include your booklet or info-pak offer on the chapter page. Or perhaps you can offer a laminated card of 3 organizing tips. Then state on the card that they can either go to your Web site or call you to receive your "complete," free info-pak of organizing tips.

    Please note: Many organizers have tried to hand out a gift certificate for a free, one-hour sample of their time to strangers. Generally, this offer is an offer to someone who is already a prospect; it is not the best offer to try to generate a prospect. While you may get a few strangers accepting this type of offer at this stage, it's too soon for most people. Your results will most likely be very low.

  - ✓ **Know what numbers to expect:** For every 200 samples distributed, you may expect:

    Handed out
    Minimum: 50 may take the sample / 1 may request the idea-pak
    Expected: 51-75 may take the sample / 2-3 may request the idea-pak
    Outstanding: Over 75 may take the sample / Over 3 may request the idea-pak

    Mailed out (obviously all 200 will get your sample)
    Minimum: 1 prospect response

Expected: 2 prospect responses

Outstanding: Over 2 prospect responses

♦ **In-Person visits (business, organizations, residential, etc.):** When you're face-to-face with your potential prospects, you can instantly build rapport and gain trust, plus you have their direct attention.

✓ **Door-to-door method:** Remember the old Avon method—someone ringing your bell and announcing herself as the "Avon Lady calling!"? Times have changed, but if you're in a safe community and you're willing to use this method, it can be very powerful. However, I must stress to be sure you're in a safe area if you choose to utilize this method, especially in residential areas.

✓ **Business visits:** If you're a very confident person, you might try to use this method with businesses or organizations. The face-to-face approach can be very strong, but it should only be used if you're excellent at qualifying someone—she must be genuinely interested in getting organized. Be sure you talk to the  decision-maker and tell her what you're offering immediately and how it can help her increase productivity, reduce workplace stress, or increase the bottom line. Remember, you're not trying to "sell" your services. At this initial prospecting stage, you're going to offer the decision maker your free idea-pak or booklet and hopefully build a little rapport.

✓ **Approach the person in "helping" mode:** You might consider saying something like, "I have a free gift that will help you and your staff increase productivity, reduce stress and increase your bottom line. It's a booklet that contains dozens of tips to help you and your staff manage time better." This is one case where you can give the person your information immediately." Make sure you qualify the person. Don't just hand out your info-pak at random.

✓ **Know what numbers to expect:** This depends on how many people you can visit in a day. Don't just give them your info-pak, or booklet, or audio cassette. Try your best to qualify them first. Remember, unless you pre-qualify them, you'll get a bunch of "unqualified" people taking your booklet, just because they're too embarrassed to say no when you're standing in front of them. Response rates are based on every 100 decision makers you speak with:

Minimum: 1-39 prospect responses
Expected: 40-60 prospect responses
Outstanding: Over 60 prospect responses

♦ **Internet:** There are many places on the Web where you can announce your offers and/or promote your own Web site. You can advertise on other Web sites, you can visit other Web sites and join in discussion forum conversations, you can write articles for Web sites and list your offer below your articles, you can write an ezine and offer it to potential prospects and so on. We'll talk a bit more about Web promotion later on in this guide.

♦ **Interviews (print, radio, television, Internet, etc.):** Is your subject matter, offer, product, service or business newsworthy? With the right slant, every business can be interesting. The media is always on the lookout for interesting stories or information to relay to their viewers, listeners or readers.

✓ **Offer your expertise:** You may offer your expertise to the media and find yourself being interviewed on the evening news or on a radio broadcast. Many successful marketers make excellent use of publicity and interviews to help deliver their message to their market. Don't forget to make mention of your offer.

✓ **You have to be proactive:** If you want to be interviewed, don't sit home expecting it to just happen. You must send out press releases and/or contact the media to discuss how an interview might interest their audience.

✓ **The possibilities are endless:** I have been interviewed by so many publications, including Delta In-Flight Magazine. A reporter from Delta interviewed me on the telephone for one hour. That resulted in my interview being printed and read in Delta's magazine on all Delta flights for two months and my offer was read and responded to by thousands of people.

✓ **Know what numbers to expect.** The potential here could be extremely high. If you're interviewed in a national magazine, the response rate could be in the thousands. For local publications, the response rate could be dozens or hundreds. Just remember, the response rate is going to be extremely low if you forget to ask to have your offer included with the article or broadcast. It's imperative. Expected numbers are:

National print media or broadcast publication (circulation per million):
Minimum: 1-199 prospect responses
Expected: 200-499 prospect responses
Outstanding: Over 500 prospect responses

Local print media or broadcast publication (circulation per 10,000):
Minimum: 1-10 prospect responses
Expected: 11-25 prospect responses
Outstanding: Over 25 prospect responses

Electronic publication (Web site or ezine: based on 1,000 visitors or subscribers):
Minimum: 1-10 prospect responses
Expected: 11-25 prospect responses
Outstanding: Over 25 prospect responses

♦ **Networking:** Everyone knows about 250 other people. Each of those people knows about 250 other people. The potential number of contacts for direct business or referrals is enormous.

✓ **Organizations to network in:** You might consider taking advantage of business networking events at the Chamber of Commerce, women's groups, business organizations, etc. You may directly find prospects at these events or you might meet someone who knows a person who may be a prospect for you.

✓ **Virtual networking:** You can also network online, in online discussion forums or chat sessions. This can be a very effective way to draw people to your Web site if you have one.

✓ **Here's what's really going on:** Very often, when you're networking with people you're trying to get people interested in what you do for a living—but the recipient is also trying to get you interested in what he or she does for a living. You may get some qualified prospects here and there, but be careful. The recipient may expect you to reciprocate. You might offer your organizing audio cassette to someone and she may come right back and offer you her make-up samples.

✓ **Know what numbers to expect:** This depends on how much networking you do and if you're in the right place at the right time. Of course, you may end up speaking with someone who knows a lot of people who would love to get organized, or someone who knows an organization that pays for time management speakers. For every 100 people you network with—by handing them your business card or postcard with your free offer stated on it, over time you may get:

Minimum: 1-10 prospect responses
Expected: 11-20 prospect responses
Outstanding: Over 20 prospect responses

However, if you're offering your free idea-pak or booklet on your business card and you hand your cards to someone you're networking with and ask him/her to refer you, the number of prospects you can then get over time will increase.

♦ **Newsletters:** Free print newsletters are terrific vehicles for delivering your messages. Just make sure the newsletter targets your primary prospects and you have a strong offer.

✓ **Content-rich:** If you decide to write your own newsletter, don't make it a newsletter full of ads or full of information about your company and services. Instead, include lots of helpful tips, ideas and articles. This doesn't mean you shouldn't include a strong offer. You should. But, it should be in addition to lots of helpful information.

✓ **Here's a neat idea:** When committing to write a newsletter, most people think the newsletter has to be written every single month—forever.

Instead, write 12 issues. Rather than naming them the current month (January 2012, February 2012, etc.), name them the current issue (Issue 1, Issue 2, etc.)

Then, when you add someone to your subscriber list, you start him off right from the beginning on Issue 1. No matter when someone signs up, he'll always get Issue 1 and then every other issue thereafter. You just have to keep track of who received what issues. Once you're finished writing your 12 issues, your work is done.

✓ **Saving time by purchasing a newsletter license:** If you don't feel that you have the time to write your own newsletter, you might consider purchasing the license to a newsletter that is already written. After paying for the license, you can insert your promotional flyers in your newsletters and mail them out.

> **Great Results**
>
> News releases are an excellent form of marketing. After sending out 20 news releases, the Milwaukee Business Journal immediately responded. They were interested in interviewing me.
>
> The reporter came by my home and interviewed me for over an hour. He then sent a photographer over to take photographs.
>
> This resulted in a two-page spread—with a color photo—thousands of Web site visitors, and hundreds of sales.
>
> The really nice thing is, I only invested around $7.00 in printing and postage!

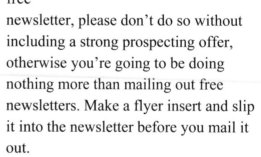

✓ **Insert your offer:** If you're going to send out a free newsletter, please don't do so without including a strong prospecting offer, otherwise you're going to be doing nothing more than mailing out free newsletters. Make a flyer insert and slip it into the newsletter before you mail it out.

✓ **Know what numbers to expect:** If you send out a print newsletter as a prospect generator, you can probably expect numbers similar to direct mail flyers. For every 200 newsletters you mail, you may expect:

Minimum: 1 prospect response
Expected: 2 prospect responses
Outstanding: Over 2 prospect responses

♦ **News releases:** The media is always looking for items of interest. With News Releases you can get your message out for little or no cost.

✓ **Make it interesting:** News releases are free, but they are not ads. If you write your news release to sound like an ad, there's a good chance it won't get printed. It must be an interesting story, tips, or a free e-book or booklet you're offering to the public.

✓ **The media will be doing a "favor" for you by printing your release:** The media is not required to print your news release. If they feel it will benefit their audience and they have room for it, they may run it.

✓ **Targeting the correct editor:** Try to send your news release to a specific editor when possible. This may increase the chance that your news release will get to the right person and be read. If you're sending out bulk news releases, then address the release "To the Editor" or "To the Business Editor" or "To the Lifestyles Editor."

✓ **Don't annoy the editor:** Don't bug the editor by calling and asking if your news release has been printed yet. Editors are busy people with pressing deadlines. If you annoy them, you may never get a news release printed in that particular paper.

✓ **Finding out if it was printed:** Unfortunately, you'll only know if your news release has been printed if you actually see it in the paper, if someone you know sees it in the paper and contacts you, or if you begin getting responses to your offer within the news release.

If you're getting response and people are asking for the specific offer you mentioned in your news release, you'll know your news release was picked up by one of the publications.

If you want to know which one, you can always ask the person in what paper they read about you, or on what radio station they heard about you.

✓ **Know what numbers to expect:** For every 100 news releases you send out, you should shoot for a 1-4% response rate. That means that 1 to 4 out of every hundred papers would print your news release. Once your release is accepted, of course, readers, listeners or viewers will then be responding to your offer.

**Media that will pick up your news release
(100 news releases mailed):**
Minimum: 1 that prints/uses the release
Expected: 2-3 that print/use the release
Outstanding: Over 3 that print/use the release

Once your news release is printed:

**National print media or broadcast publication
(circulation per million):**
Minimum: 1-199 prospect responses
Expected: 200-499 prospect responses
Outstanding: Over 500 prospect responses

**Local print media or broadcast publication
(circulation per 10,000):**
Minimum: 1-10 prospect responses
Expected: 11-25 prospect responses
Outstanding: Over 25 prospect responses

**Electronic publication
(Web site or ezine: based on 1,000 visitors or subscribers):**
Minimum: 1-10 prospect responses
Expected: 11-25 prospect responses
Outstanding: Over 25 prospect responses

♦ **Radio commercials:** You may try to use radio commercials as one of your marketing vehicles. However, for new organizers, it's probably not the way to go due to the high cost. Once your business is established, however, you might want to test some radio spots to determine how many prospects you can generate.

✓ **Stick to the important information:** You're only going to get a minute or less, so don't waste time trying to make your radio spot funny, clever or cute. Mention your free offer—a few times if possible.

Also, if you have a Web site where people can request your free offer, mention your Web site—a few times. In this case, don't even bother to mention your phone number. Most people won't have a pen in their hands and most people won't remember your phone number. Web sites are a bit easier to remember. Hint: If I had 30 seconds of radio airtime, my commercial would sound something like this:

"Want a free idea-pak filled with dozens of tips to help you get organized? Visit www.getorganizednow.com . . . Want a free idea-pak filled with dozens of tips to help you get organized? Visit www.getorganizednow.com . . ."

. . .and I'd keeping repeating this until my time was up! I'm only half joking.

✓ **Know what numbers to expect:** This depends on lots of criteria including whether or not the listeners are your target, what time of the day your spot airs, how many spots you run, how professional your spot is, if your radio commercial states your offer clearly, etc.

Based on 1,000 listeners, 5 spots, high listener time

If they have to remember your phone number:
Minimum: 1-3 prospect responses
Expected: 5-7 prospect responses
Outstanding: Over 7 prospect responses

If they have to remember your Web site and it's simple and easy to remember:
Minimum: 1-10 prospect responses
Expected: 11-20 prospect responses
Outstanding: Over 20 prospect responses

♦ **Radio programs (your own):** Imagine the credibility you can gain by having your own radio program. It's possible, but would be very challenging for a new organizer. However, once you're established, you might want to branch out and give it a try. Contact your local radio stations and propose your idea for an informative and fun show on getting organized, or consider your own Internet-based radio show!

✓ **Know what numbers to expect:** If you can get your own radio program, you can get two things: a) lots of credibility and b) prospects. Remember, if your program airs at 2:00AM, you'll get much less response then if your program airs at 10:00AM.

The radio station may not be able to promise you a particular time slot and you may even want to take a strange timeslot to get your foot in the door. But your goal should be to air your show—and state your offer—at a time when lots of people are actually listening. If you end up doing a radio show between 6:30AM and 10:00PM, you can potentially get hundreds— or thousands—of responses. Response based on 200 listeners, listening to your radio program airing between 6:30AM and 10:00PM is:

If they have to remember your phone number:
Minimum: 1-20 prospect responses per show
Expected: 21-30 prospect responses per show
Outstanding: Over 30 prospect responses per show

If they have to remember your Web site and it's simple and easy to remember:
Minimum: 1-40 prospect responses per show
Expected: 41-60 prospect responses per show
Outstanding: Over 60 prospect responses per show

◆ **Referrals:** Think of happy customers as your marketing goldmine. These are the people who loved your product or service so much, that they want to tell their friends, relatives and associates about it. You may get some referrals by not doing anything at all. However, a more proactive approach can significantly increase your referral potential.

  ✓ **Use happy customers as your sales force:** Have a compelling prospecting offer printed on your business cards, brochures or a postcard and hand these materials out to your happy customers. Tell them that you have a "very special offer" for people who are interested in getting organized, or relocating, or organizing memorabilia, etc. Ask them to hand out your postcard, business card, etc. to their family, friends and associates.

  ✓ **Use associates, friends and acquaintances as your sales force:** Have a compelling prospecting offer printed on your business cards, brochures, or postcards and hand these materials out to your associates, friends and acquaintances. Tell them that you have a "very special offer" for people who are interested in getting organized, or relocating, or organizing memorabilia, etc. Ask them to hand out your postcard, business card, etc. to their family, friends and associates.

✓ **Thank your referrals:** You might consider making an offer to your potential referrer, such as, "I value every referral I get from you. For every sale I make based on one of your referrals, you'll get . . ." The reward could be money, or discounts, or products, etc. This will give the potential referrers a reason to refer your business.

✓ **The more subtle approach:** If you'd prefer not to make a special offer to your customers for one reason or another—not everyone is comfortable doing this—then say, "I'd love it if you would hand out my business card to anyone who you feel might benefit from my free offer of _____."

Hand them your business cards or postcards and leave it at that. If you get a referral from one of your customers, which turns into a sale, be sure to send the referrer a gift—such as a gift basket or a plant—or a thank you letter.

✓ **Know what numbers to expect:** Just because you asked your potential referrers for referrals, doesn't in any way mean they are going to be thinking about your business all the time. People are busy and you can't expect them to be proactively and constantly promoting your business.

Keep an active referral system in progress. Send something to your potential referrers every single month—such as an organizing tips newsletter—so they remember to refer you. Here are some approximate numbers you might expect for every 100 potential referrers to whom you give your prospect generating business card or post card:

Referrals from happy customers:
Minimum: 1-15 prospect referrals
Expected: 16-30 prospect referrals
Outstanding: Over 30 prospect referrals

Referrals from family, friends or associates:
Minimum: 1-10 prospect referrals

Expected: 11-20 prospect referrals
Outstanding: Over 20 prospect referrals

♦ **Signage (billboards, magnetic signs, wall signs, counter signs, etc.):**
Everywhere you look there's a sign! Billboards, store front signs, in-store signs, wall signs, even magnetic car signs. Some professional organizers attach magnetic signs to their cars. Others use signs and posters at trade shows. Remember however, that using signs is a passive system. Just because your sign is posted somewhere, doesn't mean that tons of people are actually going to see it, or read it.

✓ **Make sure it can be seen.** If you use a sign, be sure your offer is clearly displayed and is big enough to be seen from a distance. If the typical person will see your sign from 20-25 feet away, be sure that you step back 25 feet and make sure the type is clear and legible.

Also, if your sign is going to be used in a dimly lit room, be sure you don't use dark, hard-to-see colors. Be aware of your background. If the sign is going to be placed on a white wall, don't make your sign white. Make it a color that will stand out.

✓ **Don't write a book:** Signs are meant to grab the reader's attention immediately. The reader should be able to get your message within a few seconds. State your offer clearly and do it with as few words as possible.

✓ **Know what numbers to expect:** For every 500 people that actually see and read your sign (not the people that just walk by; they must see "and" read it) here are some approximate response rates:

Minimum: 1 response
Expected: 1-2 responses
Outstanding: Over 2 responses

♦ **Telephone (telemarketing):** As long as you honor those who do not wish to be called (find out about your state's *Do Not Call List*), you can use the phone to build your prospect list. You may be saying to yourself, "Oh, I would never want to cold call people. I hate when telemarketers call me." Just so you know, if telemarketing didn't work, then the bigger companies wouldn't be using it.

Telemarketing is still a strong way to get response to the offers that interest people. Although it might be distasteful for some people to do, telemarketing can be very effective.

✓ **Ask for the correct person:** When you cold call, if you don't get the person you'd like to speak to, ask for the woman of the house, or the man of the house, or the business owner, etc. When that person takes your call, tell him about your special offer and how it could benefit him. Say, for example, "I have a wonderful free kit that can help you organize all the paper in your life. There's no obligation and I would love to send you one. If you would like one, I can drop it in the mail today."

✓ **Don't try to sell; build rapport:** Don't try to force the recipient to say yes. Try to build some rapport and if you're skilled at doing this, qualified people will say yes. Just know that you may have to call 10-30 people before you hear, "Sure, send it along."

✓ **A contact means you actually spoke to the decision maker:** When you call people, if you get their answering machine, just hang up. Don't bother to leave a message, because the majority of people will not call back. Try to call at a different time of the day tomorrow and make at least 5 or 6 attempts to speak to the decision maker before you give up.

✓ **Know what numbers to expect:** For every 100 decision makers that you speak to:

Minimum: 1-6 prospect responses
Expected: 7-10 prospect responses
Outstanding: Over 10 prospect responses

♦ **Television commercials (cable or commercial):** For a brand new organizer, the expense of a television commercial may be cost-prohibitive. However, once you're established and have a wide array of services and products to sell, you may choose it as one of your methods for getting your prospecting offer to the masses. Keep in mind that cable TV is a lot less expensive, although you can't reach as many people.

✓ **Know what numbers to expect:** This depends on lots of criteria including whether the viewers are your target, what time of the day your television spot airs, how many spots you run, how professional your spot is, if your TV commercial states your offer clearly, etc.

 Based on 1,000 viewers:

If they have to remember your phone number:
Minimum: 1-6 prospect responses
Expected: 7-14 prospect responses
Outstanding: Over 14 prospect responses

If they have to remember your Web site and it's simple and easy to remember :
Minimum: 1-12 prospect responses
Expected: 13-25 prospect responses
Outstanding: Over 25 prospect responses

♦ **Television program (your own):** If you're really ambitious, you may even host your own organizing tips program or time management program, either on local commercial television or on cable.

✓ **Know what numbers to expect:** If you can get your own television program, you can get two things: a) lots of credibility and b) prospects. Remember, if your program airs at 2:00AM, you'll get much less response then if your program airs at 10:00AM. If you're going to do a television show, shoot for a reasonable time of the day. The television station may not be able to promise you a particular time slot and you may even want to take a strange time slot to get your foot in the door. But your goal should be to air your show at a time when lots of people are actually watching. If you end up doing a TV show during high viewing times and you mention your offer, you can potentially get hundreds—or thousands—of responses. Rates based on your TV program airing between 6:30AM and 10:00PM are:

If they have to remember your phone number:
Minimum: 1-40 prospect responses per show
Expected: 41-60 prospect responses per show
Outstanding: Over 60 prospect responses per show

If they have to remember your Web site and it's simple and easy to remember:
Minimum: 1-80 prospect responses per show
Expected: 81-120 prospect responses per show
Outstanding: Over 120 prospect responses per show

♦ **Trade shows:** There are many opportunities available for you to rent space or a booth at a trade show. It's an excellent way to meet potential prospects face-to-face. You will have to pay for the booth and prices vary depending on what organization is sponsoring the event.

   ✓ **Finding trade shows:** Keep an eye on local newspapers so you're aware of trade shows coming up in your vicinity. Check with your local Chamber of Commerce for information on upcoming events.

   ✓ **Don't just hand out stuff:** Very often, businesses have tons of brochures and literature spread out at a tradeshow booth. This is ineffective. You'll just be handing out literature that will get dumped in the trash as soon as people leave the event—or possibly even before they leave. Rather than just handing stuff out, make an offer to your prospects. Give them cards that can be filled out with their contact information and then handed back to you, to receive your free tips-pak, or tips brochure, etc. You can then mail them your idea-pak or booklet a few days after the trade show.

   ✓ **Holding contests:** Sometimes businesses hold contests to win a prize. To do so, they just ask people to drop their business cards in a fishbowl. People usually enter contests to win the prize—not necessarily because they have a need for your services or products. This does not mean you shouldn't have a contest. Just know that many people who enter your contest are not necessarily qualified prospects. You can qualify them later when you follow up with them.

✓ **Prizes:** Some organizers try to give away a free hour of organizing consulting time as a prize. While you will get a few people who enter your contest, you'll get many more names if you offer something less frightening to people, such as a book, an audio cassette, a planner, etc. Just make sure the item is directly related to what you do.

✓ **Designing your booth:** Designing your booth can get very expensive, very quickly. Be careful of spending more money on designing your booth, than you can possibly make back later.

Keep it simple. If you already have colors you use for your business cards and/or stationery, use those colors for your booth, this way everything will be consistent. Signage is important. If you're trying to get a message across, make a large sign that can be seen easily from a distance. Anything you can include that will be interactive, like a computer demo or a game, will draw people to your booth.

Some people like to include aromatherapy candles for a nicer atmosphere. Just realize that the most important thing you should concentrate on is your offer. No matter how lovely your booth is, if your offer is weak, your response rate will also be weak.

✓ **Know what numbers to expect:** For every 200 people who stop by your booth, these are the number of people you can expect to fill out your free offer request card (contest entries not included):

Minimum: 1-20 prospect responses
Expected: 21-50 prospect responses
Outstanding: Over 50 prospect responses

♦ **Web site (your own):** More and more people are turning to the Internet for information about products and services. The time is rapidly approaching when all businesses will need to have a presence on the Web, or they'll be left behind. Don't be left in the dust.

✓ **Very inexpensive:** Whether you're just selling your organizing services locally or you have many products and services that you're selling locally, nationally and internationally, a Web site is a cost-effective way to market your business. You can have a full-color site. No postage involved. Lots of interaction. Lots of opportunities.

✓ **Choose the right type of Web site:** You can't create a Web site and then expect sales. It takes work to build an effective, income-producing Web site. So, it's very important to determine what your main goal for having a Web site is. If you're using it for credibility purposes and to send people there who you come into personal contact with, you may opt for the "Image/brochure style" Web site. However, if you're planning to make money from your Web site, you'll need to develop a "content-rich" Web site. We'll be discussing this later on in this guide.

My Offer

Since I started my business, my main offer has been my "Get Organized Now! Idea Pak." It contains over 50 tips and ideas to help organize your home, your office and your life.

It only took me a few hours to compile the tips. I first had a print version for people who I was promoting to offline. It was on one piece of legal size paper and was folded in fourths.

Then, I went to an electronic version, typed as a text document, for those people that are online. I have never changed my offer and I don't plan on changing it anytime in the near future. I did the work once, and I use it over and over again. The results have been remarkable. I get approximately 65,000 people asking for my electronic idea-pak each year!

✓ **Know what numbers to expect:** Approximate estimations are based on the number of new unique visitors you get coming to your Web site:

- Minimum: 1-10% prospect response
- Expected: 11-20% prospect response
- Outstanding: Over 20% prospect response

♦ **Ezine:** A free ezine can be an effective way to generate prospects for your products or services. An ezine is an email newsletter, which is sent out to "opt-in" recipients—people who request to receive it— on a regular basis.

✓ **Content-rich and send often:** If you're planning to make your Web site a profitable one, a regular ezine is essential. The majority of your ezine must include helpful tips and you should also include a small section recommending your products or services. Ezines should be sent out once or twice a month—at minimum, but preferably weekly.

✓ **Promote your offer:** In order to get people to sign up for your ezine, you must proactively market its availability. Some of this can be done by getting people to visit your Web site and promoting the free ezine prominently. In addition, you can announce your ezine on various sites throughout the Internet. Plus, don't forget about the offline methods to get people on your list, such as mentioning its availability in your marketing materials, on your business cards, during a presentation, etc.

✓ **People must opt-in:** If people have requested to receive your information from you, or your email newsletter, or updates on your Web site, that means they've "opted-in" or have agreed to receive your messages. They may have seen your Web site, or heard about you from a friend, etc. In this case, you're free to use email as a marketing vehicle.

✓ **Know what numbers to expect:** Approximate estimations are based on the number of "new" unique visitors you get coming to your Web site:

Minimum: 1-5% prospect response
Expected: 6-10% prospect response
Outstanding: Over 10% prospect response

♦ **Free workshops or seminars:** If you can stand up in front of an audience and present organizing tips, or time management tips, etc. then you have a great way to generate prospects for your business. To get assistance with your public speaking skills, read some books that specialize in public speaking or visit Toastmasters International: www.toastmasters.org

✓ **Content-rich:** An hour's worth of useful tips may be all it takes to generate lots of prospects for your business. Remember, this is a "tips" presentation; not a "sales" presentation. Don't be afraid to tell people exactly what to do. Just because you tell them how to get organized, doesn't mean they'll remember what you say, understand what you say or want to do what you say. I never hold back any information and I generate lots of prospects and sales from my free presentations.

✓ **Number of attendees:** I use this marketing vehicle all the time and while some of the audiences are below 20 people, many of them are 100 people or more.

- ✓ **Who? Where?:** Be creative. Free seminars can be offered to bookstores, libraries, Chambers, organizations, businesses, churches—the possibilities are endless. Do your best to obtain a free meeting room.

- ✓ **Slides? Overheads?:** I've done presentations both with and without audio/video equipment. This depends on where you're doing the presentation, if it's worth making slides or transparencies or a Powerpoint presentation for the number of attendees, what equipment is available, etc.

    If you're given the choice, go the extra step and include slides, transparencies or a Powerpoint presentation. It will increase the professionalism and the interest of your presentation substantially.

- ✓ **Know what numbers to expect:** I've done hundreds of free seminars for 20 people or less, 90% of which resulted in thousands of dollars in new projects. There's lots of potential here, if you feel comfortable talking in front of a group.

    Asking people to attend a presentation—even a free one—is asking a lot more from prospects than requesting your free booklet. Therefore, you aren't going to get as many responses as you might for your other offers.

    To determine the approximate response you can expect, take the vehicle response numbers you already learned in this guide—for direct mail, postcards, flyers, etc.—and divide them in half.

    If you do a presentation where the attendees are invited by the organization, such as a Chamber of Commerce, or a church, for every 50 attendees you can expect the following number to request your free idea-pak or booklet at the presentation:

    Minimum: 1-10% prospect responses
    Expected: 10-20% prospect responses
    Outstanding: Over 20% prospect responses

Your call to action

Different people respond to different offers in different ways. That's why just giving someone the option of responding to your offer by telephone is going to eliminate some of those people who would have contacted you if you gave them a different method to respond.

When I see something I want, I don't have too much of a problem picking up the telephone and asking for it. However, there are lots of people who just won't do this. Remember, many people are afraid that if they call, they will have to speak to an aggressive salesperson.

So, your best bet is to always offer people a few different ways to respond. Allow them to call, fax, email, visit and/or mail.

Your sense of urgency

As a professional organizer, you're probably well aware of the incredible tendency people have to procrastinate. Even if you offer something very enticing, many people will place your offer in a pile of papers which is bound to get lost for months, if not forever.

By putting a sense of urgency in your offer, you'll get people to take action right now. Include phrases such as "Call within 10 days and you'll also get," or "Offer valid for September only," or "Only 100 left. Call today," or "Offer ends on January 15," or "Hurry. Supplies Limited," or "Offers ends soon."

Tracking your marketing pieces

It is vital for you to track exactly what marketing pieces are working for you and which are not. This way, you're only investing your money in the ones that are bringing in response and not wasting your money on those that don't bring in response. Attach a fictitious tracking code to each of your marketing efforts. For instance, include a fictitious code in your state Yellow Pages ad, such as "Ask for Idea-Pak #12," and another fictitious code in your local Yellow Pages ad such as "Ask for Ext 22," etc.

Do the same for your newspaper ads, your flyers, your letters, etc. If it's a marketing piece your prospect will be mailing or faxing in, make sure it has a printed code that identifies that particular marketing piece.

Use the Prospect Report and Marketing Results Log forms in this guide.

When people call you, immediately ask them for the code number on the marketing piece they're holding. Jot the number down on your tracking log. You'll know exactly where all of your leads are coming from. Keep these numbers in a safe place and refer to them often. This is the only way you'll know which vehicles are producing results and which are not.

Creating your offer (info-pak, tips booklet, report, etc.)

Your offer should almost always include free tips related to what you are selling. For instance, if you're selling hands-on organizing services, your info-pak might be called, "32 Tips To Help You Organize Your Home," or "27 Ways To Get Your Office Filing System Under Control." If you're selling time management consulting or workshops, you might choose a title like, "14 Secrets To Eliminate Procrastination" or "21 Ideas To Increase Your Staff Productivity."

Don't just send out a brochure or a letter. Remember, in order to get the highest number of people responding, you must include a compelling offer.

> **I generated over $4000 in organizing projects from one free presentation**
>
> I've had phenomenal response to my free workshops. Out of all the marketing vehicles, this vehicle is definitely on my "Top 5 List."
>
> For instance, I once did a presentation to a group of Ph.D.'s who belonged to a counseling group. There were only 18 people who attended this workshop.
>
> I put together a one-hour organizing tips presentation and used Powerpoint to come up with some overhead transparencies as visuals.
>
> This simple presentation resulted in over $4,000 in sales, including referral sales, over a 2 month period—all for a tiny $25 investment in handout materials.

In addition to your tips, you can also include some or all of the following:

- a cover letter
- your brochure
- a few business cards
- client testimonials
- press clippings or published articles

- an issue of your newsletter
- your biography
- a description of your services/products
- possibly some average price ranges

Here are two popular ways of doing this:

1) Prioritize these items—cover letter first, tips right behind your cover letter, any other pages after these items—and place everything in a #10 envelope or a catalog envelope. Be careful. The more paper you add, the more postage you'll have to attach.

2) Place these items in an attractive presentation folder. If you use this method, put the free tips on the left side of the folder and your cover letter on the right side of the folder, so these are the first two papers the prospect will see when he or she opens the folder. You might also wish to put a label on the front of the folder, if it's not already imprinted, with your company name, logo and contact information.

Chapter 7
Generating Customers

Getting response

Once you have an effective offer out there and you begin to receive responses, you are at the beginning of building relationships, which you will be working on converting into first-time sales, repeat sales and referral sales.

As you get calls, if the people are friendly and/or talkative, take the time to listen, talk to them, ask questions and begin building friendly relationships.

Be sure to get the information you'll need to follow-up with them. This will include their name, address, phone number and perhaps their email address. (Note: if you're prospecting online, you may *only* need their email address.) You should then store this information in a computer database, contact manager, or in a notebook or index card file. You should also record the proper information on your Prospect Report and Vehicle Results log.

Within a day or two, mail the booklet or info-pak you promised. Include the free tips, a thank you letter, a brochure if you have one and some information about the service or product you're selling. Whatever you do, don't wait a week or two before you mail this information out. It's very important to be prompt. If you're not, the person may lose interest in your offer.

In addition, take a few moments to record when your first follow-up date will be, whether that follow-up will be by phone, mail, email, etc. For organizing or consulting services, follow-up phone calls will most likely be the most effective way to get your foot in the door.

What services or products do my prospects want?

People are constantly looking for solutions to their problems. Your job is to find out what their problems are and come up with ways you can help solve those problems and make a profit.

Many people think that they can come up with a service or a product and then sell it. It really doesn't work that way. Just because you want to sell something, doesn't necessarily mean that the people in your marketplace want to buy it.

That's why it's so important to a) know who you're selling to and b) know what they want to buy.

Following-up

Effectively converting a prospect into a customer takes time, experience and skill. Most people get all the way up to this step and then end up losing the sale. They're afraid of the gatekeeper. They're afraid of rejection. They don't know exactly what to say. They're not sure how to handle objections.

Follow-up phone calls are one of the most effective ways for professional organizers to get in the door. If you're selling organizing services or consulting, having the skill to follow-up with people using the telephone, is very important. You could follow up by mail, or with a postcard, but those methods are generally going to be much weaker than a phone call.

If you're selling products, like filing systems or books, you can certainly follow-up with other sources in addition to the telephone, such as direct mail letters, print newsletters or ezines.

When you're first starting out, the follow up process can be both exhausting and disheartening. If you don't follow-up correctly, you'll get lots of responses like, "I'm really not interested," or "No thanks."

Once you begin to gain the necessary follow-up skills you need, however, you'll realize that for every so many prospects you call, you will be able to get an appointment. For example, depending on your skill level, you may have to contact anywhere from 5 to 25 prospects, to make one sale. Once you determine your follow-up ratio, for the most part, you'll be able to use that same ratio in the future. Let's say you get 1 appointment for every 10 prospects you contact. You should then make 2 appointments for every 20 prospects, 3 appointments for every 30 prospects and so on.

Getting past the gatekeeper

If your prospects are people in business, very often there will be somebody taking their phone calls—often an administrative assistant or a receptionist. These people, also known as gatekeepers, will do their best to block you from getting through to his/her boss. A business owner or manager can't be interrupted by sales calls all day long, so the gatekeeper provides this much needed service for his/her employer. There are some techniques you could use to get past the gatekeeper. You can read about these techniques in any good sales book.

One good method I've found is to call when the gatekeeper isn't there. Call before 8:30 in the morning, or call after 5:00 at night. Very often, the business owner or manager picks up his or her phone when the gatekeeper isn't there.

Some business people use their voicemail as an electronic gatekeeper. You can try to leave a message; some people will call you back; others will not. For those who do not, don't get insulted. Your prospects are busy with a million other things and they're not going to go out of their way to call you.

I usually don't leave voicemail messages for prospects. I call them back later. If you must leave a message, make it as enticing as possible so you have the best chance possible to get a call back. Use other methods in addition, such as direct mail, postcards, or newsletters.

How often should I follow-up with my prospects?

This depends on a number of variables, including your skill, the cost of the service you're trying to sell, the type of service you're trying to sell, how interested a particular prospect sounds, etc. However, it is important for you to follow up regularly. For prospects that sound hot, try to get the appointment on the first or second follow-up call. Once per month is probably a good start for all other prospects that are warm.

Realize also that it could take anywhere from 1 to 12 follow-ups to actually get an appointment. If you can't get the appointment in 12 follow-ups, you've probably overestimated the interest level of this prospect.

There are a number of marketing books available on handling objections, such as "the price is too high," "I'm not ready right now," "I'm still thinking about it," etc. If you find that you're constantly getting hit with objections that you can't respond to effectively, you should seriously consider brushing up on your follow-up skills.

What should I say when I follow up?

When following up, it's very important to sound natural. You could certainly have a regular script that you use, but it should not sound like you're reading. Practice using a tape recorder, or perhaps rehearsing with a friend, until you feel it is natural enough to use on a prospect.

Never call a prospect and say, "Are you ready to buy yet?" This is very pushy and will turn off many of your prospects immediately. Once your prospects are turned off, you can pretty much forget about getting an appointment from that point on.

Never call a prospect just to say, "Just calling to see how everything is going." This is a waste of your time and a waste of your prospect's time. When you call, offer something that will get you closer to the sale.

Generally, for professional organizers, it's very difficult to get the sale, without first meeting with the person. If you can get the sale without this step, good for you. If you can't, your next goal should be to meet your prospect in person.

You can try to ask for an appointment. However, this may be too big of a leap for many prospects. If it is, you can experiment with other offers to get closer to the sale. Some examples are . . .

♦ offer to give them a 20-minute free tips presentation at their home, home office or business

♦ offer to give them an hour's worth of your time for free

♦ offer to schedule a free needs analysis, either in person or on the telephone

You'll notice that all of these offers are focused on getting you in front of your prospects, which is exactly what you want. As you share your tips with them, they will get to *know, like and trust you.* During your tips presentation you can, of course, tie in some of your services/products and how they can help your prospects solve their problems.

Keep detailed notes about each prospect you contact, so you're prepared for the next call. If your prospect tells you anything personal, such as an upcoming birthday, be sure to send her a birthday card when the date rolls around. Or if the prospect tells you he enjoys golf, you might consider sending him an interesting article about golf. This will show the prospect that you really care.

Do I have to offer a "free" consultation/needs analysis?

It has always been my recommendation to offer potential customers a free consultation or needs analysis. This is a good time for you to become familiar with your prospect's problem and determine what solutions you'll be able to offer.

A free analysis is actually a vital part of your sales system. It helps build rapport and gives your prospect the opportunity to get to *know, like and trust you*.

If you decide to charge people for a needs analysis, you're going to dramatically lower your number of appointments, which will lower your number of sales. The majority of people will not pay for a needs analysis. It's just like asking someone to pay for a sales presentation. Most professional companies that truly wish to help people offer a free consultation. I recommend that you do too.

Do I have to do a needs analysis in person?

You will get a better idea of what a particular job is going to entail if you meet with your prospect in person. There's no doubt about that. If the person is close enough in proximity, I would suggest you hop in your car and do a free, face-to-face consultation. This will give you the opportunity to meet the potential customer, determine his/her needs, more accurately price out the job and start building a solid relationship.

However, this is not always possible. Let's say you get a call from a prospect who is over 90 minutes away. In this case, you might decide to meet him in person if you feel this is almost a sure-shot job. Or you might decide to test your needs analysis skills over the telephone and save yourself the trip. If you can convert a prospect to a customer right on the telephone, that's excellent.

Chapter 8
The Appointment

What do I do when I meet my prospect for the first time?

When you first meet or speak to a prospect about an organizing or consulting job, it is extremely important that you do everything you can to make sure the prospect feels at ease. Try to begin with some friendly talk—perhaps about the weather, or a ball game, or the town, or something enlightening you just heard on the radio.

Don't ever start off complaining about anything—even the weather. Attempt to say something very positive or uplifting. Then, ask a simple question to get your prospect talking to you. For instance, "I just love this town. How long have you lived here?" or "What beautiful weather we're having today. Have you had a chance to get outside at all?" Keep smiling and be friendly.

If the prospect says something like, "I'm embarrassed to even show you my mess," put her at ease as quickly as possible. Say things like, "Please don't worry about it. I'm here to offer you some help," or "Believe me, this job isn't as overwhelming as it might seem to you right now."

Don't say things like, "Oh my . . . this seems like a really huge job," and don't allow your body language to reflect these words either. A prospect will pick up on raised eyebrows in an instant and if he or she begins to feel uncomfortable, there's a good chance you're adding an obstacle to the sale.

Confidentiality

One other very important aspect of putting prospects at ease, is ensuring them that the organizing jobs or sessions you conduct and any materials you see or things you hear, will be kept completely confidential.

Many prospects, especially when it comes to organizing, are concerned that their personal information might be given to someone else. Do everything you can to make sure the prospect trusts you. Never release the names of your prospects or customers, or any information about them, without a written agreement that is signed by both the prospect/customer and you.

How do I conduct a needs analysis?

Properly assessing the situation takes a little bit of experience, but in time, you'll be able to look around and get a good sense of what needs to be done. You have four major goals that you must try to accomplish during your needs analysis:

1) To make sure you put the prospect at ease.

2) To assess the situation.

3) To offer a solution that sounds irresistible to the prospect.

4) To close the sale.

Prior to coming up with a price and a proposal for your services or products, determine exactly what problem your prospect needs solved. You can't ask the prospect what he or she needs. You're the expert and the prospect is looking to you for a solution. First, you must determine exactly what the problem is. Is this person just a messy person, or is he unfamiliar with effective paper flow systems? Does this person have too much to do, or does she have a difficult time prioritizing her projects?

Be sure you're always "listening" to your prospects' problems. Really try to understand what they are telling you. Very often, the true problem is hidden. The answers to these types of questions come with knowledge of your field. Be prepared for each Needs Analysis. As the prospect is telling you what his/her problems are, jot down any notes on an Assessment form. Having a standard form is very important. You should be able to check off the problem areas quickly, rather than writing long essays about the problem(s). If you're spending all of your time writing, you're not really listening to your prospect.

Be aware of your surroundings. Are you sitting in the area that needs to be organized? If so, you might want to make a quick sketch that you can refer to later. Does this client have filing cabinets? How many drawers are there? If you're going to be helping this person with his filing, this is good information to jot down.

> **Control the Situation**
>
> After consulting with a client to help her manage her time, she showed me her husband's office. It was completely disorganized. She asked me if I would assist her in getting it organized.
>
> Her husband overheard our conversation and said, "I like it the way it is. It doesn't need to be organized."
>
> My response was, "I'm sorry, but I'd prefer not to get in the middle of this. You guys talk it out, and if you both decide you need help, give me a call and I'll meet with both of you to determine a good plan of action you can both live with."
>
> You don't have to accept every organizing job—especially those that make you uncomfortable for one reason or another.

In some cases, you might need to ask the prospect to show you what she's using as her current system. Ask if you can look inside her filing cabinet to get an idea of her current filing system. Or, if you'll be conducting time management consulting, talk to the prospect a bit about what her main concerns are. Empathize with her.

In all cases, be sure to jot down notes. In most cases, you'll be happy you did. You'll now have something to refer to when pricing out this job, or if you have to contact this prospect later on.

Don't, in any way, indicate to the prospect that this is going to be a "huge" job. The last thing you want to do is scare him/her, because if you do, there's a good chance you won't get the job.

What do I do if I don't want the job?

If, after you assess the situation, you don't feel like you can help this prospect for one reason or another, tell the prospect right there and then. Don't let the situation drag on and certainly don't take on a job you're not comfortable with.

You may be asking, "Why would I ever turn down a job?" Here are a few possible situations:

♦ **You don't have the skill.** Let's say you were expecting to do a simple filing job for this prospect, but as it turns out, you determine that this person actually needs a project management system. Since you don't have expertise in this area, you wouldn't want to test out your efforts on a paying client. Instead, you might want to tell this prospect that you'll have to refer her/him to someone with more experience in this type of situation.

♦ **You aren't comfortable with the situation.** Sometimes, a wife may want to organize her husband's desk area, but the husband is totally against it and doesn't want anyone touching his stuff. The wife might insist that you come to her home, while the husband is at work and just do the job without him knowing about it. Since this is a touchy situation and you don't want to come in between a relationship squabble, this may not be the best type of job to take on. You can tell the prospect that you don't feel very comfortable with this type of situation.

♦ **You are uncomfortable with the surroundings.** Perhaps you don't feel safe with the person asking for your help, or you're concerned about a large pet the owner won't put in the yard, or the area you're being asked to work on is infested with insects. In any of these cases, you'll be doing yourself a big favor by turning the job down or maybe referring the job to someone else.

There are many different possibilities, but the bottom line is, you should feel good about the job you're taking on. If you don't, something is wrong and I recommend you seriously consider turning down a job you're uncomfortable with.

Do I need to offer a proposal?

Many professional organizers waste countless hours coming up with a customized proposal for each new project. In fact, some organizers will actually leave the prospect's home or office, work for hours—or days—on a proposal, send the proposal back to the prospect and then wait while the prospective customer decides if he/she wants to go ahead with the job.

For most small to medium size organizing jobs, this is a very ineffective approach. If you actually have some canned proposals with you, with areas that you can check off, there are two major benefits:

♦ You write "one" proposal that you can use over and over again. No need to ever come up with a new one.

♦ You can make your proposal to the prospect during the Needs Analysis, rather than sending it to him afterwards. Very often, he will decide—right there and then—if he wants your services or products.

This approach is much easier for both you and the prospective customer.

However, on larger jobs, the prospective customer may ask you for a detailed proposal. Larger companies and government institutions may even require a proposal—usually because the job needs to be approved by someone in a higher rank. In this case, you should have a standard proposal on your computer, created using your word processing program, that you can adjust according to the needs of your prospect.

Don't waste time recreating the wheel. Each proposal you do does not have to be unique. If you want it to feel more personal, use your word processing program to actually fill in the person's name in standard places throughout the proposal. Remember, every moment you're spending doing this sort of administrative work is time you could be using to market and grow your business.

How do I write a proposal?

♦ Your proposal does not have to be a literary masterpiece. It should be a method of communicating what someone will get by signing up for your service.

♦ **Summarize the goals:** Write 2-3 sentences summarizing your overall project goal.

♦ **Define the problem:** In bulleted points, list the problems that you've come up with based on your Needs Analysis.

♦ **List the solutions:** In bulleted points, list the solutions that you are proposing. Don't reveal "everything." Each point should be no more than 3-4 sentences long.

♦ **Keep it short.** Nobody wants to read a 10 page proposal—and nobody will. Keep your proposals to 1-2 pages.

♦ **Use simple language:** I can't emphasize this enough. Don't use jargon or 50 cent words. Pick up a copy of Woman's Day or Good Housekeeping. Look at the words they use for their copy. Use the same types of words.

♦ **Proofread:** Read your proposals 2-3 times at minimum, to be sure you catch any spelling errors, grammatical errors, punctuation errors, etc. before they reach your potential customers. If possible, have someone else proofread for you.

♦ **Close and include signature lines:** Be sure you always include space at the end of your proposals for your signature, the prospective customer's signature and the date.

Offering an irresistible solution

If, after the assessment, this sounds like the perfect job for you to assist this prospect with, it's time to come up with an irresistible solution—one that will be too good for the prospect to turn down.

Getting a high conversion rate takes time, skill and experience. In the early stages, don't be discouraged if you are only able to convert 1 out of every 10 prospects into customers. That would actually be an excellent start and would equal a 10% conversion rate. As you become more skilled at sales conversion, each month you should shoot to convert a higher percentage than you converted the previous month.

Unless you're a superstar, it's going to be nearly impossible to convert more than 60% of your prospects into customers. After all, not everyone who is a prospect is going to be able to afford your services, be interested in your services, etc. However, always strive for achieving at least a 40-50% conversion rate over time.

Closing the sale

So many people who are attempting to sell their products and services never ask for the sale. If you've read any sales books or magazines, you've learned that this is one of the biggest mistakes you can make. If you don't ask for the sale, chances are, you're rarely going to get the sale.

There is a famous phrase in sales that is as easy to remember as ABC: **A**lways **B**e **C**losing. This means that every time you're doing a presentation to a prospective customer, you should either a) close the sale immediately or b) get closer to closing the sale.

I rarely leave an appointment without trying to close the sale right then and there. Once you say, "Why don't you think about it and call me back if you decide to go ahead," or "I'll send you a price in the mail and if you're interested, just email me," there's a good chance you'll never hear back from this prospect again.

In most cases, it is not recommended that you leave the prospect's home or office and then spend hours thinking about and creating a formal proposal. A proposal can be extremely simple, like the example in this manual, and can be done ahead of time. In most cases, this is all that's needed. Remember, people lose interest quickly. They may be really hot about getting organized today, but if you allow them to think about it for a week or two, they may lose heart, their priorities may change or they'll get distracted and forget about you.

So, do everything you can to get the sale immediately—today—before you leave the prospect's home or office, or before you hang up the telephone.

Sandwich your regular price in between the solutions. Then give them some bonus solutions at the end that you'll add on a complimentary basis. For instance, paint a picture of how wonderful their life is going to be when they're able to find something in a few seconds or when they can schedule effectively. In between painting that picture, explain exactly how you're going to help them. Then, briefly show them your prices. Keep painting that picture.

Finally, say that if they agree to this job today, you'll toss in some other complimentary bonus things, such as a continuation plan, or file maps so they can find all their paperwork, or a book, or a 20% discount. Choose one or two to offer them, so you don't confuse them, but also so they have a strong reason for signing up today, instead of putting it off. Procrastination is a sales killer. You've got to kill it first.

Use your proposal form and check off, or write, everything they're going to get in a bulleted list format as he or she is watching you. Write out, or highlight the complimentary bonuses—be sure to place a value next to each bonus. Then, write the regular price, cross it out and write in the special price.

Last, circle the final price in red.

The goal is to get the client saying to himself/herself, "This is great. By agreeing to this, I'll be getting so much, for so little." No matter what price you propose— $50 or $5000—this is the way your client should feel.

The next part is critical to getting an immediate decision. Say, "How does this sound to you?" and wait to hear what the prospect has to say. Don't say a word. If you were really good, the client will often say, "Sounds great. When can we start?" and you can discuss the starting date and have them sign the proposal immediately. If this happens:

1. simply smile
2. shake the person's hand
3. tell the prospect how excited you are about the job and how happy you are to be able to help
4. schedule a day and time to begin
5. get your deposit
6. thank the client and leave

If, on the other hand, the prospect objects, you have some more work ahead of you. You can try to answer some of these objections on the spot. However, it's very important that you try to "read" the prospect at that point.

If the prospect really seems adamant that he's not interested, you may want to reconsider if you want to spend the time trying to convince this person that he needs your services. You won't want to waste a whole lot of time on someone who isn't interested, when that time could be better spent on finding someone who is truly interested. In other words, if a prospect says, "I'm not interested in your services at all," thank him and leave. It's unlikely that you'll be able to convince him that he needs something he doesn't want.

If the prospect seems somewhat interested, but not quite ready, you could tell this person you will give him some time and then follow-up with him. You might say, "My offer, including the bonuses/discounts, is good for the next 7 days. I'll call you on (say a specific day/time). Is this convenient for you?" Almost all the time he or she will say, "Sure, that will be fine."

Please understand that many people are not going to re-read your information, brochure or proposal, or even think about your proposal over the next 7 days. They're just much too busy and distracted. However, it's a great idea to send prospects a thank you note immediately after your meeting. The thank you note will get their attention and remind them about you and your proposal one more time. Include a note that says, "I'm looking forward to talking to you on (your scheduled follow up date/time). If you have any questions at all, call me at 555-5555."

Handling objections

Don't mistake an objection for a lost sale. While it is important that you don't spend time with someone who isn't interested, it is even more important to recognize an objection from someone who *IS* interested. Here are some common objections and ways to handle them:

OBJECTION 1: "Your service/product costs too much." Don't get defensive. Don't say, "Well it's a lot of work and my service is worth it." That type of come back is nothing more than an opinion that won't be believed or appreciated. Instead, make the price seem much more reasonable by breaking it down. For instance, let's say the price for a file organizing session comes out to $450. Your discussion might sound something like this:

YOU: "If you could have a cost-effective filing system that allows you to never lose a piece of paper again and allows you to find everything you need when you need it, you would probably say yes right now, correct?"

PROSPECT: "Yes. If it were cost effective."

YOU: "Is it safe to assume you're losing at least $25 per day in lost time and productivity because you don't have an effective filing system?"

PROSPECT: "Probably more than that!"

YOU: "Let's imagine you're going to have a great filing system in place for 5 years or more. That comes out to less than 25 cents per day, for an effective filing system that saves you $25 per day!"

PROSPECT: "Hmmm, 25 cents per day to save $25 per day. Now that you put it that way, it seems like quite a bargain."

♦ **OBJECTION 2: "I can get it from someone else for less."** Whatever you do here, don't begin a price war. Your conversation might sound like this . . .

YOU: "That might be true. Although I wonder if you'll be getting everything that you would get from *my* service/product. Let me list everything for you."

At this point, begin making a bulleted list of everything you offer. If you already have a bulleted list with you, review each item and check each one off as you go along.

PROSPECT: "Your services do seem complete. Is the price you gave me the very best you can do for me?"

YOU: "My prices are already discounted as low as I can possibly go, but if you sign up for my services today, I will give you two complimentary follow-up sessions to help you get used to your new system. In addition, I will give you a copy of my book to reference for years to come. These two additions are valued at over $125. How does that sound to you?"

♦ **OBJECTION 3: "I want to think it over."** This may be a brush-off. Or, it may be procrastination. If it's procrastination, try to overcome it by offering something that will get them to agree to the job right now.

Your discussion might sound like this. . .

YOU: "Ok, that's fine if you would like to think it over. However, my experience has been that most people don't really find the time to think it over. Let me see if I can help you pinpoint your concerns."

PROSPECT: "Okay."

YOU: "Just so I can get it straight in my mind, what are your biggest concerns right now?"

Then begin asking questions and waiting for answers after each one.

"Are you interested in the service?"

> ### Make your Guarantee Strong
>
> I always stand behind my services and products 100%. That's why I always offer a very strong guarantee.
>
> Of all my organizing project customers, not one of them has ever asked for his/her money back.
>
> With products, there are always going to be some returns. Perhaps it didn't fit his needs or it wasn't what she expected.
>
> I have a very low return rate on my products—less than 2% on average. I'm perfectly willing to refund anyone who isn't completely satisfied. This type of strong guarantee helps me to sell thousands of dollars worth of services and products.
>
> Always guarantee your services and products to ensure the highest sales possible.

"Are there one or two elements you are not sure of?"

"What parts of the service do you like the most?"

"Which parts of the service do you like the least?"

"Wouldn't you rather make a decision while the information is fresh in your mind?"

Nine times out of ten, the true objection will come down to money. If that's the case, go back to the first scenario. If it's not the case, discuss any objection the customer comes up with in a calm, rational, understanding tone.

Restate their problems and frustrations. Restate the solution, the total cost, bonuses and special rate. Restate the cost broken down into small segments.

In addition, you might make an additional offer that a very interested person would not refuse, such as . . .

YOU: "Since I know this is such a difficult decision for you and I understand that you feel it's a bit outside of your budget, I'm going to try to make it a little bit easier. If you sign up today, I will personally buy you $50 of my time. That means that this entire job will be only $400.

Plus, I will add a written continuation system so that your filing system will still be working beautifully 5 years from now. How does that sound to you?"

If he still wants time to think it over, at this point, you should accept his wishes. Set a date and time to follow-up and thank him for his time. Later on that day, send him a thank you note in the mail and follow-up on the scheduled date.

You might even extend your special rate offer for 10 days.

A formal proposal

The one situation in which you might not be able to ask for the sale immediately, is if you're proposing to do a job for a large company, a government office, or anywhere else where the person you're speaking to is not the decision maker.

Every so often, someone may ask a staff member or assistant to meet with you about the situation. In this case, you'll probably be asked to send back a formal proposal.

I still wouldn't recommend you waste hours creating and writing up a proposal. A one to two page proposal with a cover letter, detailing what this job is going to entail and how much it's going to cost, should be sufficient for most organizing or consulting jobs.

The longer your proposal is, the less chance you're going to have, that somebody will a) read it or b) read it in a timely manner. Say what you have to say in as few words as possible. Don't make the prospect work for you.

Once you create one formal proposal, you should be able to use that proposal over and over again. Do it on your computer in a word processing program and every time you need to submit a proposal to someone else, just make any necessary adjustments, print it out and submit it.

Please, remember to follow up. Don't expect to get a call back from whoever you submit a proposal to. If they do call before you follow up with them, great! Just don't ever wait for them to call you. The more you follow up, the more sales you'll end up closing.

Your guarantee

If you believe in your services and/or your products, you should feel comfortable with offering your prospects a strong guarantee. Exactly what you guarantee is, is up to you, but you should know that the stronger the guarantee, the more likely you'll be to get the job or to sell your products. Here are some guarantees that you can offer:

♦ **100% One-Year, Money-Back Guarantee:** We want you to be completely satisfied with any products you purchase from Get Organized Now! If, for some reason, you feel one of our products is not for you, return it for a full refund, minus shipping and handling.

♦ **We guarantee our services:** If, on the completion day of our organizing session, you feel that you didn't receive exactly what was outlined in our original proposal, we will be happy to work with you at no additional charge, to achieve those promised goals.

♦ **Satisfaction Guarantee:** If you feel you need further information regarding our time management sessions, or a refresher course, call me anytime within 30 days. I will be happy to assist you free of charge, either in person or on the telephone.

Quite often, your strong guarantee will be the clincher of the sale. If you're willing to stand behind your product or service so strongly, it must be good!

Chapter 9
Pricing Out a Job

If you're about to quote someone for a first-time job, there's a good chance that you're going to underestimate or overestimate the time and cost. This is okay, because as you get more and more jobs, you'll be able to come up with a pricing formula that works well for you. The amount you charge depends on a number of factors.

What can I charge for hands-on assistance or consulting?

If this is your first job, I would suggest you start off with a formula that is simple and easy to determine, without lots of calculations. An hourly charge is usually the best way to help you determine a job cost.

Hourly charge

If you're a professional organizer just starting out, you'll probably want to initially charge anywhere from $35 to $50 per hour. However, the last thing you'll want to tell prospects is that you charge $35 per hour, without giving them any indication of how long the job is going to take. Most prospects are not going to feel comfortable signing up for a service with an hourly fee and an indefinite time frame. In other words, they won't know whether the final job is going to cost them $35 or $3500!

Anytime you quote a prospect an hourly fee, be sure to give the person a time range so they know approximately how much this job will cost. For example, if you charge $40/hour and estimate that the job will take between 6 and 10 hours, you can tell the prospective client that the final price will be between $240 to $400 dollars.

In this case, if you work over the 10 hours, I would not recommend that you charge more than you originally estimated—$400 maximum. Charging more will do nothing more than anger the customer and pretty much discourage any possibility of you getting future business or a referral from this person.

Just realize that on your next job, you should pad the time you think it's going to take. It's a lot better to quote more and charge less, then to quote less and charge more.

Project charge

If you're a professional organizer who has been in business for at least a few months and has had some paying jobs, you might consider working out "project charges" rather than "hourly charges." For example, if you know that it takes you around the same amount of time to organize a 2-drawer filing cabinet no matter whose home or office it is in, you might charge a flat fee of, for instance, $200, to unclutter and organize any job you get that involves a two-drawer filing cabinet.

Or, if you know that it generally takes the same amount of time to organize a clothes closet, your fee for organizing one clothes closet might be $125.

Again, it takes a bit of experience to come up with some project costs, but in the long run, it will save you time, plus the customer will always know exactly how much the job is going to cost.

More experienced organizers who become leaders in their field and have written books, do public speaking and/or deliver seminars and workshops, can often charge more for their services, because of their experience, expert status and prestige. In this case, you're only limited by your own time, motivation, imagination and creativity.

I'm not sure I'm comfortable with my rate

First of all, it's imperative that you keep in mind that your customers are not only paying for your time—they're also paying for your expertise. If you don't think your services are worth $35 per hour, then they're probably not going to either. Make your services so special and have total confidence in them. This way, you will have no problem quoting that price. If you're going to work for $10-$20 per hour, then you might as well work for somebody else. You can easily get a job for that kind of money. You have to "think like a business owner" if you're planning on making your business a very successful one.

Be consistent in your pricing

Develop a pricing scheme that you're going to use to compute all of your organizing project costs. You won't want to charge one person $300 for a 6 hour filing job and then charge someone else $450 for the same type of job. This may put you in an awkward situation in time, especially if the client who paid more finds out that she paid you much more than another customer.

How do I estimate how long it will take to complete a job?

Time estimation is always one of those questions that is tough to answer. There are so many variables to consider. Are you doing home organizing or business organizing? Are you giving hands-on assistance or consulting only? Are you doing a paid workshop? If so, on what subject, how many hours will you be speaking and how many people will be in attendance? How quickly can you get the job done based on your energy levels? Do your energy levels change based on the time of day you're performing the job? How much experience have you had and are you able to base your estimated time on past jobs? Are you dealing with someone that has a difficult time throwing things out? Are you working with someone who has lots of questions or no questions at all? Is this a paper heavy job? Do you understand how to categorize these papers, or do you need to learn a bit about the types of categories you'll need to set up? The questions are limitless.

Again, experience plays a big part in being able to properly estimate the time a job is going to take. Many organizers just starting out will actually do some free organizing jobs to gain experience and to help them get used to some of these variables.

During your practice sessions for hands-on organizing, for example, sort through a pile of paper or organize a closet and keep an accurate time check of how long each step takes. For instance, let's say you're organizing a closet. Keep a time check of how long it takes you to empty out the closet. Note how long it takes for you to discuss with your "client" what items can be donated. Jot down how long it takes you to categorize and replace everything that will be put back into the closet.

Once you have some averages, you'll then be able to multiply the time it takes you by the number of piles, the number of cabinets, or the number of closets.

One other important point to note is that many organizing jobs cannot be done in one fell swoop. If you have a project that's going to take 12 hours, you may consider breaking it up into two or three sessions of a few hours each. This will depend on the energy levels of both you and your clients and any time limitations imposed.

The A-B-C Method

With a little bit of experience under your belt, you might consider coming up with your own pricing plan—3 basic prices, based on 3 simple criteria. This type of pricing plan helps you to easily price out a job and also helps the prospect decide if he or she can afford the job cost you're proposing.

Your pricing plan (based on $50 per hour) may look something like this . . .

Personal Organizing Assistance or Consulting

A.	B.	C.
Small Job	Medium Job	Large Job
Less than 8 hours	8-15 hours	16-24 hours
$400	$800	$1200

Workshops or Seminars (with a minimum of 5 attendees each)

A.	B.	C.
Less than 2 hours	2-3 hours	4-8 hours
$20 per attendee	$35 per attendee	$50 per attendee

Don't "nickel and dime" your prospects

There's one thing that is a big no-no when it comes to pricing out a job— "nickeling and diming" someone to death. This means that you list 50 little charges on your proposal, rather than including most of these charges right in your price.

For example, let's say you have to drive a few miles to get to your prospect's home or office and you want to charge for your fuel. Don't list $4.23 for fuel costs on your proposal. Or perhaps you want to charge for your meals at a fee of $5.00 per day. Don't list six $5.00 meal charges on your proposal.

Don't nickel and dime your prospects. Include whatever you feel you need to include in your total proposed fee.

Who pays for the supplies my client's job will require?

Any costs for file folders, labels, dividers, trays and other organizing tools needed to complete a job should be paid by your customer.

If you choose to have these supplies on hand whenever you have an organizing job, be sure you indicate the cost of the supplies in your client job proposal so the potential customer is aware of this additional charge.

Don't mix it in with your organizing price quote. It should be on a separate line so the customer can immediately see the break down. Otherwise the customer may think you're charging $450, when your bill was really only $400 plus $50 worth of supplies. Some organizers prefer this method since they always use the same types of folders, tools, etc. and feel more comfortable having them all at their disposal when needed.

I've always preferred to first determine exactly what supplies the client will need during an initial consultation. Then, as soon as I get the client to agree to the job, I actually sit down with them and my office supplies catalogs. I help them choose the items they need.

The client calls the supply companies to order these tools while I'm sitting there. This way I know he won't procrastinate and I know the tools will be there during our organizing session. The client then pays for the supplies with his credit card and asks to have the supplies delivered to his office or home. The method you choose is completely up to you and what you feel comfortable with. There is no "one right way" to do this. Choose a consistent method and use it.

Here are some of my favorite supply companies:

Lillian Vernon .... www.lillianvernon.com

Stacks and Stacks .... www.stacksandstacks.com

The Container Store .... www.thecontainerstore.com

Organize.com .... www.organize.com

Ikea.. www.ikea.com

Solutions .... www.solutions.com

Target .... www.target.com

Office Depot... www.officedepot.com

Staples .... www.staples.com

Who pays for traveling costs?

Every now and then, a prospect may call and ask you to do an organizing job or workshop that is not very close to where you live. Perhaps it might even be in another state. You should be prepared to determine whether or not this is something you might like to do and to what degree. If you are agreeable, what would you charge for your traveling costs?

Should I charge for my driving time?

Whether or not you charge for driving time is up to you. The way I usually determine whether or not I would charge a client for driving time has always depended on the amount of time it would take me to get from point A to point B and back.

Generally, if the job is less than 30 minutes each way, I would waive any driving time charges.

However, if it takes more than 30 minutes to get there and then to get back, I charge half of my regular hourly consulting charge per hour. So, at my current rate of $75 per hour, I would charge $37.50 per hour of driving time. This would generally help to cover my time, fuel and wear and tear on the car.

What if I have travel expenses?

On occasion, you may get an out-of-town prospect who needs your help. This won't happen too often for regular organizing jobs, since the client is responsible

for traveling fees—airlines, trains, car rentals and hotel accommodations—which are generally cost prohibitive.

However, it may occur on occasion—more so if you specialize in things other than organizing projects, like if you're a public speaker.

Before you agree to do an organizing job or workshop that is going to require you to travel via airplane, train, bus or ferry and that will also require you to rent a car and/or pay for a hotel room, first research all the necessary costs.

Then, be sure to get a signed proposal and a deposit from your client to cover these costs and/or any fees incurred from a client cancellation.

Chapter 10
Customer Psychology

Helping people get organized is not only about helping them get physical clutter out of their homes or setting up filing systems. Rather, it is helping them have a better life, less stress, more time for themselves, their family and so on. Always keep the bigger picture in mind and it will help you work with customers so you can provide them with the best organizational systems suited to their needs.

Will you be able to help everyone you come in contact with? Probably not. But if you have the expertise and skill you need in your particular specialty and you have enough marketing savvy to get the word out about your company, you will certainly be able to help a large number of people.

Here are some common customer personalities and possible solutions for handling them:

1) **Larry Learner:** Larry wants to learn from you, is not resistant, asks questions, is helpful and is open to new ideas. He works with you to come up with effective solutions to his organizing problems. Larry is a pleasure to work with.

   The flip side of this is that Larry will probably not need your services after your initial organizing session or consultation. He now knows enough to keep his home or office organized or to manage his time better.

   Since you probably won't be hearing from Larry again, be sure you collect a good testimonial for your files. Also, keep in touch with him for possible referral business.

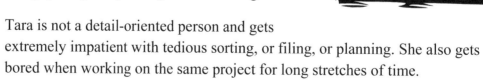

2) **Tara Tasmanian Devil:** Tara is extremely excited and is in a big rush to get this project completed as quickly as possible. She doesn't really think about what you're saying or doing, but is convinced that the project isn't moving along quite quickly enough for her liking.

   Tara is not a detail-oriented person and gets extremely impatient with tedious sorting, or filing, or planning. She also gets bored when working on the same project for long stretches of time.

Try to talk to Tara and explain why this project cannot be rushed. Explain that all effective systems take some time to develop and you wouldn't want to charge for something that wasn't planned and thought through.

Use the "Rome wasn't built in a day," phrase. Try to get her to relax. Perhaps suggest that you can work on one part of the project for an hour, such as filing. Then, during the next hour, work on clearing a desk. This will help keep Tara energized, but will also prevent her from getting bored.

3) **Peter Puppet:** Peter pretty much agrees with whatever you say. If you tell him to jot something in his calendar, he does so without even thinking about it. If you tell him to sort his photos a certain way, Peter just does it without questions or comments. If you say that something can be tossed, he just tosses it.

However, since Peter never asks any questions and never thinks about what you're saying, he is not really learning. This means that the problem will get fixed for the moment, but the second you leave, he is going to be right back in his original situation.

This is a good situation if you want to get Peter on a "continuation plan"—a plan in which you go to Peter's home or office every few months and help him do the job all over again. This can be a very profitable situation for you and even though he just does what you say, he is easy to work with and willing to pay you to keep him organized.

Don't try to convince Peter that he has to understand everything you're saying. Obviously, he doesn't want to understand the reasoning. He just wants an organized office, a clutter free home, or a schedule that he can keep up with.

4) **Edith Eternally Confused:** No matter what you suggest or how easy you're trying to explain the solution, Edith has no clue what you're talking about, what you're doing, or why you're doing it. In fact, she always looks bewildered and confused.

If you're making everything as easy to understand as possible and Edith still cannot grasp what you're trying to say, you might have to accept that. Don't try to convince her that she has to understand before you move on.

Get Edith organized as best as you can and tell her that it's okay if she doesn't totally understand. Then, work out some kind of continuation system so you can keep her on track in the future.

5) **Oliver Overwhelmed:** Oliver is the type of person who works with you for 15 minutes and then states that he, "Can't bear to do any more." The thought of going any further is just too overwhelming for him, even if you've been working for no more than 15 minutes.

Oliver needs to be reassured that the problem is not as bad as it may seem. Paint a picture for him, so he's aware of how wonderful everything will be when his office, or calendar, or time is more organized.

Oliver also needs to be urged to keep going. Just keeping pushing the "baby steps" philosophy and say, "It's not so bad. Look at all we're accomplishing."

6) **Suzy Scaredy Cat:** Suzy is indecisive and afraid. If you tell her that something can be tossed, she puts it aside and says, "let me think about it." If you tell her to move her desk to the other side of the room, closer to the filing cabinet, she'll say something like, "let's put that thought aside until later." If you tell her to set some goals with you, she doesn't want to because she fears she will be a failure.

Suzy needs to be reassured that it's ok to feel uneasy about some things, but that change is necessary to be able to get anything accomplished. Get her to begin making small decisions and then work your way up to the more difficult decisions. For instance, it's relatively easy to convince someone to toss a flyer for an event that is already a month over. However, it's more difficult to convince someone to donate the extra bed that hasn't been used in 10 years.

7) **Bobby Bashful:** Bobby feels he is "the most disorganized person in the entire world"—or some variation of that.

You are there to soothe his fear. Convince him that disorganization is a problem shared by millions of people to some degree or another. Tell him that once the job is broken down into smaller pieces, it will feel like less of a monster.

Help him feel at ease. Help him feel hopeful for a better life. Do everything you can to ensure that Bobby does not feel embarrassed or stupid.

8) **Donna Deserter:** Donna is someone who, even after agreeing to work with you side by side, decides that you should do the job on your own. She either tells you this flat out or skirts the issue by doing other things—dealing with the children, talking on the telephone or telling you that she has to work on something important and there's no sense in the both of you working on the same job.

In some cases, you might be able to handle the job on your own without arguing with Donna. For instance, if you're working on a home filing project, you may be able to do the job perfectly well, with or without her by your side.

However, if you feel you cannot do the job effectively without the customer by your side, then tell her straight out. Say, "I'm sorry, but this job requires you to work with me. I cannot make effective decisions about your paperwork—or clutter or whatever—without you." If she still resists, you might consider telling Donna that you cannot do the job and then leave.

9) **Connie Conversationalist:** Connie is constantly talking to you about something—her family, her job, her friends, the holidays—and no matter how long you're there, you're not accomplishing anything.

Do everything you can to pull Connie back to the project at hand. It is very important that she's focused and it's also important that you're able to remain focused.

When Connie begins to tell a story, tactfully say, "I'd love to hear all about that later. Let's just concentrate on this one thing first, so we both have time to enjoy that story when we're done."

10) **Sammy Sentimentalist:** Sammy is sentimental about every object he picks up. Either that object is directly attached to a particular person or event, or the object kicks off a memory of something unrelated. The sentimentality is lovely, but it's taking up lots of time. Plus, you can't get Sammy to part with anything he has sentimental attachment to, which seems to be everything he owns.

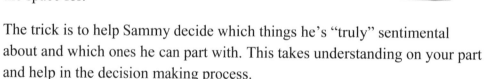

Whatever you do, don't quickly recommend that Sammy part with the things he's "truly" sentimental about. Try to come up with a "keep one-donate one" solution. Or perhaps you can convince him to use the Rotation box solution. He might even take some photos of the things he really enjoys, but doesn't have the space for.

The trick is to help Sammy decide which things he's "truly" sentimental about and which ones he can part with. This takes understanding on your part and help in the decision making process.

11) **Florence For-the-Moment:** Florence doesn't necessarily care if a system she's currently using will not be good for the future. She figures, "As long as it's working now, it's fine." So, rather than looking for long-term solutions, she's basically looking for a few quick band-aids.

You can try to talk to Florence about how coming up with a more long-term solution will end up saving her time, money and effort later. If you can convince her to just be patient, you'll be able to help Florence with some more permanent solutions so she doesn't have to worry about this in the future.

If you can't get her to agree, help Florence out with the simple problem at hand. Be sure you record your suggestions and mail her a copy so she can't say later that your systems aren't working anymore.

12) **Alvin Arm-Crosser:** Alvin is totally resistant to all of your ideas, no matter how effective you know they can be. No matter what you suggest, he disagrees with you and it's either a struggle or an impossibility to get anywhere.

Alvin's problems are much deeper than needing to get organized. In many cases, it's probably a good idea to tell him that you don't feel the job is working out and move on.

Unless you have a degree in psychology and you're willing to spend hours trying to change him, then you should probably find someone who is more willing to work *with* you, rather than *against* you.

13) **Sandra Satisfied:** Sandra has lots of organizational dilemmas, but only wants your help in fixing one or two of them. Also, the solution doesn't have to be the best solution in the world, as long as it's bearable. For instance, she may have piles all over her office, but she really only wants to get the top of her desk under control. Once you clear Sandra's desk, you attempt to recommend that you both move on to her desk drawers. But she doesn't want to.

While you should recommend the solutions you feel that people really need and explain why they need those solutions, that's basically all you can do. You can't force Sandra to want her desk drawers organized. She has to want it on her own. Help her with the project at hand and follow up with her later to determine if she's interested in you helping her go any further.

14) **Uma Undesirable:** Every once and a while, you might run into a very undesirable situation. Uma's house might be infested with insects for example. In this case, if you don't wish to proceed with the job, give Uma her deposit back and recommend that she hires a cleaning service. Or, Uma's home may smell really bad. Or you're allergic to the cat hair that's embedded in the rugs. Or this client makes you ill, uncomfortable or unsafe. The money you can get from this job isn't as important as your health or well-being. Don't take on any job you do not want to do. Tell Uma you don't believe you can help her and leave.

15) **Edgar the Enemy:** Edgar does not want your help. Perhaps a boss, spouse or relative hired you to help him. Basically, Edgar looks at you and says, "no way, not a chance, over my dead body."

Don't waste your time trying to convince him. Instead, speak to the person who hired you and say that if Edgar is not willing to help you help him, then you can't do the job. Short and simple. Don't allow yourself to get in the middle of marital disputes, employer/employee relations or any other arguments. It's not worth it.

Chapter 11
Getting Paid

Should I charge a deposit?

Once a prospect agrees to an organizing job or seminar, it is always a good idea to ask for a deposit. This will help ensure that this client is serious about paying for your services. Be sure the check clears before you begin the job. This is especially necessary if you've never done work for this particular customer before. Be sure you give her a "paid" receipt for her records.

> **Make it Easy**
>
> For any organizing job I've ever had, I always charge $100 deposit.
>
> It makes it easy for both me, and my client.
>
> No calculations needed, and I never had any one seem surprised that I was asking for it.

I almost always ask for a deposit first. The only times I've waived it are those times when I'm doing a job for a client that I've already done a number of jobs for in the past. In other words, I now know him well enough to expect that I am definitely going to get paid in full for any session I assist him with.

When you charge a deposit, be sure you subtract the deposit from the job cost once it is paid—the remaining amount is the fee, minus the deposit.

How much should I charge for a deposit?

Generally, 15-20% of the total job price is a sufficient deposit. If the total job cost is going to be around $200, charging a deposit of $30-$40 would be appropriate. If all of your organizing jobs are estimated between $500-$1000, you might consider a standard deposit of $100 on all jobs, just to make it easier to remember with no calculations necessary.

When do I get paid?

Please don't make the mistake of leaving your client's home or office and then billing them. While some people will pay you the full amount and will pay you on time, others will not.

For those that do not, you'll waste hours just trying to get paid and in some cases you'll never get paid. It will cost you too much to take any further action (getting a collection agency and attorney), so you'll probably never pursue further action. In the end, you'll most likely never get paid for the job.

I strongly suggest you get paid at regularly scheduled intervals, either on a daily basis if you can complete the job in a few days, a weekly basis if you're going to complete the job in a month, or on a small project basis—for example, breaking the job that needs to be done to organize a home office into 5 distinct mini projects. At the end of each scheduled interval, ask the client for payment while he's standing in front of you. Don't bill him. Ask him for a check, money order, or credit card if you accept them, right then and there.

This will ensure that 1) you get paid for every job you complete and 2) that you don't have to work for endless days before reaping any of the monetary rewards of your business.

In addition, if you're also selling organizing books or products, always get paid before you deliver the merchandise and don't accept C.O.D.'s.

How should I get paid?

When you're first starting out, accepting cash, checks or money orders is the preferred choice of payment. When customers pay you, be sure you give them a hand-written receipt before you leave.

Once you're established, you might consider talking to your bank about obtaining a merchant account so that you can accept credit cards. If you have a Web site or you're planning to have one in the future and you wish to have the ability to accept credit cards from your Web site, be sure you check with your bank about the future integration that will be necessary.

Be very careful about the companies you deal with to obtain a merchant account. There are lots of shady companies involved with this sort of thing and many scams. Your best bet is to work with a trusted bank—preferably, your own.

What should I do about payment problems?

If, for some reason, the customer's check bounces after the job is completed, you will then have to take steps to get paid. Since I always break organizing jobs down into a few days each and get paid at each interval, the most I would ever lose would be a day or  two's worth of work. However, you should know that I've never received a bad check for an organizing project and I never had a client not pay his or her bill in full. I'm just telling you this so you can safeguard yourself.

If a customer's check does bounce, the very first step would be to call that client, tell her what happened and ask her to submit payment to you within 7 days. Don't make the person feel embarrassed. Remember, this might be an oversight and there's a good chance she will take care of it immediately.

If however, you don't get paid within 7 days, you will have to begin sending payment due letters to this person, each one a bit stronger than the last. The basic notes should say:

♦ **1st Attempt: Send by regular mail**
"I have recently contacted you about a payment you made by check. I've just been notified that you have insufficient funds to cover the payment. Please submit payment in the amount of (whatever) within 7 days."

♦ **2nd Attempt: Send by registered mail with return signature**
I have contacted you previously regarding a payment you made by check that resulted in insufficient funds. Your payment in the amount of (whatever) is now 30 days past due. Please submit your payment upon receipt of this letter to avoid further action.

♦ **3rd Attempt: Send by registered mail with return signature**
Your account with our company is now seriously past due. Please submit payment of (whatever) within 5 days or this matter will be turned over to our collection agency.

♦ **Final Attempt: Send by registered mail with return signature**
We've contacted you several times to remind you of your seriously past due account in the amount of (whatever). This matter has been turned over to our collection agency and you will be hearing from them shortly. Please submit payment immediately to avoid any further legal action.

At this point, you will have to speak with legal counsel to determine if this matter is worth pursuing any further. Very often, legal action costs more than the amount of money you're attempting to collect and further action might not be worth it.

It's up to you to decide whether to proceed with legal action or to cut your losses. Be sure you keep all correspondence with this customer and all signed postal receipts you receive back in the mail.

Chapter 12
Your Customer List is a Goldmine

Repeat sales

Once somebody purchases one of your services and products, it's then your job to get repeat sales from this customer. What else do you have that this person might be interested in? How can you add on to that first sale? It's 10 times as easy to sell to a current customer, than it is to sell to someone who has never purchased from you before.

Keep in touch with your customers on a regular basis. Put them on a monthly newsletter list. Send them articles you feel might interest them. Send them birthday, anniversary and holiday cards. In short, make them feel special—and always make special customer offers to them, such as discounts, add-ons, or special customer rates during the holiday season.

The Power of Advocates

I treat my advocates like the gold they represent.

They hear from me on a regular basis. I send them things they would be interested in. I give them special discounts. I even do some jobs on a complimentary basis for them.

Some of my advocates have brought in thousands of dollars in sales for me, with their purchases and referrals.

It's worth every penny and every ounce of time to make them feel as special as they truly are!

Continuation plans

If, at the end of your first customer session, you feel your customer may need regular assistance, you may discuss getting him on a continuation plan. A continuation plan is basically a plan in which you return to the client's home or office every month, every 3 months, every 6 months and so on to help him weed out his filing cabinet, rid his office of clutter, help him manage his time or do whatever it is you've been doing with this person.

If your hourly rate is generally $60 per hour, you may offer to meet with him for 1-2 hours at regularly scheduled intervals for half of your rate—$30 per hour—as long as he contracts with you for a year. Continuation plans are a great way to ensure your customers stay organized and to also continue to bring a more steady income your way.

Turning your customers into lifetime customers and advocates

Just because a person buys from you once, doesn't mean she's going to become a lifetime customer or an advocate. You have to work at this to make it so. A lifetime customer is someone who buys from you again and again. If you want someone to keep purchasing from you, you have to make her 1) lots of special offers and 2) feel extremely special.

An advocate is someone that loves your products and services so much, that she tells everyone about you. You should do everything in your power to keep this customer thrilled with you—even if you do some complimentary jobs for her. She'll bring in more money for you than you can imagine!

Here are some ideas:

- Send personal greetings, notes and holiday cards (handwritten; not computerized)

- Send articles you know your customer would find interesting—something related to her personally, such as her hometown, family, school she attended, her hobbies and so on

- Send discount offers, like exclusive customer discounts towards the purchase of your products and/or services

- Send small gifts, related to your products and/or services, to let him know you're thinking of him—such as a timer, new style of file folder, etc.

- Call her on special occasions, such as birthdays or anniversaries

- Get to know his spouse's name and his children's names. When you call or write, mention his family members by name

- Give her tickets to an event you feel she may be interested in

- Invite him to lunch

- Do something special for her kids

Chapter 13
Building Your Credentials

Your USP

According to www.wikepedia.com, your USP (a.k.a. Unique Selling Proposition OR Unique Selling Point) is a marketing concept that was first proposed as a theory to explain a pattern among successful advertising campaigns of the early 1940s. It states that such campaigns made unique propositions to the customer and that this convinced them to switch brands.

The term was invented by Rosser Reeves of Ted Bates & Company. Today the term is used in other fields or just casually to refer to any aspect of an object that differentiates it from similar objects.

Today, a number of businesses and corporations currently use USPs as a basis for their marketing campaigns. This is something you can do for your business. What exactly sets you apart from your competitors?

If you say you can organize anything, there are likely a bunch of other organizers in your area who do exactly the same thing. However, if you specialize in organizing garages, for example, and you market this fact well, you'll likely get most if not all of the garage organizing jobs in your area.

You want your specialty to represent your experience, knowledge and passion.

Perhaps you want to focus yourself on Residential Organizing. Ok, so that's pretty basic. But what if you do Residential Organizing with a Feng Shui approach? That makes you different. That's your USP.

Rather than just focusing on organizing one's schedule, you might specialize in helping those who have ADD or ADHD with their schedules—medical conditions that affect sufferers with the ability to focus on tasks.

Your USP could be as simple as you offering a 2-hour free follow-up session with every organizing job you do.

Your USP is something special and enticing—something that will get a prospective customer to choose you over another organizing professional.

Your portfolio

Keeping a collection of client testimonial letters, articles you've written, interviews about you or your company that were printed in publications and photographs of work projects, is an excellent promotional tool to have on hand. It is also a record of all of your business achievements.

If all of these materials are kept in one place, such as a file folder in your filing cabinet, or in 3-ring binders, you'll always be able to pick and choose which ones you wish to use in your marketing pieces. Plus, whenever you need something for the media, you'll have everything at your fingertips.

Client testimonials

Try to get a client testimonial from every single job you complete to the customer's satisfaction. You might choose to ask the client to write up a few words and send them to you. Of course, some people will procrastinate on this and it may be months before you see the testimonial, if ever.

If, during your session, the client says something that you can use as a testimonial, immediately ask her if it's okay for you to quote her later on. If the client agrees, immediately write it down and ask her to sign it.

Sometimes a client can't find the words or the time to write a testimonial, even though he or she would like to. In such a case, you might consider asking the client to check off some sample testimonials that he wouldn't mind agreeing to. Come up with 10 standard sayings and ask him to check off all that apply. Plus, give him 1-2 additional blank lines in case he can think of anything else. Be sure you ask him if you can use his testimonial later and have him sign the agreement stating that he allows it.

Some standard testimonials you can use might be . . .

"Thanks for doing such a great job. I feel more organized than I have in years!"

"I appreciate you helping me get my filing system under control. I can't believe how easy it is to find things now!"

"I love my new organized closet! Thank you so very much!"

"Your time management course has really opened my mind to new goals and opportunities. Thanks!"

Case studies

As you work on an organizing project for someone, take notes. When you get back to your office, type these notes into a word processing document in your computer.

List the problems and what solutions you provided.

Later on, you'll be glad you did. You'll be able to reference it when you're writing, compiling a presentation or preparing for an interview.

Before and after photographs

If you're doing hands-on organizing projects, it's a very good idea to take both before and after pictures of your work. You can use these in your portfolio for a) securing future jobs and b) examples during media interviews. Keep these organized in photo albums with detailed notes next to each photo.

Video and audio clips

Whenever you're going to be on television or on the radio, be sure you record the segment—or get someone you know to do it for you. You will want to keep these records for your portfolio. Whenever I'm on television or the radio, I ask at least two people to videotape the episodes for me. For instance, my husband may tape the segment at our home, while a neighbor might tape the segment at her home.

This is a good idea because just in case something goes wrong with one of the recordings, you'll always have the other as a back-up. If nothing goes wrong, you'll then have two good copies—one for yourself and one you can use if you wish to show the clip(s) to the media.

Client letters and cards

I have so many letters and cards from happy clients that my files are bursting with them. However, I'll never let them go. They're a testament to all the work I've done and they continue to increase the value of my portfolio.

Chapter 14
Using the Media

The media can be a huge help to you and your business. Unlike advertising, publicity does not require payment. If you can make a few good media contacts, you can get on radio programs, television programs and news segments. You can also write for national and local magazines, have interviews written about you and have press releases written about your business. The possibilities are endless.

I love the media folks. They have and continue to help me grow my business. I've been on local and national news programs. Articles have been written about my business in local, national and international newspapers, magazines and online publications.

My name, Web site and tips have been included in Access Magazine, Better Homes and Gardens, Woman's Day and Country Living—just to name a few. I've been interviewed countless times by companies such as Delta Airlines In-Flight Magazine and the Milwaukee Journal Sentinel.

All of this publicity was . . . free!

In addition to this, I've written articles that have appeared in hundreds of print and online publications such as Lifestyles Magazine, OTC Beauty Magazine and the Dollar Stretcher. Plus, I've had my press releases announcing my free tips info-pak printed in newspapers across the country. Press Releases have also announced upcoming workshops in places like Barnes and Noble, the public libraries and town chambers.

Believe me, there's no limit to how the media can help you and your business if you're 1) proactive in getting media contacts and 2) proactive in coming up with stories or angles to communicate to the media that will interest their particular audience.

Creating a press kit
If you're planning to utilize the media, having a professional press kit on hand is an excellent idea.

Your press kit should include some or all of the following:

♦ a cover letter
♦ a bulleted list of your areas of expertise
♦ a photograph (have this done at a professional photographer's studio)
♦ your brochure
♦ a few business cards
♦ client testimonials
♦ press clippings
♦ published articles
♦ major accomplishments (such as information about a book you have written or an organization you have a high position with, etc.)

Place these items in an attractive presentation folder. You might also wish to put a label on the front of the folder if it's not already imprinted, with your company name, logo and contact information.

Before sending press kits to a random list of people in the media, you should call first to make a contact and build a relationship. Then, send the press kit.

Believe me, if you send your press kit out blindly, it will most likely get tossed in a pile or in the trash can. Just like you have to target your prospects, it's also important to target the media that will be most helpful.

Media assignments

When you get a media assignment, it is a good idea to accept it, even if it's a bit inconvenient. Once the media begins to call you, if you begin turning down opportunities, you're unlikely to get another call from that person again in the future.

For instance, if you have a client session at 8:00AM on Tuesday and the local news calls you and asks you if you can appear on one of their programs on Tuesday at 8:00AM, do your best to say, "Yes, I will be there. Thank you." Then, call your client and ask if you can meet at 6:30AM or 9:00AM instead.

If you agree to do an interview at a certain time, be prepared and be on time. If you agree to write an article for a particular newspaper by a certain date, get it done ahead of deadline.

I can't emphasize this enough. If people in the media find it difficult to deal with you, they won't. Make a good impression now and in the future. It's well worth it.

Articles, Press Releases, Ads—What's the difference?

Article: An article is a literary piece of interest that can include tips, such as 10 tips to help you organize your office, 7 ways to help you find more time, or general information on a particular subject of interest. You write your own article, or a reporter can interview you and write it for you. You do not pay to have an article printed and the newspaper may or may not use it. If your articles are good, you may even be able to secure a regular "column" in a newspaper or magazine.

Press Release: A press release is something newsworthy that you announce to the media—generally something that is timely. This may be the results of a poll, a free workshop that's coming up that will interest the residents in a particular city, an event that will help a certain cause such as raising money for cancer research and so on. A press release may even be an announcement of a new company, a new book or a new product. You do not pay to have a press release printed and the newspaper may or may not choose to print it.

Press releases can be sent individually to newspapers or magazines, or distributed through a press distribution service. Your press release will only be printed if the newspaper or magazine sees it as something that will truly WOW its readers. Be careful. There is a fine line between a press release and an ad. If you try to blatantly advertise your services or products, your press release will not be printed. Publications are not in the business of advertising you, your company or your products and services for free. If you send press releases frequently, you might consider joining PR Newswire www.prnewswire.com or a similar service.

Ad: An ad is a "sales tool." You come up with your own ad, or someone from the newspaper does this for you. It showcases you, your business and what you sell. You PAY for your ad and the newspaper prints it.

How do I get into the major media?

Once you're in business for awhile and you begin getting "known" you may get reporters contacting you—without you doing a thing. This is the easy route and the reactive approach. It's also the one that doesn't happen all that often, but is nice when it does.

The more proactive approach is to contact editors. You might send a press release offering editors your media kit. You might send a free copy of your book if you've written one.

If you can get into the local newspaper and on the local radio and TV stations, you can use that information in your press releases to boost your credibility and land an interview with a national TV program or magazine.

Once you've gotten "in the door" with the media, if you interview well, you may find that you're getting more media calls.

Once you know a reporter, you can likely contact him or her directly over the phone to determine what else you can do for them.

I must warn you though. If you just do the interviews and never require that your web site is mentioned in the piece or on air, you can certainly use that information to build up your portfolio, but it's likely not going to do much to increase your bottom line.

Very often, the media will say, "I don't think I can include your web site in our article" or "It's not really our format to include your phone number or your business name." In those cases, think long and hard whether spending the time doing the interview is worth it.

While some readers or viewers may actually take the time to look up your name, most will not. The purpose of your interviews, besides building credibility, is to generate prospects for your business.

Get something in return for your time and expertise. Get the media to mention your web site if you have one, or your business phone number. If you have written a book, try to get the media person to mention your book and where readers or viewers can obtain a copy.

How do I prepare for a media interview?
Sometimes the media will call you and expect you to take an interview immediately. I always try to get a general idea of the subject matter and the target audience first before we start. This way, I'm somewhat prepared for the types of questions I'm going to be asked.

When an interview is not immediate, but rather scheduled for another day, I ask the interviewer to email me a list of possible questions. In this case, I can be very prepared and even have some notes to refer to during the interview.

In some cases, the reporter will even ask you to come up with the subject matter or questions for the interview, and email or fax them ahead of time. This is always nice, as you can then steer the interview in the direction you wish.

Knowing the subject matter well will help ease some of the anxiety you might feel prior to an interview—especially the first one ever. As with anything else, the more you're interviewed, the more comfortable you're going to feel.

My other advice is, prior to being interviewed, to always have a cool or hot beverage on hand. When your throat gets dry, you'll have immediately aid. In addition, having a pen and paper in front of you can help also. In doing so, you'll be able to take quick notes if necessary.

If at all possible, try to get the reporter to email you the link to the actual interview or ask a family member to record the radio interview for you. Once you can hear yourself, you'll be able to evaluate how you did and what you would change when you have an interview opportunity in the future.

Many people are surprised at how many times they repeat the same words or how many "uh's" or "ah's" are in the final segment.

Finally, keep a reminder in front of you that reminds you to promote (gently) your web site, newsletter, book, etc. Otherwise, you'll have given a lot of yourself and your time, without getting anything in return.

How do I get on a radio show?

You can send a press release about what you can offer to a radio show producer or you can call them and give them the scoop on what you can offer their listeners.

I've found that radio interviews are fairly easy to get. Radio stations are always looking for good interviews for their listeners—if you contact an appropriate radio station for what you're offering.

Chances are, a hard rock station is not going to let you share home organizing tips. But an information radio station will probably welcome your tips with open arms.

You will need to have a good speaking voice to get accepted. Practice on family and friends first. Have them interview you and record the interview. Make adjustments for any "ahs" and "ums." Listen for any words you say over and over again, and fix that before calling a radio station.

Also, know that when you're on a radio station, it's sometimes a taped show—but mostly they're LIVE shows. There will be no going back if you make a mistake, so be sure you know your subject well.

Where are radio shows done, and how?

Sometimes, radio shows are done at the radio station location. Most of the time, they're done over the telephone, from the comfort of your home or office.

Be sure you do the interview from a land line (not a cell phone) whenever possible. In addition, if you have CallerID, be sure to turn that off before your radio call.

In some cases, the radio personality will call you and give you instructions on when the show is about to begin, and any openers they want you to start with. In other cases, you'll have to call the radio station and wait for your segment to begin.

In general, radio segments are short and there will be advertisements in between. You'll be asked a question or asked to describe something, and you'll respond. Be concise and clear.

How do I get on some of the popular organizing shows on TV?

In order to get on some of the bigger shows, the first thing you should aim to do is get on TV on a local level—such as a news broadcast. Call you local TV station and let them know what you can offer their viewers.

Perhaps you can show them a new way to organize files or maybe you have a bunch of great holiday tips you can share. Be sure you get someone to record you when you're on TV!

Once you have done a few TV segments, you can contact the producers of the show you're trying to get on. Be sure you list what you can offer them, so you have some good ideas when you speak with them.

It's likely they'll have you send a copy of your prior TV appearances, so be prepared to do so.

Once you've appeared on TV, if you have a good TV presence and personality, it will be easier for you to get chosen for future appearances.

If I'm accepted on TV, who pays my travel expenses?

While producers will occasionally pay for your travel expenses, in general getting to wherever the show is being produced will be up to you. You'll likely have to pay for your own airline tickets, your own hotel accommodations, your own meals, etc., so be sure you're prepared to do so if you're chosen.

Will I get paid for my TV appearances?

Again, this is up to the individual show you're on. Sometimes, yes. Sometimes, no. Be sure you ask before agreeing to be on a show if getting paid for your appearance is important to you. If you don't get paid, try to get your web site, books, etc. mentioned on air. Get something for the money and time you're putting into entertaining this program's viewers.

Chapter 15
Getting On The Web

Should a professional organizer have a Web site? I have to adamantly say, "Yes." Businesses that are not planning on getting on the Web are going to be left behind in the future. Even if you're not exactly sure what you would use your Web site for, I'd recommend that you begin learning and researching so you're ready for the future. A successful business owner thinks of today, "and" tomorrow.

The types of Web sites

First, you should determine what kind of Web site you'd like to start off with. Here are 4 common choices:

♦ **An Image Web site:** This type of Web site is not for the purpose of generating prospects or sales. It is a place where you could send customers and potential customers, so that they see you as more professional. You will also be able to tell your family, friends and associates that you have a Web site which will, perhaps, give you an ego boost and help you feel more confident. People will also have the opportunity to learn about your products and services at your Web site.

Your Web site would have the name of your company, a few services you offer and contact information, just like a print brochure would.

It can be very low-cost to start an Image Web site and it is extremely low-maintenance. However, it also has the least sales and profit potential.

♦ **A Store Web site:** This type of Web site will allow you to display your products or services and will

---

What's your goal?

Many professional organizers choose the "Image" web site format because they're only selling their services to a local market. This is fine. However, it's then unlikely to be a money-making web site.

If you expect to make any kind of money from your site, consider writing a booklet or a book, creating a product(s) or reselling someone else's product(s).

My goal was to make lots of money from my web site. So, I wrote a book, created a number of products, have others sell my products through my affiliate program, and sell products created by others.

We're making an average of $4000 per week from the site alone—and that excludes any consulting or workshops I'm doing in addition.

give potential customers the opportunity to buy something you have directly from your Web site.

This type of Web site can be a bit more expensive to start, since it requires more detail and is higher maintenance than an Image site. In order for potential customers to buy from you using credit cards, you will need the proper technology that will allow you to accept credit card payments.

You should know that just because you have a Web site, doesn't mean that people are going to 1) know where your site is, or 2) buy from it. While you may get a few sales here and there, this type of Web site uses the "one-step" marketing approach, which as you've already learned, brings in very little, if any, response.

♦ **A Free Service Web site:** This is the type of Web site in which you can include some organizing articles and/or free electronic services, such as an automatic reminder service, search engine or an electronic organizer.

There are a few purposes for this type of site:

✓ You can do this out of the goodness of your heart and be an advocate for helping people get organized.

✓ You can do this as a service for your current customers, so they have something to reference after you do an organizing job for them, after you consult with them, or after you sell a product to them.

✓ You can do this to generate advertising dollars.

If you can get a substantial number of people drawn to your Web site on a regular basis to take advantage of the free services you offer. You can then attempt to get other companies to run ads and ad banners on your Web site and then pay you advertising fees. In other words, the sales potential is from the advertisers and not from the people visiting your Web site.

This type of Web site costs a bit more to start, since you need the proper technology set up. It's high maintenance. The person maintaining your site always has to troubleshoot problems that people may be experiencing with the technology.

Plus, it needs your full-time attention. Not only will you have to draw people to your site, but you'll also have to convince advertisers that you have enough traffic to warrant them buying ad space.

♦ **The All-Encompassing, Relationship Building Web site:** This type of Web site includes all of the above and more. It's an Image, Store and Free-service Web site that potential customers visit on a regular basis, brag to their friends about and use it to make purchases.

This is the type of Web site that I have for Get Organized Now! To get an idea of what I mean, pay my Web site a visit. The Web address is: www.getorganizednow.com

You'll notice that I've easily taken care of image. I am proud and eager, to tell people that I have a Web site and I offer my credentials to anyone who is interested.

I display my products and services and give people the opportunity to buy from me using checks, money orders, Pay Pal, or credit cards.

My site is content-rich. I offer tons of free information including clinics, articles, slideshows, a weekly ezine, a discussion forum, monthly checklists, recipes, inspiration, free quick tips, free motivational quotes, a blog and more.

All of these elements work together to form a Web site that attracts well over a million visitors each year and is extremely profitable.

This type of Web site takes a bit more money to start and is high-maintenance. However, the profit potential is enormous. If you can market your products and services nationally and internationally, there is no limit to your income potential.

What do I have to do to have a Web site of my own?

In order to have a Web site, someone has to develop the Web pages you're going to have on your site. A Web page is just like a page in a book. For instance, if you go to my Web site (www.getorganizednow.com), you'll notice that I have a bunch of Web pages—Articles, Inspiration, Quick Tips, Checklists, etc. In all, I haven't counted them in awhile, but I probably have over 750 Web pages on my site and that's not counting all of my discussion forum pages. You don't have to start off with this many pages. It's just that I've been doing this for awhile. A compilation of all of your pages constitutes what is called a Web site.

You need someone to develop your Web pages. Your final choice is really dependent upon a) the money you wish to invest, b) the time you wish to invest and c) the control you wish to have over your site.

♦ **Use a web designer:** You can certainly use the services of a Web designer to create your Web pages for you. You tell the Web designer what you're interested in having on your Web site and he/she develops those pages for you.

The amount of money it will cost depends on the individual designer and the complexity you desire. You might commission a high school student to design your pages for you at a very low cost (under $200) or you might hire a very talented designer to design your pages for a very high price (over $1000). Of course, there are many options in between. You can even have a family member design a site for you for free.

> ## Please don't duplicate other Web Sites
>
> While it is certainly recommended that you learn from the content and design of other Web sites, it is inappropriate and often illegal to copy content and design.
>
> For instance, we put tons of work into the Get Organized Now! and Give to Get Web sites and our pages are copyrighted.
>
> At one point, we noticed that someone tried to steal our page design. He immediately ceased using our page design when he heard from our legal department.
>
> So, always avoid this type of situation by coming up with your own unique content and design.

I will warn you that most Web designers are not marketing experts. In other words, if you're going to choose this option and your goal is to make money from your Web site, I highly recommend you learn everything you can about an effective marketing strategy, lay out on paper exactly what you want your site to include and then tell the designer that is what you want. If you don't, you might end up with a pretty site—or a not so pretty site—that won't fulfill your Web site goals.

I also recommend that you learn at least a little bit about Web programming code (html). You need this knowledge to protect yourself. For instance, your Web designer may charge you $75 for a simple change on your Web site that may only take all of 5 minutes to do. Without a little bit of html knowledge, you can really get taken for a very expensive ride.

♦ **Use template software/service:** You can go to your local computer shop and pick up Web site template software and use ready-made templates to create your Web pages on your own. Tell the store clerk you wish to create a Web site and you need Web site building software. He or she will help you choose something appropriate.

You can also use an online Web template service. Check out: www.vodahost.com/partner/idevaffiliate.php?id=10275_1_3_9

First fill in the electronic templates and you can have a Web site in less than an hour.

You often get a few basic pages from these online Web template services for free. Many make their money by placing ads on your Web site. Some give you a Web site for free, but charge you for hosting services (explained later). Of course, most also offer options that you may, eventually, want to consider purchasing depending on your goals, such as shopping cart capabilities if you want to give potential customers the opportunity to purchase anything from your site.

While you have some control as far as adding graphics or changing text on your canned Web site, you don't have as much flexibility as you would have if you knew how to create a Web site using html Web code.

♦ **Do it yourself:** This is the option that my husband and I took to design our Get Organized Now! and Give to Get Marketing Web sites. It's definitely more time consuming and requires more knowledge, but we have total control over everything on our Web sites.

If you choose to go this route, you'll first need to develop an effective marketing strategy. Visit our sites and notice all of the important elements. Then, get yourself a good html book from your bookstore and little by little, create your own site.

We created our sites and maintain them ourselves. Depending on what your strategy is and the complexity of your Web site, the time it will take you to do this depends on your skill and motivation.

If you're a quick learner, learning html code for a very basic Web site can take as little as a week. The more complex you want it to be, the longer it will take you.

Plus, of course, you're going to be going through a number of revisions and additions after your initial design.

Realize that your first design should never be your final design. It just doesn't work that way. Continuous improvement is the name of the game. No matter how long your Web site has been around, you should be thinking and making improvements on a regular basis.

I add to the content—not the format—of my Web site every week, so that people who've been to my site come back for fresh content. If I never changed the content, they would never come back. That wouldn't be very good for sales. This takes me about an hour, once each week.

We wouldn't have done this any other way, as we feel it's very important to have control over this end of our business. Believe me, we delegate other parts of our business, but with this area, we've decided that it is so very important that we prefer doing it ourselves.

How should my site be designed?

There's no way that I can provide an entire design course in this manual, but here are some Web site design basics:

✓ Use white or very pale colored backgrounds. Avoid dark or patterned backgrounds that make your words difficult for people to read. Don't use white type on black backgrounds for the same reason.

✓ Justify left. Don't justify right or center all of your text. This is amateurish and difficult to read.

✓ Use upper and lower case letters. Don't use all capital letters. THIS IS KNOWN AS SHOUTING. While you might want to use capital letters for a few headings, they should not be used for your regular body text.

✓ Text belongs on a nice, clean background. Never put text over graphics or busy backgrounds. It's very difficult to read. It doesn't matter how light or faint the background may be. It's still very difficult to read.

✓ Avoid frames—not the picture kind; the html kind. Many servers and search engines are not compatible with them.

✓ Avoid animation unless it has a very specific purpose. It's distracting. We use it minimally. Plus, it may crash some visitor's computers due to incompatibility.

✓ Don't use large graphics on your Web site. They take a long time to load. This means large in dimension and in file size. Each of your Web site pages should load within 10-15 seconds. If they don't, people won't wait.

✓ Be consistent in the design of your Web pages. Use the same format, colors and placement of your elements. If you have a set of side or top links on your home page to your other pages, use the same link format, font and placement on every single page. When you select a font for your headings, use that font for all of your headings. The same applies to your body copy.

✓ Don't use fancy fonts. You won't know if your visitors have a particular font on their computer and if they don't have the font you use, you won't know what they're seeing on their screen. Stick with Arial and Times New Roman, since everyone has these on their computer and they are easy to read.

✓ Your links to other pages should be "blue" and underlined which is the standard color and format for links. Don't try to get creative by using other colors. If you do, some people won't know that they're links to be clicked on.

✓ Don't assume that people will know what you want them to do. If you want them to click somewhere, you may have to actually say "Click here to see Article A."

✓ Keep your pages to a maximum width of 600 pixels. If you don't, many people won't have their browser window maximized and will only see a portion of your Web site at any time. They will have to scroll left and right to read your copy and see your entire page. Many of these people won't take the effort and will just leave your site.

✓ If you're going to use a photograph of yourself, be sure it is appropriate. If you're helping to organize offices, a photo of you in business attire would be best. If you're helping to organize homes, you can use a photo of you wearing more casual attire. Think of what you're doing and try to match an appropriate photo to that specialty.

✓ Improve your pages. Don't remove them. Users get annoyed when they bookmark a page, then return a month later to find you've removed the page.

✓ It is especially important for a professional organizer to have an organized Web site. Think about it before you do it. Each page should be dedicated to its own specific topic. You don't want to have a hodgepodge of topics and elements on any one page. Think of organizing your Web site the way you would think of organizing someone's home.

✓ Your Web designer may suggest some fancy elements on your Web pages, such as JavaScript or Shockwave. We recommend you stay away from these. While they may look cool—when they work—many of your visitors won't have the proper software to view the animations. You may even crash some of your visitor's computers. They won't be happy and they won't be back. It's best to keep it simple.

What about Web hosting?

Once your Web site is developed, you have to determine who will host it. This means that you have to actually rent virtual storage space on the web to store your Web pages. Without a Web host, nobody will have access to your Web site. It's not a choice. It's a requirement.

If you're having a Web designer design your site, he/she may have some Web host recommendations for you.

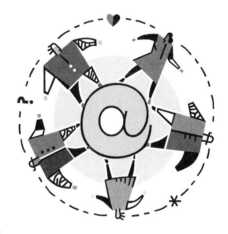

Initially, I used a free Web hosting service called Xoom (in case you look for them, they're no longer in business.) The reason the service was free, was because I was required to have a big banner ad across the top of each of my Web pages. I felt this was an excellent place to start as I was able to develop and improve my Web pages without paying a monthly hosting fee.

Once my site began to grow, however, the free service wasn't the right choice for me anymore. First, the site would occasionally be down—meaning people were not able to get to my site because of technical difficulties on my host's end— which was not good for business. Second, the free host wasn't able to handle all of my Web site traffic—people coming to the Web site. Third, the free host wasn't able to provide me with the technology I needed for a powerful shopping cart system so that people could place credit card orders through my site.

Now, please understand. I'm certainly not saying anything bad about the service I used. For a free service, I felt they were excellent—probably beyond excellent. They really helped me to get my Web business off the ground. However, after 6 months, I was ready to upgrade to a more powerful Web hosting service. So, at that point, I decided to look around some more. I finally decided on a Web host based on a referral from one of my colleagues. It cost me $9.95 per month at the time.

Shortly after, I discovered that I made the wrong choice, which is fine. You may not realize something is not going to work out for you, until you try. It turned out that this new Web host could not handle all of my Web traffic because the business was growing so rapidly. Our site would actually shut down frequently from all of the activity. The technical support was lousy—and that's to put the situation mildly.

This really came to a head when one of my press releases was picked up and printed in Access Magazine—which is a national magazine. At the time, they had over 9 million readers! We had so much traffic on the Sunday that the paper came out—over 5,000 visitors at once—that our Web site actually shut down our Web host's server. Of course, that was the end of the $9.95 per month hosting service. They couldn't handle our rapidly growing needs either.

Finally, we decided that in order to really grow our business, we'd have to invest a little bit more money and go with a reputable Web host that could easily handle our Web traffic. We went with a company called Hosting.com. They were able to provide us with what we needed and we're still with them to this day. For more information, visit:
www.hosting.com

We initially went with their Mini Web hosting package, which was around $40 per month. Since then, we've had even more traffic and had to upgrade four times for lots more space. But at this point, we're very happy with the service that Hosting.com provides us.

The bottom line is, you get what you pay for. You can always start out with one of the free or low cost Web hosts—that is, as long as you know that if you're planning to grow your Web site, you'll have to upgrade to one of the better hosts later.

If you're really motivated and it's within your budget, you might want to just bite the bullet and start off with a company like Hosting.com right from the start. It will save you headaches and aggravation in the future.

What about a domain name?

When a company hosts your Web site, you automatically get an IP address. This number identifies your "address" on the Web. An IP address would look something like . . . http://216.55.24.77.

However, obviously you would not want to tell someone your Web site is 216.55.24.77. So, you have to get a company to coordinate a Web site name such as www.getorganizednow.com with your IP address. The name you choose is called your domain name.

To register my domain name, I contacted a company called Network Solutions. However, these days, most Web hosts will do this for you. Plus, many also offer a break on the domain name fees. I initially paid $70 for 2 years and now I pay a renewal fee every 2 years after that.

What about a discussion forum?

If you visit my Web site you'll see a link called FORUM. This takes you into my discussion forum where people can visit my site and share questions and ideas with other site visitors.

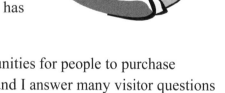

This is very important for me because it gives people a sense of community and friendship. That means they come back to my site every single week—some of them come every single day. It has developed into one big family over the years.

This also means that I have many more opportunities for people to purchase something from my Web site. My moderators and I answer many visitor questions and people appreciate it so much that they purchase my products and services.

If you choose to have a forum, it's very important that you have a regular presence on the forum. First, you have to delete any posts that are inappropriate. Second, you have to watch that there is no negativity happening on the board, which is a big deterrent to people coming back to your forum again. Third, you have to be available to answer questions and share ideas.

If people never see you on the forum, that means they have no expert to learn from. If they have no expert, they'll go somewhere else.

Keep this in mind when deciding whether or not you want a forum. It is a wonderful marketing tool, but to keep it running smoothly and to answer questions regularly, you'll have to dedicate a solid hour or two each week until you have reliable, professional moderators helping you out.

I have approximately 10 volunteer moderators who help me out with each of the topic areas since I have so many visitors participating on the forum. I'd never be able to answer every single organizing question that comes up. There's just not enough time in the day to do that and everything else you must do to run a successful business. Bottom line: Find excellent moderators once your forum is up and running and you have significant traffic.

That said, if you're going to have a forum, I suggest you get the same type of forum as I have. You can purchase it for around $300 from a company called Ultimate Bulletin Board (www.ubbcentral.com). I actually installed this myself, but it was more headaches than it was worth. Take my word for it and have them install it for you, even if it costs you a few hundred dollars more. Believe me, it will be worth every single penny.

Later on when you have to upgrade—and you will have to upgrade every few years—pay the forum people to upgrade it for you unless you're extremely technically capable.

How can I accept credit cards on my Web site?

If you're planning on selling products or services from your site, it's essential to have credit card capabilities. If you don't, you're really limiting your profit potential. Initially, when I started out, I was only accepting checks and money orders. Once I began offering credit card payment capabilities, my sales quadrupled. Enough said.

When I first began accepting credit cards on my site, I used a wonderful company called CCNow (www.ccnow.com). By using CCNow, I didn't need my own merchant account. I signed up for their service and followed the instructions on their site for getting set up. It was very simple.

Once it was set up, people who came to my site just ordered what they wanted. I would immediately get an order notice from CCNow detailing the person's name, address and what they ordered. I would then send the customer his or her merchandise. Twice per month, CCNow sent a check to me for all of the orders. It didn't cost a dime to set up, but CCNow deducted 9% from every order placed on my site as the fee for using their services.

This worked out beautifully for a while, but as we sold more and more products from the site, that 9% fee began to get a little bit expensive. At that point, there was no reason to continue paying that high of a fee.

Plus, CCNow would not allow us to sell intangible merchandise. In other words, we were able to sell our books and planners, but we were not able to sell organizing services or advertising space using their credit card system.

It was time to upgrade. We had to get our own merchant account from our bank, a payment processor to process credit card transactions and a shopping cart system to provide the interface for people to place orders on our site.

When you're ready to do this, you'll need to go to your bank with a business plan detailing how much money you're making now and what your financial projections will be for the next 5 years. Once they approve your merchant account, you'll then have to work with them to find a payment processor and a shopping cart system—that are compatible with your needs, your merchant account provider, your Web host and with each other.

In the long run, doing this will save you money as well as make you money. Plus, you'll be able to accept credit card payments for intangibles as well as tangibles.

Just for your information, we currently use a company called Authorize.net (www.authorizenet.com) as our payment processor and Virtual Cart (www.vcart.com) as our shopping cart service. We highly recommend both.

What should I have on my Web site?

The information and elements you have on your Web site depends on what your ultimate goals are. However, here are a few suggestions for inclusions:

- **Contact information:** Your company name, your name and any other contact information you wish to display. If you include an "About" page, you can describe your credentials, how your company can help someone get organized, your experience and so on. If you're a member of NAPO, you might want to include the NAPO logo. You can obtain this from the NAPO Web site. You might also consider including a photograph of yourself throughout the site. This adds personality and credibility.

- **A strong offer:** I actually have two strong offers on my Web site. I offer both a free "Get Organized Now! Idea-Pak" and a free, weekly "Get Organized Now! Email Newsletter." You should know that I consider these elements to be the most important elements on my Web site. When people ask for these items, I immediately get their email addresses so I can contact them over and over again. Without a strong offer, you won't be able to get people to give you their contact information and since most sales only come after repeated follow-ups, you'll have a very low chance of ever selling them anything.

- **Free tips articles:** Most people want to see free, helpful information when they come to your Web site. Displaying organizing articles on your site will give people something fun, interesting and helpful to read when they visit. I like to have lots of articles on the site. Since people can't read all of my articles in one sitting. They come back to my site again and again to continue reading the rest of them.

  You can either use your own articles or you can ask permission to post someone else's. If you post someone else's article, be sure you 1) get permission to do so and 2) include the byline that the author requests.

  Tips articles (10 tips for . . ., or 7 ideas to help you . . .) are the type that are easiest and most interesting for people to read. Look at any *Woman's Day* or *Better Homes and Gardens* cover and you'll immediately see tips articles listed.

- **Other free information:** The more free information you include on your Web site, the more enticing it's going to be. On my site, I include a number of additional free things including slideshows, tips, checklists, motivational quotes and a discussion forum.

- **A referral system:** If you can get others to refer your Web site to their family members, friends and associates, that can be a very powerful way to generate hundreds of additional visitors to your Web site. You or your webmaster can create your own referral system using a cgi script. There are also some free "tell a friend" services available if you do a web search, but be careful—everything free comes with a price.

♦ **A Web poll:** People love to participate in polls. This added element is a great way to get people involved on your site. You come up with a question and some possible answers. People then come and vote. The system calculates the percentages based on the votes. We use Web site Gear (http://poll.websitegear.com/). It costs approximately $10.00 to $20.00 per month depending on the services you wish to purchase.

♦ **A helpful links page:** This page would contain links to other Web sites that you feel would benefit people. This is also where you would put links to other Web sites that want to do a link exchange with you.

♦ **Product and service information and/or a store:** Include a listing or catalog of your services and products. Also, be sure to be very clear as to how people can obtain these services and products. If they can pay by credit card, make it as easy and clear for people as possible. Give people the option to pay by check, money order, Pay Pal and/or credit card, plus a variety of ways to get their payment to you—over the Internet, by mail, by fax, by phone—and you'll increase your chances of getting more sales.

♦ **A strong guarantee:** On your products and services page, you should seriously consider adding a very strong guarantee. This will help eliminate the risk-factor that people are so afraid of. I offer a 100% money back guarantee on all of my products and services. I believe in everything I sell and I'm willing to back everything with a strong guarantee. In turn, people feel very comfortable buying from me, because they know that if they're not completely satisfied they can return their merchandise for a refund.

If your services and products are excellent, you should end up with a very low return rate. Every business that sells products gets returns. There's no way that your product is going to fit the needs of everyone you sell to. My return rate is less than 2% on average, so offering a strong guarantee is well worth it for me.

♦ **A tracking system:** It is imperative to track the number of visitors you get visiting each of your Web pages. This is the only way you'll be able to make good marketing decisions. For instance, if you put a brand new page up describing one of your services and very few people are visiting that page, you'll then know that something must be done to improve that number of visitors you can get to that page. Or, if lots of people are visiting your free articles page, you might consider displaying something you're selling right on that page.

Know your numbers. If you don't, you're wasting your time and you're making decisions by guessing.

There are many tracking tools available throughout the Web. Some are free and some are paid. Your Web host might even offer something you can use. We use two free tracking tools: Site Meter (www.sitemeter.com) and Google Analytics (www.google.com/analytics). We have a different Site Meter tracker on every important page on our Web sites and we track and record the numbers on a weekly basis.

Basically, you want a tracking system that will tell you how many "unique visitors" go to each of your Web pages. Don't go with a tracking system that just gives you "hits" or "page views." It's very important to get one that tracks "unique visitors." Here are the definitions of these 3 common terms:

✓ **Hits:** This tracking system counts the number of files that are retrieved from your Web host's computer server per Web page. Your html code is one file, plus every graphic on your page is a separate file. In other words, if you have 21 graphics on your page and you get 10 visitors, it will register 220 hits—10 file "hits" for your html code, plus 210 file hits for your 21 graphics. This number is so misleading. It makes it look as if you've had 220 visitors, when in reality, you've only had 10. Some sites use this term to over-exaggerate the site's popularity. Don't do this. It's dishonest. Plus, people who do understand the difference will think you don't understand anything about usable Web numbers.

✓ **Page views:** This number includes all the "visits" to a particular page; not just the "unique" visitors. In other words, if someone comes to your home page on your site and clicks on another link and then returns to your original page again, they're counted each time. If they come back to that page 10 times, they represent 10 page views. This number is used very often by advertisers, since it is important to them to know how many times a particular ad on a page is seen, even if it's seem multiple times by the same person.

✓ **Unique visitors:** This number is exactly what it states—the number of unique people who visit a particular page on your Web site. If they go to another page on your site and then return to the page they started on, they are not counted again. This is the number you should make all of your decisions from since it most accurately represents how many people are visiting your Web site and each of its pages.

Create a Web marketing byline

Your Web marketing byline, also known as your signature line, is one of your primary keys to driving visitors to your Web site.

Basically, your Web marketing byline consists of your name, your Web site name, your Web site address and your free offer.

One of my marketing bylines looks like this:

by Maria Gracia - Get Organized Now!
www.getorganizednow.com
Want to get organized? Get your FREE Get Organized Now! Idea-Pak and Ezine, to help you organize your home, your office and your life, at the Get Organized Now! Web site.

When potential prospects see your free offer, they should be enticed enough to go to your Web site and then take advantage of your offer—a free idea-pak, a free newsletter, a free e-book, etc. Of course, when they request your offer, you'll then receive their email address—which is what you'll use to follow up with them. This is how you'll build your list of potential customers.

When you submit an article for publication, post a message to a discussion forum, write an email, etc., your Web marketing byline should almost always be included after your message.

How can I promote my Web site?

Actively promoting your Web site is very important. People will not be able to find your Web site, among the millions of other Web sites, on their own. The amount of Web site promotion you do is completely up to you. I try to fit in as much Web promotion time as possible into my schedule, because I want to draw thousands of people to my site every single month.

Any time you promote your Web site, you should promote your "free offer." If you're offering a free newsletter, promote that. If you're offering a free e-book, promote that. If your offer is strong and enticing enough, you'll get people visiting your Web site. There are hundreds of ways to promote your site. Here are just a few:

♦ **Search engines:** One of the first things you should do is submit your site to the major search engines. This way, anybody who is looking for information about getting better organized will be able to find you. When you visit the

search engines, be sure you read the submittal instructions carefully on each one. This will help you get listed. Some search engines will list your site immediately. Others take weeks—or months. Occasionally, you'll even have to contact the search engine administrators to determine why your site hasn't been listed, even though you may have submitted once or twice already.

Since many search engines are a free public service and they get hundreds of thousands of submittals each month, you have to take care to be very tactful when you're writing a note to them and not appear that you're either frustrated or angry that you're not yet listed.

Don't expect to be listed in the number one spot on the search engines. This will depend on many criteria. However, there are things you can do to improve the ranking of whatever listing you get. You might want to subscribe to the Search Engine Watch Email Newsletter to keep on top of the latest Search Engine News (www.searchenginewatch.com).

Some of the major search engines at this time are:
- ✓ Google..................www.google.com
- ✓ Yahoo..................www.yahoo.com
- ✓ Alta Vista.............www.altavista.com
- ✓ Excite..................www.excite.com
- ✓ Lycos..................www.lycos.com
- ✓ AOL ....search.aol.com

- ✓   Go.......................www.go.com
- ✓   Live ....www.live.com
- ✓   Ask ....www.ask.com

♦ **Article submittals:** How are your writing skills? A great way to promote your site is by writing articles and submitting them to various publications. Always include your Web marketing byline under the article.

  ✓ You can submit your articles to other email newsletters. Very often, newsletter publishers are looking for free content. In return, they allow you to include your Web marketing byline at the end of each article. When people see your article and notice your byline, they will have the opportunity to visit your Web site.

  ✓ You can also submit your article to Web sites throughout the Web. Again, many people are constantly on the lookout for free content to use on their Web sites.

  ✓ Articles can also be submitted to Article Announce services and other Web sites where people are actually looking for free articles. One of the popular ones is Idea-Marketers (www.ideamarketers.com). Another popular one is Ezine Articles. They can be found at: http://ezinearticles.com. Learn how to search the search engines to find similar types of sites that will accept your articles for publication.

  ✓ Don't forget the good ole' print media. Submit your articles to print magazines, newspapers and other publications for publishing consideration. Don't forget to include your Web marketing byline and offer. If your articles are picked up, you have a good chance of getting hundreds—even thousands—of visitors to your Web site.

♦ **Link exchanges:** One of the ways that search engines determine how high you'll end up in their listings is by determining how popular your Web site is. This is not based on the number of people who actually visit your site. Instead, it's based on the number of people who include a link to your site, from their site.

A great way to get listed on other Web sites is to do a link exchange. They link your site. You link their site. In exchange, you both get visitors from each other's sites and your popularity rating increases.

- **Banner ads:** Banner ads are nothing more than display ads—graphical representations of what you're offering on your Web site. These ads are usually rectangular in appearance. You probably see them all the time as you're surfing the web. Some are even animated.

  I recommend that you don't waste a lot of time with free banner exchanges. Dozens of banners on your page will just make your site look junky and will reduce the number of return visitors.

  You might test some paid banner ads on sites that get an enormous amount of traffic. You'll then have to determine how many visitors—your results—you get from your banner ad on any particular site and if it's worth running in the future. I caution you however, to track your visitors. Banner ads can be very expensive to run if you're not getting good results.

- **Participate in forums or newsgroups:** Throughout the Web, you will find discussion groups on various topics. Many of these sites will allow you to post messages on their forums as long as they're not blatant advertising messages.

  For instance, you might find a forum that you know your target audience frequents. Let's say that scrapbookers are one of your targets and you land upon a scrapbooking Web site with a forum.

  One of the people has posted a message about getting her scrapbooking materials organized. You can then post a message containing a few tips to help this person—tips that are unrelated to your products/services. Then, right before you post your article, you include your Web marketing byline with your free offer and Web site address. This will help you come across as a helpful person, plus it will drive traffic to your Web site.

  Different discussion forums and newsgroup have different policies regarding Web marketing bylines. Some allow you to include your free offer, some allow you to include your Web site only and others don't allow you to include your Web site, or your free offer. Therefore, I caution you to read each Web site's or Newsgroup's guidelines and adhere to them.

  If you don't, there's a chance your post/message will be deleted—or worse, you'll be banned from the forum.

♦ **Electronic press releases:** There are many sites on the Web that will allow you to submit free press releases containing "newsworthy" information. Look for them using your favorite search engines.

In addition, there are also press release services that will submit your press release to hundreds or thousands of online and offline publications. These are paid services, however, so be sure you track your response to determine if this vehicle is worth it for you, or not.

♦ **Ad swaps:** Do you have an ezine? If so, people may be willing to swap ads with you. You include their ad in your ezine and they include your ad in their ezine.

Don't swap ads with just anyone. First, think about your target audience. Does the person you're considering doing the ad swap with have your target audience on his or her subscriber list?

In addition, when you do ad swaps, be sure they're an "even" swap. If you have 5,000 subscribers on your newsletter list and the person you're considering doing a swap with only has 500 subscribers, this is an uneven swap. They'll probably benefit way more than you will.

You can also work out a "ratio" swap. In other words, if you have 5,000 subscribers and you find a list with 10,000 subscribers, you might offer the list owner a 2 for 1 ad swap. In other words, you'll run that person's ad in your next "2" ezine issues, if he/she runs your ad in one issue of his/her ezine issues.

♦ **Free-for-all ads (a.k.a. FFA's):** There are many places on the Web where you can submit free classified ads.

While you may get some visitors from your ads, I must caution you of two things I've discovered. First, when I first started out on the Web, I submitted my free classified ad to many of these FFA sites.

I did get some visitors, although I didn't find them to be as qualified as I would have liked them to be. I also discovered that spammers—people who send unsolicited junk mail to your email box—would hang out at these types of sites just waiting for me to place my free ad so they could get my email address and add it to their spam lists. When I did so, I quickly noticed that my email inbox began to fill up with spam—lots of get-rich-quick and adult-rated emails.

Second, the ads found on many of these FFA sites are very tacky. I decided that I didn't want to associate my business with any of those types of ads. In fact, except for a few FFA sites, I have stopped using them altogether. Your results may differ, of course, but this was my experience.

- ◆ **Contests:** Sometimes there are Web sites that are running contests for their subscribers. You might consider donating one of your services or products as one of the prizes, in exchange for some free promotion.

Before you do this, be sure your target frequents that particular Web site and also be sure the site gets a substantial number of unique visitors on a daily basis. In other words, don't do it unless you foresee getting a large number of visitors to your Web site from it.

- ◆ **Web interviews:** On occasion, you might come across someone who conducts print, audio or video interviews on the Web. This might be a great way to get many visitors coming to your site. Answer the interviewer's questions and make sure you mention your site and your free offers.

- ◆ **Offline marketing:** Web marketing doesn't only have to be conducted on the Web. Promote your Web site and your free offers whenever you can—on your stationery, on your business cards, on your magnetic signs, in print articles, in print interviews, in your ads/flyers, on the radio, to your family/friends/associates/prospects/customers, etc. There is no limit to the possibilities.

Send it often

If you're going to have a Web site, I strongly recommend you have an ezine. It's the best way to keep people returning to your site again and again. You need repeat visits to increase your sales potential.

I write a weekly ezine that is published on Sundays for my Get Organized Now! subscribers. This means I'm contacting my readers a minimum of 52 times per year. My newsletter for professional organizers goes out weekly too—again 52 contacts per year.

Every time I send out an ezine, I get tons of sales. Sales then taper off a bit until I send my next newsletter out.

Since I've been tracking my numbers, I always know about how many sales to expect from every single newsletter I publish.

How do I create a free ezine?

An ezine is a newsletter that you send out using email. I suggest that the majority of your ezine be comprised of free, helpful tips. Of course, you could mention one or a few of your products and services in the ezine. Just don't make the entire newsletter sound like a sales pitch. If you do, people will unsubscribe. Here are some tips regarding creating and sending your ezine:

♦ There are two different ezine formats you can choose to use: either plain text or html formats. Html format is much nicer because you can add colorful graphics, bold headings and other custom formatting to your ezine. Unfortunately, there are still many people who use email software that cannot read html format. That's why I've chosen to send both. I create two versions of my newsletter—one in text and one in html. I then copy and paste both versions into my newsletter host's template. The system automatically detects which version to send based on what various email providers accept.

♦ I strongly recommend that you write your ezine using a program called Textpad, instead of using your word processing program. Word processing programs contain all sorts of codes that when pasted into an email and then sent, could potentially be unreadable or difficult to read by the recipient.

Textpad (www.textpad.com) can be downloaded for free. You can then submit payment to them after your evaluation period. It's a very inexpensive program and well worth it.

After typing your ezine in Textpad, always remember to "convert to DOS" before pasting your newsletter into your email or listserv service you're using. There is an option in Textpad that will allow you to do this. This will eliminate any chance of "bad characters" being transported in your email.

♦ Keep your line lengths to 60 characters or less. In other words, make sure none of your lines go over 60 characters, by pressing your return key when you're at 60 characters or getting close to 60 characters. Many email programs will only display 60 characters per line, before breaking to the next line. If yours goes over the limit, some people will see strange line breaks when they receive your ezine. This looks unprofessional and will be extremely difficult to read.

♦ Subscribe to my newsletter at www.getorganizednow.com or my husband's newsletter at www.givetogetmarketing.com to get an idea of proper ezine newsletter formatting. Make your headings stand out with capital letters. Break up sections with lines, or asterisks for easier reading. Keep your paragraphs down to no more than 4-6 lines each.

♦ In your ezine, be sure to put some teasers to draw people back to your Web site. Once they are there, you can guide them to your store where they can read about your services and products. For instance, every month I update my monthly organizing checklist on my site. Every month in my ezine, I mention that this monthly checklist is available on my Web site. This, in turn, draws people to the site. Of course, besides the checklist, there are also ads for my products on the checklist page that draw people into my store page. A percentage of those people always make a purchase.

♦ There are a number of different ways to send out your ezine. Some people do this right through their email program. Others use something called a listserv.

The more subscribers you have, the more need you'll have for a listserv. While most email programs have a limit to the number of subscribers you can send to at one time, a listserv will allow you to send your ezine to hundreds—even thousands—of people on your list at one time, with the click of your mouse.

I used to use a free service called Topica as my listserv

(http://lists.topica.com/). I then moved on to a paid service called Sparklist (www.sparklist.com), but they turned out to be quite expensive. As of this printing, I'm now using a service called AWeber (www.aweber.com) and am currently happy with what they provide. Their prices are extremely reasonable.

As people subscribe to your ezine, their email addresses are all stored on your list. Every time you want to send out a newsletter, you "post" a message—meaning that you copy and paste your ezine you've just written into your listserv's posting section. At that point, you can send your newsletter out to a subscriber list of 100 or a subscriber list of 100,000—all with one mouse click!

There are certainly other listservs on the market—some free, some paid. Look around to see which one serves you best.

What is a blog, and should I have one?

A blog (a.k.a. web log) is a website or an entry on a web site with regular entries of commentary, descriptions of events, or other material such as photographs or video. On some blogs, readers can also leave comments.

My blog can be found on the following link:

http://getorganizednow.typepad.com/get_organized_now_weblog/

As you'll be able to see, I include information on my family, the book club I belong to, my scrapbooking hobby, travel, events, general tips and more—all of which I usually relate back to the subject of organizing.

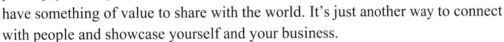

Should you blog? It's up to you, whether or not you enjoy writing, and whether or not you feel you have something of value to share with the world. It's just another way to connect with people and showcase yourself and your business.

Chapter 16
A Future of Possibilities

No matter what type of professional organizing you're already doing now, there's no limit to the opportunities that are available to you in the future. When I first started as a professional organizer, I knew that I didn't want to limit myself to only doing organizing projects and seminars. That's why I jumped out of my box, wrote a book and created a bunch of great organizing products that are being sold not only throughout the country, but around the world. Who knows what other wonderful opportunities the future will hold!

Getting out of your box

You can certainly do very well just doing simple organizing projects. However, if you get out of your box, here are just a few ideas of what you may be able to do in addition to your current professional organizing services:

♦ **Create an organizing tips booklet.** You can then immediately call yourself an "author." Come up with 30 or 100 or 225 two to three sentence tips.

It's fairly simple to come up with tips to include in your booklet. Just remember to always start each tip off with a verb. For instance, "put" your belongings away as soon as you walk in the door to avoid clutter. Or, "give" the clothes you rarely use to a charity organization.

If you feel you can, make the outer cover yourself using a heavier stock—you can use regular 20 pound white stock for the inside—or ask your printer to create one for you. Then, utilize a program like Microsoft Publisher or go to your local printer and have them put your tips into booklet format.

You now have an item you can sell for a few dollars each, use as a free prospecting offer, sell in bulk to larger companies to give to their customers or employees as gifts, and/or use as a promotional item. Plus, you now have "author" credibility.

When you write a booklet, you don't even have to go through the trouble of obtaining licenses. Make sure it has a copyright notice on it so it won't be copied freely. If you wish, you can obtain an official copyright from the copyright office for a fee. (See "Write a Book" in this guide.)

♦ **Write a book.** Seem like a daunting thought? If you break the project down into small steps—just like we teach our clients—it's not as bad as you think. Within a year, you could be an author with lots of credibility under your belt. You'll automatically gain an incredible amount of respect from customers and the media.

There are two ways to write a book. You can either attempt to get your book published by contacting a publishing house or you can self-publish.

✓ **Getting Picked up by a Publisher:** I do warn you that it's not easy to get picked up by a publisher, especially if you've never written a book before. It's not impossible, but it's not easy. If you contact a publisher that happens to agree to publish your book, they will pay for the printing of the book and some of the marketing. That, however, doesn't alleviate you from having to market your book.

You see, publishing firms only have so much money in their budget to market their authors' books. They put the bulk of that marketing budget into sure-shot authors, like Mary Higgins Clark. They're not going to invest that sort of money in an unknown author.

In addition, if you plan on going this route, you should read a few reputable books that tell you exactly how to go about doing this. You have to be very careful. If a publishing company calls you expressing interest in your book, find out who is responsible for paying for the printing. If they say "you are"—run away. You've most likely just spoken to a "vanity" publishing firm. Vanity publishing firms are nothing more than printers trying to land big printing jobs, with you footing the bill. There's a great chance you're going to lose more money than you make.

When dealing with a publishing firm, ask many questions and make sure the final contract that is drawn up is going to be a good agreement for you. Who owns the final rights to the book? Who has the final audio rights and/or CD rights? Who has overseas rights? How much will you have to pay your publisher for copies of your book if you'd like to sell some on your own? Do you have to edit the book as the publisher wishes? Who gets final say concerning the title, jacket cover and copy? Can you print excerpts of your book in your marketing material? How much money will you make per book?—by the way, it's generally only a few dollars each.

✓ **Self-Publishing:** This is the route I took when I wrote my original *Finally Organized, Finally Free* and, recently when I wrote, my new *Finally Organized, Finally Free for the Home* and *Finally Organized, Finally Free for the Office* books.

When you self-publish, you must pay for the printing and design of the book and you must market the book on your own. However, you have full control over the rights of your books, how many you sell and how much profit you can make from each one. There's no red tape. Everything is your decision. The best thing is, it's not as difficult as it may seem.

It took me about 6 months to write my original book, but I sold thousands of copies. It took about a year's time to write my two newest books, which are selling very well. I expect to sell many thousands more over my lifetime.

Once you write your book, it's a matter of compiling everything into a nice looking format, getting it printed and bound—and then marketing it. Initially, you may wish to stick with a small printing firm—even a company like Kinko's could help! When I first started, I had my books printed through a local printing company a few miles away from where I live. Eventually, when you're going to purchase in bulk, you can go with a bigger printing firm. I use Bookmasters, Inc. (www.bookmasters.com).

One of the great things about self-publishing is that you can start off by printing a very small amount of books at a time. Yes, it may cost you a little bit more to do a run of 50 or 100 books, but that's much better than having 4,000 books printed and not making any kind of a profit until years later. In the beginning, I was only getting 50 books printed at a time. Soon after, that went up to 100 book runs, 200 book runs, 500 book runs, 1000 book runs, 5000 book runs, etc. It all depends on how many books you're selling and how much storage space you have.

As far as profit goes, I've been able to get some of my books down to about $5.00 each in printing costs. So, if I sell a particular book at $25 and am only paying $5, that leaves me with a profit of $20 per book sale.

Once you write your book, you have to apply for an ISBN, LCCN, Copyright and Barcode. Some printing companies, like Bookmasters, Inc. will do this for you.

You'll need these elements so that you can sell your book from bookstores and so that you can get your book into libraries around the country. The main things you need are as follows:

* **ISBN-International Standard Book Number**
Approximate cost $200
Obtain from: www.bowker.com

* **LCCN (Library of Congress Catalog Number):**
Free
Obtain from: http://pcn.loc.gov/

* **Registered Copyright:**
Approximate cost: $25
Obtain from: www.copyright.gov

* **Bar Code:**
Approximate cost $25
Obtain from: www.fotel.com

◆ **Create a product.** Do you have an idea for a product that you think people would love to purchase? Listen to your customers and prospects so that you can determine what it is that people really want.

Within two years, I developed a bunch of products including, *Finally Organized, Finally Free*, the *Get Organized Now! Easy Organizer*, the *Holiday Planner*, the *Easy Bill Paying System* and the *Ultimate Guide for Professional Organizers,* in addition to a few print newsletters.

Some other product ideas might be e-books, audio cassettes, video cassettes, CD's, planners, filing systems and computer software. Once you determine what you want to create, you must then determine what materials you're going to need to create it. For my business, so far I've been sticking with "informational type" products, which mainly consist of printouts, binders, pocket folders and index tabs. You can also create a "digital" product that doesn't require any materials at all. Your customer just downloads the book or course from your web site.

If you choose to create something a little more involved, like a filing system or a computer program, there's going to be more legwork involved just to get it manufactured. Don't forget that when you sell products, somebody has to assemble, pack and deliver the boxes to the post office. In the beginning, my husband and I were assembling, packing and preparing the boxes for shipping right in our living room. Then, each morning, we had to pack up the car and head to the post office—sometimes we had to make 2-3 trips!

Once it started to get to the point where our home looked like UPS and the postal clerks sighed every time we walked in with 25-35 boxes to ship, we decided to bite the bullet and delegate this responsibility to a fulfillment service. Now, we email the daily orders to our fulfillment service and they take care of assembling, packing and shipping. They send us a bill at the end of each month and we gladly pay it. Believe me when I say that the investment is *well worth it*.

As far as profit goes, I make anywhere from $10-$50 profit on each product I sell—and I sell tons of product each month—all from my Web site!

♦ **Sell somebody else's products or publications.** I'm very choosy as to what I'll sell on my Web site. Generally, I stick with the products and publications that I create. However, I do sell a few products that other people have created that I truly believe in. This is called an Affiliate Program.

One of my hot sellers is an informational debt-reduction program offered by Leo Quinn. (If you join Leo's affiliate program, please let him know I referred you: www.leoquinn.com) Leo can actually help people pay off their mortgage within 10 years without having to pinch pennies, get a second job or cut back spending in any way. It's an excellent program and I'm proud to offer it to my subscribers. I simply send my subscribers to Leo's sales page and many of them buy. Sales made from my newsletter referrals earn me anywhere from $30-$60 profit on each program I sell. Sometimes I sell 25-100 programs from a single newsletter!

If you're not already signed up to my Get Organized Now! Newsletter, I urge you to do so. You'll be able to see what I'm selling and the types of affiliate programs I associate with. You'll see them listed under "A Word from our Sponsor"—typically four affiliate ads per newsletter.

There are affiliate programs all over the Web. In a nutshell, when you join an affiliate program, you sell their products (digital or other) and you make a commission on each one you sell. Look for affiliate programs that match your goals and then do all you can to make a profit with them. At Get Organized Now!, we pay 51% commissions! If you're not already signed up to our affiliate program, you can do so on the following link: www.getorganizednow.com/affiliate.html

♦ **Get other people to sell your products and publications.** There are many people in the world who would love to try to sell your products and publications for profit. In other words, you could start your own affiliate program. This takes a little bit of thought to determine exactly what the procedure is going to be, but this could be very profitable for you. Remember, in order to get somebody excited about selling your product or book, you have to make it worthwhile for them. Even if you're giving away 30-50% of your profit, likely that is money you would have never had.

We use Clickbank as our affiliate provider. (www.clickbank.com). Once you have everything set up, Clickbank practically takes care of everything else for you—including payment to those selling your products.

♦ **Consulting and Presenting.** You can consult with people on clutter control, time management, goals, and so on. You can do this with individuals, small groups or large groups. Once you're very successful, you can even consult with and coach other professional organizers to help them grow their businesses!

♦ **Joint ventures:** A joint venture is when you work with another business or organization, so that you both benefit. For instance, you might team up with a real estate company. Realtors want client homes that are up for sale to be in ship-shape condition so that the homes will be more enticing to homebuyers. You might draw up a joint venture with a realtor in your town. He/she secures organizing jobs and pays you for your services.

You, in turn, help the realtor by assisting with whatever organizing projects he or she secures.

♦ **Bartering:** This is when you conduct an organizing service in exchange for another business service. For instance, you might help your local printer rid his office of clutter if he agrees to print your business flyers for free. This is a great way to build your business on a shoe-string.

♦ **Build your empire.** As you grow, you might need to contract out some of your services. You might even choose to hire employees. Perhaps your service will expand to include concierge services or party planning, for example. Keep an open mind, because there will always be new and exciting paths for you to travel.

Cause marketing

This type of marketing is done to help out a particular cause, such as an organization for heart disease, or the boy scouts, or the community, while your business benefits at the same time—either you get exposure in the community or you are actually able to generate some prospects.

In this case, you might be asked to donate your organizing services or products. For instance, you might be asked to donate a copy of your book as a door prize. Perhaps, you may be asked to donate a few hours of your organizing services as part of a fantasy auction. Or maybe, you'll be asked to speak at an event without getting paid.

Cause marketing takes time—sometimes a lot of time. You have to decide which cause marketing is going to be beneficial to you and which will not be. It's great for you to donate your services or products to causes you believe in—and perhaps on occasion you'll even do this with no intention of any personal gain. However, in most cases, the cause you're involved in should be with the intention of helping the cause "and" marketing your business—a true win-win situation.

Your idea file

I highly recommend that you have a method to capture and store all of your business ideas. Very often, ideas may come to you as you're walking down the street, when you're driving your car, or when you're eating dinner. Jot these ideas down, record them on a tape recorder, or store them electronically on a computer or a palm pilot.

Every day, review your ideas and determine which ones you would like to implement. Then, make sure they end up on your To Do list and/or in your Future Project Files.

How do I go about getting more speaking engagements?

If you want to speak in front of groups, wonderful. If you have conquered the fear of speaking in public, you can do just about anything!

Offering free speaking engagements in the hopes of generating prospects for your business will be easier than securing paid workshops.

You can simply call around town and offer your free talks to libraries, church groups, Chambers of Commerce, businesses, social clubs and more. If you have some good credentials to show, and good social graces, you'll likely get plenty of opportunities to speak for free.

If you're expecting paid speaking engagements, start small. Some universities, businesses and other groups will be willing to pay you if you offer them a fairly good deal. You can try just calling and seeing if you can get a few speaking engagements right on the phone.

Another possibility is to send out letters to the decision makers, along with your media kit. Be sure you make good offers to generate prospects. Don't forget, even if you mail letters, you'll still need to follow up with phone calls.

Don't expect $1000 paid speaking engagements right off the bat. You'll need to get experience first. Once you've done at least a dozen organizing presentations to small groups, then you might begin to pursue larger groups and more money for your expertise.

The more speaking engagements you do, the more of a chance that someone will find out about you and contact you about doing a presentation at her business or an organization she knows of.

Set up speaking parties

I'm sure you're familiar with Mary Kay, Tupperware, Tastefully Simple, AtHome America, Silpada and other home-based businesses. These businesses all follow the "at home party" system. There's nothing saying that you can't do exactly the same thing!

You can set up similar types of parties in your own home and book parties through attendees at their homes. At your house, you'd be the party host, offering organizing ideas and suggestions. The idea is to make people feel comfortable, laugh and have fun. Perhaps you'd have treats and beverages and prizes! An organizing home party can be just as fun as a make up party or a kitchen goods party.

If an attendee books a party from you, you can give that person a special gift when she holds the party for you—such as an organizing basket of goodies, or organizing books. She invites her friends to the party and provides the food and beverages—usually cake, chips and dip and a beverage such as lemonade. You, as usual, offer your organizing tips and ideas, have little games so attendees can win prizes, etc.

At the end of your session, you can offer your organizing services or products to the attendees for purchase. Perhaps even offer 1 free hour of organizing to each attendee interested just to get your foot in the door.

Who says organizing can't be fun?!

What is this "home staging" thing all about?

According to realestateabc.com, professional home stagers are practiced in the art of preparing a home for resale. They work with the "flow" of a home, eliminate clutter, edit and arrange furniture, and even assist in enhancing curb-appeal. With the aid of a professional home stager, your house can make a notable first impression on potential homebuyers.

Since many professional organizers focus on getting rid of clutter and coming up with excellent storage solutions, many have latched on to this wonderful "extra" opportunity of home staging.

In addition to your organizing knowledge and expertise, to be a home stager you'll also need a bit of design know-how. There are actually classes for learning how to be a home-stager and certifications. However, if you're good at organizing and good at designing, you can certainly add home staging to your list of credentials.

Any testimonials you can get for your home staging abilities and successes should be added to your portfolio. While this is definitely a more advanced stage of professional organizing, it can also be a very lucrative one.

If you're thinking of doing this, try teaming up with real estate agents in your area. They may hire you to organize and stage homes, so they can sell them quicker. If you do a good job, chances are they'll contact you over and over again.

The other possibility is looking around for "For Sale By Owner" signs. In these cases, you can send a letter to the homeowner, or knock on their door for that matter, and make an offer to them. Perhaps you can give them a "10 Ways to Sell Your Home Quick" booklet, filled with tips and ideas.

Of course, one of the ideas would be to hire you as an organizer and a home stager!

I think I'd like to write a book. What do I need to know?

This is a big question, and it would take an entirely separate book to go through all the logistics. But as a guideline, first write one sentence defining what your book is going to be about. Then, come up with chapter titles. Make a file folder or computer document for each of the chapters, and begin tackling the writing of your book chapter by chapter.

As previously mentioned in this book, although you can certainly pursue getting your book picked up by a major publisher, I'm a big believer in self-publishing. With self-publishing, you have more control over how much you make from your book, and how long you make that money. You are responsible for all aspects of marketing your book so be prepared to work hard to sell it.

I currently use Bookmasters, Inc. to print my books. Their web site is:

www.bookmasters.com

Before printing, you will need to obtain an ISBN, LCCN, Copyright and Bar Code. Bookmasters actually handles this for you. Some book printers do not and you'll have to handle all this footwork yourself.

Ordering in a low quantity, such as 100, will bring your per book cost up dramatically. You can pay, for example, $12 or more for a single book of 150 pages depending on your book cover, type of paper, etc. However, ordering in a higher quantity often saves you a bundle of money—perhaps bringing the price per book down to $4 or $5, again, depending on your criteria.

I usually order in quantities of 1,000. I could save even more by ordering 5,000, but you also have to consider storage options. In addition, if an error is found in one of my books, I can correct it after 1,000 are sold, rather than waiting for 5,000 to be sold.

As far as your book cover, it is recommended you find a book cover designer to handle this for you. For Finally Organized, Finally Free for the Home, I used Cathi Stevenson of Book Cover Express (www.bookcoverexpress.com). I was very happy with her work.

If you require an index, I strongly recommend you don't attempt this yourself. I tried this with the first edition of *Finally Organized, Finally Free* and it was a nightmare. Since then, I've used WordCo Indexing Services (www.wordco.com). They were also a pleasure to work with and did a super job.

You should also have your book edited. I farmed this work out and have used several different people to edit my various publications. Never edit your work yourself. It's always better to have a second or third set of eyes.

If you go the route of getting picked up by a publisher, there are countless books in the library and bookstores to teach you how to do so. Please note that it's not that easy to get published.

If you're one of the lucky ones, your publisher will pay to get your books printed and will help you get them into bookstores. You will only get a few dollars for each book, but if you're fortunate enough to get on Oprah or something amazing like that, you'll make up for that small amount per book in volume. Your publisher will expect you to attend book signings and to promote your book as much as possible.

The only problem is that when the next latest and greatest book comes out, and if and when sales on your book fizzles out, the publisher will refocus their time and energy, and won't continue to put their energy into your publication.

This is the major reason why I like self-publishing my own books. I will give them the time and energy they deserve—forever!

What about creating my very own product?

I highly recommend it, if you've come up with an idea that is certain to sell. I've put my time and efforts into creating "informational" products. I started with my books, and then created binder-type products, such as my Easy Organizer, Bill Paying System and Holiday Planner. A recent product I've created is also an informational product—My Oh-So-Organized Filing System. I also have several "digital downloadable" products.

You've probably noticed a few other products I sell on my site and in my newsletter. I find great products from time to time that are manufactured by other companies and I resell them.

I haven't created, for instance, a storage container that would require a product designer and manufacturer. This is definitely a more involved process that requires you to seek patent information and requires you to pay someone to "make" it for you. If you're going to go this route, first be sure there's a market that is going to buy your creation. I would suggest having just a few made initially if possible and see if you can sell those.

Don't just ask your friends if they'd buy your creation. They'll probably say YES, just to make you feel good. You've got to try to sell your creation to people who you don't know, and who don't know you. Be sure you do your research, before investing your life savings.

Once you come up with something that sells like hot cakes, you'll know there's a market for your wares!

Conclusion

Now that you've discovered what you need to know about starting, running and growing your professional organizing business, it's time to think about your objectives and what you'd like to implement so you can reach all of your personal and business goals.

This may seem like a lot of information, but if you do a little bit each day, you'll have the potential to grow your business exponentially.

Set some business goals for the next few months, for a few years and for 10 years from today. Adjust them as needed. Remember, you should always be in "continuous improvement" mode.

Work every day to achieve your goals.

If you're dedicated and persistent, your knowledge, skill and motivation will increase and your rewards will be plentiful.

Be sure to check out all of the vehicle examples, forms and bonus products included in this guide. I've included a nice variety that you can use for your professional organizing business.

Please continue to visit all of our Web sites:

- Get Organized Now!:
  www.getorganizednow.com

- Get Organized Now! for Professional Organizers:
  www.getorganizednow.com/po.html

- Give to Get Marketing:
  www.givetogetmarketing.com

They are constantly being updated to provide you with the information you need for maximum business success.

I wish you every success possible—in your business and your life!

Maria Gracia

Chapter 17
Sample Marketing Vehicles

Don't recreate the wheel. It took us years to develop these marketing vehicle formats. There's no need to redo the layouts of these items. When you're done, your marketing vehicles should look exactly like these—but with your offers and information, of course. You have our permission to mirror these formats exactly, with your own business information, logos, etc.

FRONT (3 1/2" X 2")

(BACK 3 1/2" X 2")

Business Cards to Generate Prospects

FRONT :

1. Put your logo here if you have one.
2. Put you name and title or credentials here.
3. Direct them to your Web site with a free offer.
4. Put your address here.
5. Put your phone, fax and e-mail here.

BACK :

6. Put your offer here. Tell them what they will get.
7. Describe your offer in more detail in a bulleted list of teasers.
8. If possible, include a graphic illustration of your Info-Pak.
9. Give them more than one way to respond.
10. Call to Action and Tracking Code. Tell them what to do. Tell them there is No Obligation.

184

SIMPLE LISTING EXAMPLES

GET ORGANIZED NOW!
611 Arlington Way.............. **555-555-5555**

① GET ORGANIZED NOW!
611 Arlington Way.............. **555-555-5555**

GET ORGANIZED NOW!
www.getorganizednow.com
611 Arlington Way.............. **555-555-5555**

GET ORGANIZED NOW!
Get Your Free Idea-Kit at our Web site
www.getorganizednow.com
611 Arlington Way.............. **555-555-5555**

GET ORGANIZED NOW!
Call for Your FREE, No Obligation,
Get Organized Now! Idea-Kit #13
611 Arlington Way.............. **555-555-5555**

1 COLUMN BOX AD EXAMPLES

GET ORGANIZED NOW!
FREE ORGANIZING IDEA-KIT
www.getorganizednow.com
611 Arlington Way...........**555-555-5555** **②**

GET ORGANIZED NOW!
CALL FOR YOUR
FREE ORGANIZING IDEA-KIT
611 Arlington Way...........**555-555-5555**

GET ORGANIZED NOW!
FREE ORGANIZING IDEA-KIT
www.getorganizednow.com
Includes Description of Our Services & Pricing
611 Arlington Way...........**555-555-5555**

GET ORGANIZED NOW!
RESIDENTIAL OR BUSINESS
CLUTTER CONTROL – PAPER MGT
CALL FOR YOUR
FREE ORGANIZING IDEA-KIT #13
611 Arlington Way...........**555-555-5555**

1 COLUMN DISPLAY AD EXAMPLES

Yellow Page Ads to Generate Prospects

1. Simple Listing. You can add your web site, or offer your free Idea-Kit to encourage even more Prospect Calls. Track your ad with Idea-Kit #13.

2. One-Column Box Ads. You can promote your Free Idea-Kit, your web site or your general service with your Idea-Kit. Track your ad with Idea-Kit #13.

3. One-Column Display Ad. A display ad is much more expensive, but it allows you to grab attention and include more information about your offer. Track your ad with Idea-Kit #13.

4. One-Column Display Ad with Idea-Kit Graphic. You can get even more attention and response by including a graphic of your Idea-Kit. Track your ad with Idea-Kit #13.

❶ FREE to Business Owners

Call Today to Receive Your Free,
No Obligation "Organize Your Business" Booklet

❷ Your FREE "Organize Your Business" Booklet Will Include:

✓ FREE - 9 Simple Steps to the Perfect Filing System

✓ FREE - The Secret Tool to Help You and Your Staff Find Anything in Your Office in Under 15 Seconds

✓ FREE - 12 Sure-Fire Tips to Slash New Employee Training Time **❹**

✓ FREE - 23 Productivity Ideas to Help You Get a Lot More Done In a Lot Less Time

✓ Plus, a Description of Our Office Organizing Services and Prices **❺**

For More Free Organizing Tips, Visit: www.getorganizednow.com

Call Today: 555-555-5555 Ext 30 **❻**

❸ FREE ORGANIZE YOUR BUSINESS

Or Mail to: **Get Organized Now!** **❼**
611 Arlington Way, Watertown, WI 53094

Name: _____

Company: _____

Address: _____

❽ City: _____ ST: _____ Zip: _____ **❾**

Phone: _____

4 1/4" x 4 1/2"

This is the size of a standard Business Card

FREE "Organize Your Business" Info-Pak

It's FREE to Business Owners

It Includes: • 5 Steps to the Perfect Filing System • Find Anything in 15 Seconds or Less • Slash Employee Training Time • Get a Lot More Done in a Lot Less Time • and Much More

Get Organized Now!
611 Arlington Way, Watertown, WI 53094
For More Free Tips, Visit: www.getorganizednow.com

Call 555-555-5555 Ext 32 - There's No Obligation

3 1/2" x 2"

Small Space Ads to Generate Prospects

1. Name your Target Prospects to ensure you get their attention.
2. Put your offer here. Tell them what they will get. Tell them there is No Obligation.
3. If possible, include a graphic illustration of your booklet.
4. Describe your offer in more detail with bulleted teasers.
5. Direct them to your Web site with a free offer.

6. Call to Action & Tracking Code. Tell them what to do.
7. Give them more than one way to respond.
8. Give your prospects a form to fill out for ordering.
9. Use a bold coupon border so they will know at a glance that there is an offer to send for.

FREE To Business Owners

Who Would Like Their Staff to Get Twice as Much Done in Half the Time!

(1)

Get Your Free, No Obligation "Organize Your Business!" Booklet Today

(2) *Here's what you'll receive in your free "Organize Your Business!" Booklet:*

✓ **9 Simple Steps to the Perfect Filing System**

✓ **The Secret Tool to Help You and Your Staff Find Anything in Your Office in Under 15 Seconds**

(3)

✓ **12 Sure-Fire Tips to Slash New Employee Training Time**

✓ **23 Productivity Ideas to Get a Lot More Done In a Lot Less Time**

✓ **Plus, You'll Receive Our Affordable, Office Organizing Service Description and Prices**

For More Free Organizing Tips, Visit:
www.getorganizednow.com

(4)

(5)

Dear business owner,

It's getting more and more difficult to keep up with the daily demands of running a business today.

The "paperless" society turned out to be a joke, and new employees are taking longer and longer to bring up to speed.

Organizing your office and your staff for greater productivity, is a must in today's hectic and chaotic business environment.

We can help. We've created a new "Organize Your Office," booklet filled with effective tips to help you and your staff get more done in a lot less time.

There's absolutely no obligation. Simply fill out the coupon below and fax or mail it.

Maria Gracia, Owner
Get Organized Now!

(6)

Call, Fax or Mail Today to Receive Your Free, No Obligation *"Organize Your Business"* Booklet

Call: **555-555-5555** Ext 21

(7) Fax: **555-555-5555**

Or Mail to:

(8) GET ORGANIZED NOW!
611 ARLINGTON WAY
WATERTOWN WI 53094

☑ **Yes!** Send me my **FREE**, *"Organize Your Business,"* Booklet. *I understand there is no obligation.* **(9)**

NAME (PLEASE PRINT) _____

COMPANY _____ **(10)**

ADDRESS_____

CITY _____

STATE _____ ZIP _____ PHONE _____

YOUR BOOKLET WILL BE MAILED THE SAME DAY. NO OBLIGATION. HURRY, SUPPLIES ARE LIMITED. **(11)**
© 2000-2012 GET ORGANIZED NOW!

Flyer to Generate Prospects

1. Name your Target Prospects to ensure you get their attention.
2. Put your offer here. Tell them what they will get.
3. Describe your offer in more detail with a bulleted list of teasers.
4. Direct them to your Web site with a free offer.
5. Include a personal letter here stating the problem and solution.
6. Put your Call to Action here. Tell them how to get the offer.
7. Give them a few ways to respond. Put your phone and fax here.
8. Put your mailing address here.
9. Use a bold coupon border. Remind them of the offer and that there is No Obligation.
10. Give them a form to fill out for ordering. Ask them to PLEASE PRINT.
11. Let them know that their booklet will be mailed immediately. Remind them of No Obligation again, and that Supplies are Limited to overcome procrastination.

①
611 Arlington Way
Watertown, WI 53094

555-555-5555 Voice or Fax
getorgnow@charter.net
www.getorganizednow.com

② A Special Offer to People Who Want to Find More Time to Enjoy Their Lives

Free "Get Organized Now! Idea-Kit **③**

④ Call Today 555-555-5555, Ask for Ext 20

⑤ Dear Friend,   **⑥**

Wouldn't you love to organize your home, your office and your life?

⑦ I am a local, professional organizer, and I'd like to send you a free informative, no obligation, Idea-Kit of organizing tips designed to help you get organized so that you can find a lot more time in your life for the things you love to do.

Your Free, "Get Organized Now! Idea-Kit will include:

- ✓ Fourteen important techniques for saving time

⑧ - ✓ How to reduce clutter by more than 50%

- ✓ How to find an extra 2 hours per day to relax or spend with your family

- ✓ Plus, dozens of effective tips to help you find more time

- ✓ Descriptions and prices of my affordable, organizing services

⑩ There is no obligation. Your Idea-Kit will be mailed the same day. **⑨**

Hurry. Supplies of the Idea-Kit are limited. Call today.

You can fax this letter to 555-555-5555 to receive your free "Get **⑪** Organized Now!" Idea-Kit, or fill out and mail this letter to, Get Organized Now!, 611 Arlington Way, Watertown WI 53094.

Name:_____ Organization:_____

⑫ Address:_____

City:_____ State:_____ Zip:_____

Phone: (_____)_____

Sincerely,

⑬ *Maria Gracia*

Maria Gracia - Owner, Get Organized Now!   **⑭**

For More Free Organizing Tips, Visit: www.getorganizednow.com

Direct Mail Letter to Generate Prospects

1. You can put the letter on your standard letterhead or plain, inexpensive, white paper without a letterhead.
2. Name your Target Prospects here so they know you have something specifically for them.
3. Put your offer here. This is what they will get.
4. Tell them upfront how they can get your free offer.
5. Use Dear friend, or Dear business owner, etc.
6. State your major benefit in the first paragraph.
7. Introduce yourself, and explain your offer in more detail.
8. Tell them some of the things they will learn from your free Idea-Kit. Make them enticing. List them in bulleted format.
9. Let them know that there is no obligation, and that they will receive their free kit quickly.
10. Give them a reason to act now, or they may procrastinate.
11. Give them a few more ways to respond.
12. Give them a simple form to fill out to mail or fax.
13. Sign the original so that you won't have to sign the copies.
14. Direct them to your Web site with a free offer.

1 ☑ *Yes!* Send me my FREE, "Organize Your Business," Booklet. I understand there is no obligation.

NAME _____

COMPANY _____

ADDRESS _____

_____

CITY _____

STATE _____ ZIP _____

PHONE _____

2

For More Free Tips and a Free Newsletter, Visit:
3 www.getorganizednow.com

PLACE
STAMP
HERE

4

FRONT

Maria Gracia
Get Organized Now!
5 611 Arlington Way
Watertown, WI 53094

Get Twice as Much Done in Half the Time.

BACK

FREE

ORGANIZE
Your
BUSINESS!

6

FREE to
Business Owners:

7

New "Organize Your Business" Booklet

8

Call Today 555-555-5555 Ext 18,
Mail This Card, or Fax to 555-555-5555

9

Your Free "Organize Your Business" Booklet Will Include:

☑ *FREE - 9 Simple Steps to the Perfect Filing System*

10 ☑ *FREE - The Secret Tool to Help You and Your Staff Find Anything in Your Office in Under 15 Seconds*

☑ *FREE - 12 Sure-Fire Tips to Slash New Employee Training Time*

☑ *FREE - 23 Productivity Ideas to Get a Lot More Done In a Lot Less Time*

☑ *FREE - A Description of Our Affordable Office Organizing Services & Prices*

11 **No Obligation! Just Drop This Card in the Mail Today!**

HURRY. SUPPLIES OF FREE BOOKLETS ARE LIMITED. MAIL TODAY! **12**

Postcard to Generate Prospects - Version A
Include with Your Direct Mail Letter, or Hand Out as a Stand-Alone, Prospect Generator

1. Remind them of the offer and that there is No Obligation.
2. Give your prospects a form to fill out for ordering.
3. Direct them to your Web site with a free offer.
4. Tell them they must put postage on the postcard.
5. Put your name and address on the front of the card.
6. If possible, include a graphic illustration of your booklet.
7. Name your Target Prospects to ensure you get their attention.

8. Put your offer here. Tell them what they will get.
9. Call to Action & Tracking Code. Tell them what to do to get your offer. Give them more than one way to respond.
10. Describe your offer in more detail with bulleted teasers.
11. Tell them there is No Obligation, and remind them to respond.
12. Let them know that supplies are limited to overcome their procrastination.

Door Hangers to Generate Prospects

1. Put a large FREE to get attention to your offer.
2. Tell them to call for the offer. Tell them there is No Obligation.
3. Put your offer here. Tell them what they will get.
4. Describe your offer in more detail with bulleted teasers.
5. Direct them to your Web site with a free offer.
6. If possible, include a graphic illustration of your Info-Pak.
7. Call to Action and Tracking code.
8. Put your mailing address here.
9. Give your prospects a form to fill out for ordering.
10. Use a bold coupon border so they will know at a glance that there is an offer to send for.

① *News Release*

② ATTENTION: LIFESTYLES EDITOR   FOR IMMEDIATE RELEASE **④**
                                            NO KILL DATE **⑤**

③ CONTACT: Maria Gracia
                  Get Organized Now!
                  611 Arlington Way
                  Watertown, WI 53094
PHONE: (555)-555-5555   E-MAIL: getorgnow@charter.net
FAX: (555)-555-5555   WEB SITE: www.getorganizednow.com

⑥ Free "Get Organized Now!" Idea-Kit
Filled with dozens of tips to help you get organized

⑦ WATERTOWN, WI—A free organizing idea kit titled, The Get Organized Now! Idea-Kit describes over 50 simple techniques for organizing your home, your office and your life.

Here are just a few of the many tips you'll discover: "Fourteen important techniques for saving time," "How to never forget an appointment, a deadline or a detail again," and "Three simple **⑧** tools to help you double your productivity," plus, dozens more simple tips to help you find more time.

To receive your free kit, call (555) 555-5555, Ext 21, or visit the Get Organized Now! Web **⑨** site at www.getorganizednow.com or write to Get Organized Now! Idea-Kit, 611 Arlington Way, Watertown, WI 53094.

For more free organizing tips, and a free newsletter, visit the Get Organized now! Website **⑩** www.getorganizednow.com

###

⑪

⑫
PAGE 1 of 1

News Release to Generate Prospects
Offer: Free Idea-Kit of organizing tips

1. Put the words News Release in large type.
2. If you know the specific editor, put his/her name and department here, or else put EDITOR.
3. Put your contact information here.
4. Always put FOR IMMEDIATE RELEASE.
5. For timeless releases, put NO KILL DATE. For releases that expire, put KILL: October 8, 2012 (put appropriate date).
6. Your headline should describe what the readers will get.

7. Start the release off with your city and state.
8. Double space your copy whenever possible, and start each new paragraph with a half inch indent.
9. Tell the readers how to get your Idea-Kit. Give them more than one way to respond. Use a Tracking Code.
10. Direct them to your Web site with a free offer.
11. Indicate the end of your release with ###, or -END-.
12. Put the page number and total number of pages included on each page of your release.

❶ *Article Submission*

❷ **ATTENTION:**   **LIFESTYLES EDITOR**   **FOR IMMEDIATE RELEASE** ❹
                                                     NO KILL DATE ❺

❸ **CONTACT:**   Maria Gracia
                  Get Organized Now!
                  611 Arlington Way
                  Watertown, WI 53094

PHONE: (555)-555-5555   **E-MAIL:**   getorgnow@charter.net
FAX: (555)-555-5555   **WEB SITE:**   www.getorganizednow.com

---

NOTE TO THE EDITOR: The following article may be used in your publication without obligation or payment to the author, as long as the ending author resource paragraph is printed with the article.

---

❻ 8 Ideas for Organizing Your Child's Room
by Maria Gracia

"Clean your room."

"Ugh! Oh, Mom. I'll do it later!"

This same dialog is shared by millions of parents and their children all over the world. Do you suddenly have the driving urge to get your child's room in order? Where do you start? Here are a few ideas:

❼ **1. SCHEDULE.** Schedule a specific date and time to clean out your child's room. Your daughter or son, if she or he is old enough, should be there to help.

2. DUMP OR DONATE. Have a large box on hand for items you will be donating to your local charity or selling at a rummage sale. Also, have a large plastic garbage bag--maybe two or three--for everything you will be disposing of. Your son or daughter can help here. Let them know that every item that is of no use to them, that they donate, will be helping another child. Also, tell them that it's important to discard anything that will never be used, to make room for new, useful items.

3. CLOTHES CLOSET. The clothes closet is usually a good place to start. Pull everything out until it's completely empty. Then, the only items that should be returned to the closet are those articles of clothing or other items that are going to be used again. This should eliminate clothing that doesn't fit, is worn out, and so on. If you're not sure if an item fits your child anymore, have him or her try it on right now.

❽ *Continued on Page 2*   ❾ PAGE 1 of 2

Page 1 - Article Submittal to Generate Prospects
Offer: Visit our Web site for a Free Idea-Kit of Organizing Tips

1. Put the words Article Submittal in large type.
2. If you know the specific editor, put his/her name here, or else put EDITOR
3. Put your contact information here.
4. Always put FOR IMMEDIATE RELEASE
5. For timeless submittals, put NO KILL DATE. For submittals that expire, put KILL: October 8, 2012 (put appropriate date)
6. Your article headline should be enticing for their readers.
7. Double space your article and write it in "tips" format. Number each tip and start each tip with a short, bold, description title.
8. If necessary, tell them that the article is continued on page 2.
9. Put the page number and total number of pages included on each page of your submittal.

① CONTACT: Maria Gracia
Get Organized Now!
611 Arlington Way
Watertown, WI 53094

PHONE: (555)-555-5555 **E-MAIL:** getorgnow@charter.net
FAX: (555)-555-5555 **WEB SITE:** www.getorganizednow.com

② *Continued from Page 1*

4. **BASEBALL CAPS.** Hang a baseball cap rack on the back of your child's bedroom door to keep all caps neat and organized. Ensure it's at a reachable level that your child understands the proper way to hang the caps on it.

③ 5. **SHOES.** A shoe rack can keep children's shoes organized, easily accessible and in one place. Show your child how to organize shoes, keeping all pairs together and separating dress shoes from casual.

6. **STUFFED ANIMALS, TOYS AND GAMES.** Put up shelves in children's rooms. This is usually a better solution for toy storage versus containers, because the toys won't get crushed and will be easily obtainable. Make sure the shelves are at a reasonable height so that your child can reach wanted items.

7. **PAPER.** Create a filing system for your child, to keep artwork, rock star photos, blank paper, notes from family and friends, etc. Use a portable filing container that is capable of holding hanging files and that can be transported to someplace else if necessary. The ones with handles are nice, since they can be transported to different homes, on vacation, and so on. Some of these containers have snap-shut compartments for pens, pencils, clips, and more.

8. **RESPONSIBILITY.** Teach your children to clean and organize as soon as they're old enough to do so. If you help them do this now, you will be helping them when they're old enough to move out on their own. Devise a simple daily checklist for maintenance. If you have two children sharing the same room, divide the room in half with an imaginary line. Describe this imaginary line to each child. Assign each one the responsibility of keeping their side clean and organized.

RESOURCE BOX:

④ Maria Gracia is the owner of Get Organized Now! and author of Finally Organized, Finally Free. You can get a Organized Now! Idea-Pak filled with over 50 simple tips to help you get organized, plus a newsletter and thousands of *free* tips, systems, articles, ideas and tools, etc. by simply visiting her Web site: www.getorganizednow.com

# # #

⑤

⑥
PAGE 2 of 2

Page 2 - Article Submittal to Generate Prospects
Offer: Visit our Web site for a Free Idea-Kit of Organizing Tips

1. Repeat your Contact Information.
2. I them from what page the article is continued from.
3. Continue the body of the article.
4. Direct them to your Web site with your free offer. You will get your Prospects' e-mail addresses when they request your free, Idea-Pak.

5. Indicate the end of your release with ###, or -END-.
6. Put the page number and total number of pages included on each page of your release.

① Get Organized Now!
611 Arlington Way
Watertown, WI 53094

②

**③ Call 555-555-5555 Ext 19 Today
for Your FREE, No Obligation,
"Organize Your Business" Booklet**

④

PLACE
STAMP
HERE

FRONT

⑤
JANE DOE
123 ANY STREET
ANYWHERE, USA 55555

BACK

Get Twice as Much Done in Half the Time.

⑥

FREE
ORGANIZE
Your
BUSINESS!

⑦ **FREE to**
⑧ **Business Owners:**
New "Organize Your Business" Booklet
Call Today 555-555-5555 Ext 18,
⑨ **Mail This Card, or Fax to 555-555-5555**

Your Free "Organize Your Business" Booklet Will Include:

⑩
☑ *FREE - 9 Simple Steps to the Perfect Filing System*
☑ *FREE - The Secret Tool to Help You and Your Staff Find Anything in
        Your Office in Under 15 Seconds*
☑ *FREE - 12 Sure-Fire Tips to Slash New Employee Training Time*
☑ *FREE - 23 Productivity Ideas to Get a Lot More Done In a Lot Less Time*
☑ *FREE - A Description of Our Affordable Office Organizing Services & Prices*

⑪ **No Obligation! Just Drop This Card in the Mail Today!**

HURRY. SUPPLIES OF FREE BOOKLETS ARE LIMITED. MAIL TODAY! ⑫

Postcard to Generate Prospects - Version B
Mail this Self-Mailing, Stand-Alone, Post Card to your Target Group

1. Put your Company Name and return address here.
2. Get their attention with a bold FREE! graphic.
3. Call to Action & Tracking Code. Tell them what to do to get your offer.
4. Put your postage here.
5. Put the mailing labels of your Target Group here.
6. If possible, include a graphic illustration of your booklet.
7. Name your Target Prospects to ensure you get their attention.

8. Put your offer here. Tell them what they will get.
9. Call to Action & Tracking Code. Tell them what to do to get your offer. Give them more than one way to respond.
10. Describe your offer in more detail with bulleted teasers.
11. Tell them there is No Obligation, and remind them to respond.
12. Let them know that supplies are limited to overcome their procrastination.

**①*News Release*

②ATTENTION: LIFESTYLES EDITOR   FOR IMMEDIATE RELEASE **④**
                                          NO KILL DATE **⑤**

③CONTACT: Maria Gracia
              Get Organized Now!
              611 Arlington Way
              Watertown, WI 53094

PHONE: (555)-555-5555   **E-MAIL:**   getorgnow@charter.net
FAX: (555)-555-5555   **WEB SITE:** www.getorganizednow.com

⑥ Successful professional organizer says,
"Anybody can get organized!"

⑦ "I'll have to do that . . . when I find the time."
"I can't find my . . . "
"I don't know where to start!"
"I really have to get organized!"

This common dilemma has been expressed over and over by millions of people around the globe. The good news is that *anybody can get organized.*

Meet Maria Gracia, founder of the Get Organized Now! web site. Gracia is also the author of the book, "Finally Organized, Finally Free," and the creator of a number of publications and products to help you get organized in your home, your office and your life.

⑧ Gracia says, "Disorganization can actually you into living a life filled with stress, frustration and chaos. It can rob you of the precious time you should be spending enjoying your life." She also says, "By overcoming disorganization, you can be set *free* to live the kind of life you've always dreamed of."

Gracia, who has attracted thousands of people to her Get Organized Now! web site www.getorganizednow.com, offers simple solutions on all aspects of getting organized, including time management, clutter control and goal achievement.

She stresses that getting organized can be extremely simple, when you understand the five basic steps:

1) Get motivated.
2) Set a goal.
3) Establish a deadline.
4) Designate a reward.
5) Apply effective organizational systems.

The best news of all is that by getting organized, you really can focus your time on the things you achieve your goals and dreams!

⑨ You can get a *free* Get Organized Now! Idea-Pak filled with over 50 simple tips to help you get organized, plus a *free* newsletter and thousands of *free* tips, systems, articles, ideas and tools, etc. by simply visiting her Web site: www.getorganizednow.com

⑩ PAGE 1 of 2

Page 1 - News Release to Generate Prospects
Offer: Visit Web site for free organizing tips

1. Put the words News Release in large type
2. If you know the specific editor, put his/her name here, or else put EDITOR
3. Put your contact information here.
4. Always put FOR IMMEDIATE RELEASE
5. For timeless releases, put NO KILL DATE. For releases that expire, put KILL: October 8, 2007 (put appropriate date)

6. Promise a benefit or the solution to a problem in your headline.
7. Start the release off with an attention getting teaser.
8. Provide a number of personal quotes and a few tips.
9. Use the last paragraph to tell the readers how to get your idea-kit.
10. Put the page number and total number of pages included on each page of your release.
NOTE: You will get your Prospects' e-mail addresses when they visit your web site and request your Idea-Kit.

① ATTENTION: **LIFESTYLES EDITOR** PHONE: (555)-555-5555
CONTACT: Maria Gracia FAX: (555)-555-5555
Get Organized Now!
611 Arlington Way E-MAIL: getorgnow@charter.net
Watertown, WI 53094 WEB SITE: www.getorganizednow.com

---

② **Maria Gracia can provide you with a fun and informative interview to help your readers get organized now!**

③ *Maria Gracia, founder of Get Organized Now! and the author of "Finally Organized, Finally Free," specializes in helping people get better organized to live the kind of stress-free life they've always dreamed of. She has been featured in local, national and online media, on topics about getting organized, including time management, clutter control and goal achievement.*

Originally from the east coast, Gracia had an accomplished career as a marketing, organization and management specialist with Dun and Bradstreet's Nielsen Media Research in New York. Today, she and her husband live in Milwaukee, Wisconsin where they own and operate their business.

④ *She would be happy to share systems, techniques, ideas and tips to help your audience demographics get organized, and is available for interviews. In addition, she is glad to submit complimentary articles for publication.*

⑤ *For more information, visit her web site at www.getorganizednow.com*
You can contact Maria Gracia at 555-555-5555, or send an e-mail to getorgnow@charter.net

⑥ *Photos available upon request.*

# # #

 PAGE 2 of 2

Page 2 - News Release to Generate a Media Interview
Offer: Available for interview or complimentary articles

1. Repeat your Contact Information.
2. Use a headline that tells the Editor why he should consider interviewing you for his publication.
3. Tell them about your background and your credentials.
4. Tell them that you are available for interviews or would be happy to submit articles on your specialty.
5. Tell the Editor how to contact you for further information.
6. Tell the Editor that photos are available upon request.
7. Indicate the end of your release with ###, or -END-.
8. Put the page number and total number of pages included on each page of your release.

Get Organized Now!
Idea-Pak

Organize Your Home, Your Office, and Your Life!

www.getorganizednow.com

50

Simple Tips and Ideas to Help You Get Organized Now!

Compliments of
Get Organized Now!

611 Arlington Way
Watertown WI 53094

555-555-5555 (Voice or Fax)

E-Mail: getorgnow@charter.net

Website: http://www.getorganizednow.com

❶ ❷ ❸ ❹

Idea-Pak Cover

❻

Format

Size: 8 1/2" x 11"

Inside: List Tips in 3 Columns

Fold: Letter Fold to fit a standard, No. 10 Envelope

❺

INSIDE

❼

❽ 50 Simple Tips to Help you Get Organized Now!

1. Set a goal. Before you start anything, determine its goal. If you don't know where you're going, how will you ever get there? Set mini-goals and reward yourself for successes.

2. Unclutter your desk. An uncluttered desktop erases unnecessary distractions and helps keep your mind on tasks that need immediate attention. Keep only the items on your desk that relate to your current projects.

3. Don't rely on your memory. You run the risk of letting tasks fall through the cracks. The best way to never forget an appointment, a deadline or a detail again, is to write everything down.

4. Consolidate similar activities. Instead of starting and stopping at different levels of activity, you'll save time by making all of your outgoing telephone calls together, taking care of all your errands at once, etc.

5. Clean out your files periodically. Before you go through the expense of purchasing more file cabinets, folders, etc., take the time to purge all unnecessary paperwork and materials.

Sample Tips

Idea-Pak to Generate Prospects
We promote this Idea-Pak in our marketing vehicles to attract Prospects to our business.

1. Put your company name and slogan here.
2. Put your web site or phone number here.
2. Put your Idea-Pak title here. Use a number in the title if you can.
4. Put your contact information here.
5. You can use a standard size sheet of paper (8 1/2" x 11"). Have your copy shop fold it in a standard letter fold with your title page on the front and your tips inside.

6. You can use the inside folded panel and back panel for more tips or to promote your company or services.
7. List your tips on the inside in 9 or 10 point type. Format them in 3 columns so each folded section contains a column of tips.
8. Number your tips and label each tip with a title in bold. Start each tip with a verb — Set, Unclutter, Consolidate, Clean, etc.

8 1/2" x 3 3/4"

Organizing Certificate Given to a New Prospect
to Generate an Appointment/New Customer
Offer: Free, No-Obligation, One-Hour Consultation

1. Use a certificate type border.
2. Put the Name and Value of the Certificate here.
3. Tell them what the certificate entitles them to.
4. To instill a Sense of Urgency and overcome procrastination, include a certificate expiration. (Valid for 30 Days)

5. Tell them why you are giving them this certificate.
6. Include your Web site and e-mail address.
7. Include your logo, company name and address.
8. Tell your prospects what to do to take advantage of your certificate offer.

Get . . . ● ● ● ●
Organized Now! ™

611 Arlington Way
Watertown, WI 53094

555-555-5555 Voice or Fax
getorgnow@charter.net
www.getorganizednow.com

Here's Your Free Idea-Kit and $75 Certificate

Current Date

Ms. Jane Doe
123 First Street
Anywhere, USA 00000

Dear Ms. Doe,

Thank you for requesting our "Get Organized Now!" Idea-Kit. This free packet
of tips is just our way of introducing ourselves.

My name is Maria Gracia. I am a local professional organizer dedicated to
helping people like you, get organized.

I specialize in clutter control and paper management, both of which, will
simplify your life, decrease stress and help you find the time you need to do
the things you enjoy.

In addition to this free Idea-Kit, I have included a complimentary
certificate (a $75 value) which entitles you to a one-hour organizing
consultation. Included in this consultation will be tips and suggestions to
help you better organize any specific area of your home or life.

There is absolutely no obligation.

I'll give you a call in a few days to introduce myself and to make
arrangements for you to receive your free, one-hour organizing consultation.

I just know you're going to love this content-rich, fun and informative
session. Getting organized is easy once you know the simple techniques I will
share with you.

In the meantime, if you have any other questions, feel free to call me at
555-555-5555, or fax 555-555-5555.

Best regards,

Maria Gracia

Maria Gracia
President and Owner,
Get Organized Now!

P.S. You'll find lots more organizing tips and ideas on my Get Organized Now!
Web site: www.getorganizednow.com

Direct Mail Letter to Generate Prospects

1. You can put the letter on your standard letterhead or plain, inexpensive, white paper without a letterhead.
2. Place your Headline here.
3. Date your letter.
4. Put your prospect's name and address here.
5. Put your salutation here.
6. Thank them for requesting your Idea-Kit.
7. Introduce yourself and tell them how you can help them.
8. Tell them about your enclosed $75 certificate for a One-Hour Organizing Consultation. This session will also serve as your Needs Analysis appointment. It will also give them the opportunity to get to know, like and trust you.
9. Tell them there is no obligation.
10. Tell them you will call to arrange for their free consultation.
11. Provide your phone and fax number in case they want to contact you.
12. Include a P.S. to direct them to your Web site.

❶ *News Release*

❷ **ATTENTION:**   **LIFESTYLES EDITOR**   **FOR IMMEDIATE RELEASE** ❹
                                           NO KILL DATE ❺

❸ **CONTACT:**   Maria Gracia
                         Get Organized Now!
                         611 Arlington Way
                         Watertown, WI 53094

PHONE: (555)-555-5555   **E-MAIL:**   getorgnow@charter.net
FAX: (555)-555-5555   **WEB SITE:**   www.getorganizednow.com

❻ "FREE Workshop to Help You Get Organized"

❼ MILWAUKEE, WI—In celebration of Get Organized Week 2012 (established by the National Association of Professional Organizers), two of Milwaukee's top professional organizers will be conducting a FREE "Get Organized" workshop at Barnes and Noble, Bayshore location.

❽   Maria Gracia, author of "Finally Organized, Finally Free" and Barb Friedman, a teacher of organization at Cardinal Stritch University, will be sharing some of their most effective organizing secrets to help you get organized.

❾   Gracia will focus on space management, with an emphasis on controlling clutter, slaying the paper beast and setting up an effective home and work environment.

     Friedman will focus on helping you better manage your time and productivity, with a strong concentration on eliminating procrastination and establishing priorities.

     If you've always wanted to get organized, Get Organized Week is the perfect time to begin.

     This workshop is free and open to the public as follows:

❿   Thursday, October 5, 6:30-7:30PM
              Barnes & Noble, Bayshore Mall, Milwaukee, WI

                         ###
                         ⓫   ⓬ PAGE 1 of 1

News Release to Generate Prospects
Offer: Free Get Organized Workshop

1. Put the words News Release in large type
2. If you know the specific editor, put his/her name here, or else put EDITOR
3. Put your contact information here.
4. Always put FOR IMMEDIATE RELEASE
5. For timeless releases, put NO KILL DATE. For releases that expire, put KILL: October 8, 2012 (put appropriate date)
6. Your headline should describe what the readers will get.

7. Start the release off with your city and state.
8. Start each new paragraph with a half inch indent.
9. Tell the readers a little bit about the free Workshop and a little about your credentials.
10. Tell the readers when and where the Workshop will be held.
11. Indicate the end of your release with ###, or -END-.
12. Put the page number and total number of pages included on each page of your release.

① **Get ●●●● Organized Now!™** 611 Arlington Way Watertown, WI 53094

555-555-5555 Voice or Fax
getorgnow@charter.net
www.getorganizednow.com

② Project Proposal/Contract

③ **Presented to:**   Jane Doe, 123 Main Street, Anytown, WI 55555
Date of proposal: Current Date

Main Goals: To help you organize your home office so that . . .

④
- you can find what you need within 10 seconds
- you gain an extra hour each day
- your productivity potential is maximized
- your level of stress is decreased substantially
- you feel more comfortable inviting business associates to your office

I can help you:

⑤
- declutter your office environment and 2 filing cabinets
- divide your office into quadrants so you have "4"
- specific work areas for specific projects/tasks
- create two effective filing systems (one for your
- reference files and one for your action files)
- create storage solutions for your office supplies,
- computer software diskettes, and reference manuals

In addition, I will provide you with:

⑥
- customized file maps for both filing cabinets
- 1 free, one-hour follow-up session (within 30 days of project)

⑦ Total price for this project is estimated at $900. If you sign this proposal today, I will extend a 20% discount to you, which would bring the proposed price down to $720 (that's a $180 savings). A $100 deposit is required to begin the project. This job will be completed in 3 four-hour sessions. Please read the reverse side of this proposal for specific terms and conditions.

⑧ I agree to all of the terms and conditions of this contract and wish to commence immediately. I have submitted my required $100 deposit.

⑨ Customer Signature_____ Date_____

Maria Gracia's Signature_____ Date_____

Page 1 - Project Proposal/Contract

1. You can put the letter on your standard letterhead or plain, inexpensive, white paper without a letterhead.
2. Put "Project Proposal/Contract" title here.
3. Put the name of your prospect here and the date of the proposal.
4. List the main goals here.
5. List what you will provide here.
6. List any additional things you will provide here.

7. Put the Project Price here and include a discount offer to overcome procrastination. Let them know the amount of the deposit needed to begin the job and how long the job will take.
8. Put your Call to Action here. Agreement of the terms and payment of the deposit.
9. Both you and your client will sign and date the proposal /contract here.

Project Proposal/Contract Terms and Conditions

In consideration of the services described on the reverse of this proposal by Get Organized Now!™, I acknowledge, understand and agree to the following terms and conditions:

Payment:

- Client's initial paid deposit will be subtracted from the final cost. A pro-rated portion of the balance will be required at the end of "each" 3-hour session as described below:

  Session 1: $200
  Session 2: $200
  Session 3: Remaining balance must be paid in full at end of Session 3

- Payment may be made by check, money order, cash or credit card. Client is fully responsible for any bank charges that occur due to insufficient account funds.

- Client is responsible for purchasing agreed upon supplies (file folders, labels, storage containers, etc.) necessary for the completion of this project. Get Organized Now!™ will assist client with these particulars. Supplies must be ordered and delivered to Client's home or office, prior to the first session date. Therefore, Get Organized Now!™ will assist Client with ordering agreed upon supplies on the date of signed proposal.

- Client is responsible for any travel fees detailed on the reverse of this proposal. Normally travel fees are incurred if Client is located more than 30 minutes away from Milwaukee, WI. If travel fees are not listed, none will be incurred.

Schedules/Cancellation Fee:

- Schedules shall be set by mutual agreement between Client and Get Organized Now!™ at the time of proposal agreement and deposit.

- Cancellation of a scheduled appointment must be done within 24 hours prior to the date scheduled. Cancellation of a scheduled appointment with less than 24 hours notice will be billed at 25% of the agreed upon rate and will be payable immediately.

- Client is required to be present during organizing sessions and to assist with the project throughout each session. It is very important that both parties can focus on the session. Client must make arrangements for handling incoming phone calls, redirecting visitors, etc. so that sessions are not interrupted.

Performance/Delivery Guarantee:

- Get Organized Now!™ promises to fulfill the proposed solutions within the amount of time indicated on the reverse side of this proposal, for the proposed price. If Get Organized Now!™ has underestimated the time it takes to do the job, another session will simply be added to complete the project. However, Client will not be charged more than the original proposed amount.

- Get Organized Now!™ strives to meet a 100% client satisfaction level. If we fail to meet any of the proposed solutions as detailed on the front of this proposal, please provide us with a written letter describing what solution, or parts of the solution, were not met within 7 business days. Get Organized Now!™ will then schedule a complimentary session(s) to make necessary adjustments. Failure to make a claim within this period implies that you fully accept the completed solutions at the agreed upon price.

Page 2 - Project Proposal/Contract

1. Put your Project Proposal/Contract Terms and Conditions here.
2. List the details of payment here.

3. List the details of the project Schedule and Cancellation here.
4. List the details of your customer satisfaction guarantee here.

Chapter 18
Ready-to-use Forms

Goals/Deadlines

Goals	Deadlines	Accomplished ✓

Goals vs Actual Report

YEAR:

MONTH	PROSPECTS FROM LISTS OF STRANGERS		FIRST-TIME CUSTOMERS FROM LIST OF PROSPECTS				REPEAT/BACK-END SALES FROM LIST OF CUSTOMERS				FIRST-TIME + REPEAT SALES	
	# GOAL	# ACTUAL	# GOAL	# ACTUAL	SALES GOAL	SALES ACTUAL	# GOAL	# ACTUAL	SALES GOAL	SALES ACTUAL	SALES GOAL	SALES ACTUAL
JAN												
FEB												
MAR												
APR												
MAY												
JUN												
JUL												
AUG												
SEP												
OCT												
NOV												
DEC												
TOT												

Goals Progress Graph

Year _____

Goal:

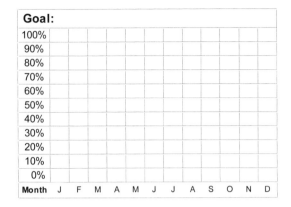

Month	J	F	M	A	M	J	J	A	S	O	N	D
100%												
90%												
80%												
70%												
60%												
50%												
40%												
30%												
20%												
10%												
0%												

Goal:

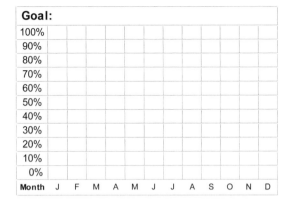

Month	J	F	M	A	M	J	J	A	S	O	N	D
100%												
90%												
80%												
70%												
60%												
50%												
40%												
30%												
20%												
10%												
0%												

Goal:

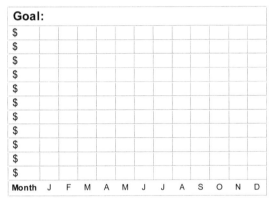

Goal:

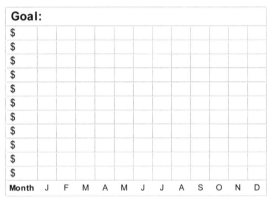

Goal:

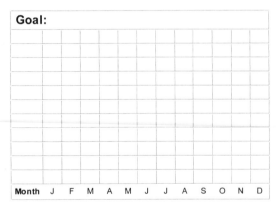

Goal:

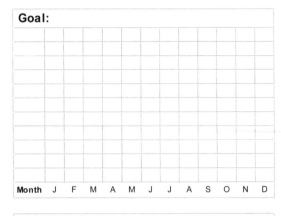

Goal:

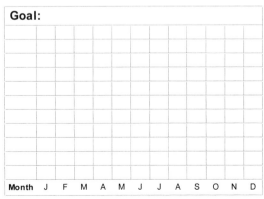

Goal:

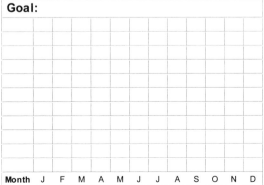

Great Ideas

Year _____

Better write down these great ideas, while they're fresh in my mind!	✓

Master List

Year _____

Transferred To My Daily To Do List

Projects or Tasks	✓	Priority Code A, B or C

Priority A: This is vital to the achievement of my goals. I must do it immediately.
Priority B: This is important to the achievement of my goals. I must do it soon.
Priority C: This is not very important, but would be nice to do if I have the time.
Important Note: If an item on this list doesn't fall into Priority A, B or C, it should not be on your list at all.

Daily To Do List

Today's Date _____

Priority A Projects or Tasks	✓
1.	
2.	
3.	
4.	
5.	
6.	

Priority B Projects or Tasks	✓
1.	
2.	
3.	
4.	
5.	
6.	

Priority C Projects or Tasks	✓
1.	
2.	
3.	
4.	
5.	
6.	

Priority A: This is vital to the achievement of my goals. I must do it immediately.
Priority B: This is important to the achievement of my goals. I must do it soon.
Priority C: This is not very important, but would be nice to do if I have the time.
Important Note: If an item on this list doesn't fall into Priority A, B or C, it should not be on your list at all.

Daily Planner

Today's Date _____

SU   MO   TU   WE   TH   FR   SA   (Circle One)

✓

Time		
6:00A		
6:30		
7:00		
7:30		
8:00		
8:30		
9:00		
9:30		
10:00		
10:30		
11:00		
11:30		
12:00N		
12:30		
1:00		
1:30		
2:00		
2:30		
3:00		
3:30		
4:00		
4:30		
5:00		
5:30		
6:00P		
6:30		
7:00		
7:30		
8:00		
8:30		
9:00		
9:30		
10:00		
10:30		
11:00		
11:30		
12:00M		

Monthly Calendar

Month/Year _____

SUN	MON	TUE	WED	THU	FRI	SAT

Daily Time Log

Week of _____

	Sun	Mon	Tue	Wed	Thu	Fri	Sat
6:00A							
6:30							
7:00							
7:30							
8:00							
8:30							
9:00							
9:30							
10:00							
10:30							
11:00							
11:30							
12:00N							
12:30							
1:00							
1:30							
2:00							
2:30							
3:00							
3:30							
4:00							
4:30							
5:00							
5:30							
6:00P							
6:30							
7:00							
7:30							
8:00							
8:30							
9:00							
9:30							
10:00							
10:30							
11:00							
11:30							
12:00M							

My Projects - Plan and Progress

Project Name	Start Date	Date Due	Percent Complete											Date Complete
			0%	10%	20%	30%	40%	50%	60%	70%	80%	90%	100%	
Step 1														
Step 2														
Step 3														
Step 4														
Step 5														
Step 6														
Step 7														
Step 8														
Step 9														
Step 10														

Project Name	Start Date	Date Due	Percent Complete											Date Complete
			0%	10%	20%	30%	40%	50%	60%	70%	80%	90%	100%	
Step 1														
Step 2														
Step 3														
Step 4														
Step 5														
Step 6														
Step 7														
Step 8														
Step 9														
Step 10														

Project Name	Start Date	Date Due	Percent Complete											Date Complete
			0%	10%	20%	30%	40%	50%	60%	70%	80%	90%	100%	
Step 1														
Step 2														
Step 3														
Step 4														
Step 5														
Step 6														
Step 7														
Step 8														
Step 9														
Step 10														

Project Name	Start Date	Date Due	Percent Complete											Date Complete
			0%	10%	20%	30%	40%	50%	60%	70%	80%	90%	100%	
Step 1														
Step 2														
Step 3														
Step 4														
Step 5														
Step 6														
Step 7														
Step 8														
Step 9														
Step 10														

Schedule for Generating Prospects

Product/Service:_____ Year:_____

Planned = X   Accomp. = Black Box   Not Accomp. = Circle

Vehicle/Activity Description	JAN	FEB	MAR	APR	MAY	JUN

Vehicle/Activity Description	JUL	AUG	SEP	OCT	NOV	DEC

Referral Log

Referred By	Person Referred
Project Price	Project Description
Referral Gift	Date Sent

Referred By	Person Referred
Project Price	Project Description
Referral Gift	Date Sent

Referred By	Person Referred
Project Price	Project Description
Referral Gift	Date Sent

Referred By	Person Referred
Project Price	Project Description
Referral Gift	Date Sent

Referred By	Person Referred
Project Price	Project Description
Referral Gift	Date Sent

Referred By	Person Referred
Project Price	Project Description
Referral Gift	Date Sent

Referred By	Person Referred
Project Price	Project Description
Referral Gift	Date Sent

Referred By	Person Referred
Project Price	Project Description
Referral Gift	Date Sent

Referred By	Person Referred
Project Price	Project Description
Referral Gift	Date Sent

Referred By	Person Referred
Project Price	Project Description
Referral Gift	Date Sent

Prospect Report

	MONTH:	YEAR:

Using Lists of Strangers

Total New Prospects Generated:

Code #	MARKETING VEHICLE DESCRIPTION	PROSPECTS	Code #	MARKETING VEHICLE DESCIPTION	PROSPECTS
1			51		
2			52		
3			53		
4			54		
5			55		
6			56		
7			57		
8			58		
9			59		
10			60		
11			61		
12			62		
13			63		
14			64		
15			65		
16			66		
17			67		
18			68		
19			69		
20			70		
21			71		
22			72		
23			73		
24			74		
25			75		
26			76		
27			77		
28			78		
29			79		
30			80		
31			81		
32			82		
33			83		
34			84		
35			85		
36			86		
37			87		
38			88		
39			89		
40			90		
41			91		
42			92		
43			93		
44			94		
45			95		
46			96		
47			97		
48			98		
49			99		
50			100		

Marketing Results Log

Service/Product:_____

Year:_____

Date	Vehicle*	Ext Code	Description (Target - Offer)	Strangers	Prospects	Contacts	Appts	Sales

AD-Ads   AR-Articles   BC-Business Cards   BR-Brochures   FL-Flyers   DM-Direct Mail   DH-Doorknob Hangers   EM-E-mail   FX-Fax   IP-In-Person

IN-Internet   IT-Interviews   NT-Networking   NL-Newsletter   NR-News Release   PB-Publicity   RD-Radio   RF-Referrals   SM-Samples   SN-Signage

TL-Telephone   TV-Television   TS-Trade Shows   WS-Web Site   EZ-E-zine   WS-Workshops

Prospect Data Sheet

Initial Contact

	Date
Name(s)	
Company Name	
Address	
Phone Number	Fax Number
E-mail Address	
Vehicle Tracking Code	Date You Sent Materials
Notes	

Follow-Up Contacts

Date	___ Reached ___ Left Message ___ Not Reached
Follow-up Method ___ Phone ___ Mail	___ Fax ___ E-mail ___ In-Person
Goal Desired ___ Make Special Offer	___ Set Appointment ___ Close The Sale
Result ___ Accepted Special Offer ___ Appointment	___ Sale ___ Not Interested Now ___ Not Interested Ever
Interest Level ___ Hot ___ Warm ___ Cold	Next Follow-up Date
Notes	

Date	___ Reached ___ Left Message ___ Not Reached
Follow-up Method ___ Phone ___ Mail	___ Fax ___ E-mail ___ In-Person
Goal Desired ___ Make Special Offer	___ Set Appointment ___ Close The Sale
Result ___ Accepted Special Offer ___ Appointment	___ Sale ___ Not Interested Now ___ Not Interested Ever
Interest Level ___ Hot ___ Warm ___ Cold	Next Follow-up Date
Notes	

Date	___ Reached ___ Left Message ___ Not Reached
Follow-up Method ___ Phone ___ Mail	___ Fax ___ E-mail ___ In-Person
Goal Desired ___ Make Special Offer	___ Set Appointment ___ Close The Sale
Result ___ Accepted Special Offer ___ Appointment	___ Sale ___ Not Interested Now ___ Not Interested Ever
Interest Level ___ Hot ___ Warm ___ Cold	Next Follow-up Date
Notes	

Date	___ Reached ___ Left Message ___ Not Reached
Follow-up Method ___ Phone ___ Mail	___ Fax ___ E-mail ___ In-Person
Goal Desired ___ Make Special Offer	___ Set Appointment ___ Close The Sale
Result ___ Accepted Special Offer ___ Appointment	___ Sale ___ Not Interested Now ___ Not Interested Ever
Interest Level ___ Hot ___ Warm ___ Cold	Next Follow-up Date
Notes	

Assessment Form

General

Name(s)/Company Name	Number of Employees
Assessment Date/Time/Location	Prospect/Customer Budget

Place To Be Organized

___ Residential	___ Closets	___ Kitchen	___ Bedroom	___ Living Room	___ Dining Room
___ Den	___ Bathroom	___ Basement	___ Attic	___ Garage	___ Craft Room
___ Boat/RV	___ Home Office	___ Business Office	___ Organization	___ Church	___ Government
___ Other (Describe)					

Problem Area(s)

___ Clutter Control	___ Paper Mgmt	___ Paper Flow	___ Filing	___ Storage	___ Relocation
___ Time Mgmt	___ Scheduling	___ Planning	___ Priorities	___ Procrastination	___ Delegation
___ Project Mgmt	___ Records Mgmt	___ Work Flow	___ Computer Clutter	___ Financial	___ Goals/Deadlines
___ Other (Describe)					

Detailed Problem Description(s)

Problem 1
Problem 2
Problem 3
Problem 4
Problem 5

Type of Solution Desired

___ Hands-on	___ Group Seminar/Workshop	
___ Consulting (In-Person)	___ Consulting (Telephone)	___ Consulting (Mail)
___ Consulting (Fax)	___ Consulting (E-mail)	___ Consulting (Group Tele-class)
___ Book or Product (Describe)		

Detailed Solution Description(s)

Solution 1
Solution 2
Solution 3
Solution 4
Solution 5

Area Sketch

Notes

Proposal/Pricing Worksheet

Offered To

Name/Company Name	Today's Date

Detailed Problem Description(s)

Problem 1
Problem 2
Problem 3
Problem 4
Problem 5
Notes

Proposed Solution Description(s)

	Estimated Completion Time
Solution 1	
Solution 2	
Solution 3	
Solution 4	
Solution 5	
Notes	

Complimentary Add-Ons

Add On 1
Add On 2
Add On 3

Proposed Price

Estimated Hours To Complete	Price Per Hour	
Subtotal (Hours X Price Per Hour)		$
Additional Expense 1 (Describe)		$
Additional Expense 2 (Describe)		$
Additional Expense 3 (Describe)		$
Estimated Price (Add Subtotal + Additional Expenses)		$
Discount		- $
Proposed Final Price (Estimated Price minus Discount)		$

Customer Data Sheet

Contact Information

Name(s)	
Company Name	
Address	
Phone Number	Fax Number
E-mail Address	

Project Log

Date of Project	Time
Organizing Project Description	
Result(s)	
Project Price	Date Paid
Notes	

Date of Project	Time
Organizing Project Description	
Result(s)	
Project Price	Date Paid
Notes	

Date of Project	Time
Organizing Project Description	
Result(s)	
Project Price	Date Paid
Notes	

Date of Project	Time
Organizing Project Description	
Result(s)	
Project Price	Date Paid
Notes	

File Map

Prepared for _____

Filing Cabinet 1	Filing Cabinet 2	Filing Cabinet 3	Filing Cabinet 4
Location	Location	Location	Location
Draw er #	Draw er #	Draw er #	Draw er #
Subject	Subject	Subject	Subject
File Number/File Description	File Number/File Description	File Number/File Description	File Number/File Description
1	1	1	1
2	2	2	2
3	3	3	3
4	4	4	4
5	5	5	5
6	6	6	6
7	7	7	7
8	8	8	8
9	9	9	9
10	10	10	10
11	11	11	11
12	12	12	12
13	13	13	13
14	14	14	14
15	15	15	15
16	16	16	16
17	17	17	17
18	18	18	18
19	19	19	19
20	20	20	20
21	21	21	21
22	22	22	22
23	23	23	23
24	24	24	24
25	25	25	25
26	26	26	26
27	27	27	27
28	28	28	28
29	29	29	29
30	30	30	30
31	31	31	31
32	32	32	32
33	33	33	33
34	34	34	34
35	35	35	35
36	36	36	36
37	37	37	37
38	38	38	38
39	39	39	39
40	40	40	40
41	41	41	41
42	42	42	42
43	43	43	43
44	44	44	44
45	45	45	45

Meeting Notes

Today's Date _____

Meeting Objectives	✓
1.	
2.	
3.	
4.	
5.	
6.	
Items Discussed	✓
1.	
2.	
3.	
4.	
5.	
6.	
Decisions That Were Made	✓
1.	
2.	
3.	
4.	
5.	
6.	
Pending Decisions	✓
1.	
2.	
3.	
4.	
5.	
6.	
Additional Notes	✓
1.	
2.	
3.	
4.	
5.	
6.	

Meeting Agenda

Meeting Name	
Location	
Date	
Time	

Attendees		
1.	5.	9.
2.	6.	10.
3.	7.	11.
4.	8.	12.

Main Objective(s)	✓
1.	
2.	
3.	
4.	
5.	

Agenda Item	Time (From/To)	Result	✓
1.			
2.			
3.			
4.			
5.			
6.			
7.			
8.			
9.			
10.			

Next Steps	Person Responsible	Deadline	✓
1.			
2.			
3.			
4.			
5.			
6.			
7.			
8.			
9.			
10.			

Meeting/Presentation Planner

General Information	
Purpose of Meeting	
Meeting Date	Meeting Time
Meeting Location (Location Name/Address/Contact/Phone)	
Room Name	Cost (inc. all equipment/amenities)
Meeting Called By	Guest Speaker(s)
Number of Attendees	Lodging/Travel Arrangements Needed? (Y/N)

✓

Attendee Notification	(Check all that apply and describe further if necessary.)
In Person	Formal Letter/Invitation
By Phone	Posted on Bulletin Board
Informal Note	Posted in Newsletter
E-Mail	Ad in Magazine/Newspaper

✓

Equipment Needed	(Check all that apply and describe further if necessary.)
Number of Tables	Number of Chairs
Slide Projector	TV/VCR
Overhead Projector	Computer
Microphone	Flipchart

✓

Table/Chair Set-up	(Describe Further if Necessary.)
Chairs Only	Tables
# Chairs Per Row	How Many Chairs per Table
# Free Aisles in Between (1, 2, 3, etc.)	Chair/Table Set-up (Describe)
Chair Set-up (Describe)	Back Table Needed

✓

Amenities	(Check all that apply and describe further if necessary.)
Water	Breakfast
Coffee/Tea	Lunch
Juice	Dinner
Soda	Snacks

Presentation Outline

Name of Presentation

Agenda - (This Is What I Believe)

Supporting Points - (Here's Why I Believe It)

Benefits	Facts (Specific Numbers)	Personal/Similar Experiences

Review - (Key Points To Remember)

Conclusion - (Therefore, My Recommendation Is . . .)

Income and Expenses

Month/Year _____

Business Income Description	Amount
Total	

Business Expense Description	Percent Allowable	Amount
Advertising/Marketing		
Auto Expense @ $ _____ per Mile		
Bank Charges		
Business Books/Periodicals		
Business Gifts		
Cleaning (Dry Cleaning)		
Entertainment/Meals		
Equipment Purchases		
Equipment Repairs		
Insurance - Business		
Insurance - Health		
Insurance - Renters/Homeowners		
Legal & Professional Services		
Mortgage/Rent		
Online Services		
Permits/Licenses		
Postage		
Printing		
Seminars/Conferences/Tradeshows		
Software		
Supplies - Clients		
Supplies - Office		
Tax - Sales		
Tax - Self-Employment		
Utilities		
Total		

Mileage Record

Year _____

Date	Destination	Beginning Mileage	Ending Mileage	Total Miles

Books to Read

Year _____

January			February			March		
Date	Book Title	✓	Date	Book Title	✓	Date	Book Title	✓

April			May			June		
Date	Book Title	✓	Date	Book Title	✓	Date	Book Title	✓

July			August			September		
Date	Book Title	✓	Date	Book Title	✓	Date	Book Title	✓

October			November			December		
Date	Book Title	✓	Date	Book Title	✓	Date	Book Title	✓

Notes

SPECIAL BONUS REPORT: $39.00

Essential Extras for Success-Driven Professional Organizers

Helping Others Get Organized:

Insider Tips and Proven Strategies from Top Professional Organizers

Provided by:

Get Organized Now!
611 Arlington Way
Watertown, WI 53094

Website: GetOrganizedNow.com
Email: getorgnow@charter.net

BONUS: Essential Extras for Success-Driven Professional Organizers

Introduction

It's one thing when you're organizing your own cabinet or desk, but completely another when you're attempting to help your clients get organized. Not only are you dealing with clutter, poor time management or paper overload, but you're also working with different personalities and emotions. You are also trying to get the job done in a reasonable timeframe to ensure the client is happy enough to pay you for a job well done and to refer you to others.

Essential Extras for Success-Driven Professional Organizers begins with the 5 universal organizing challenges and the top 10 lists for succeeding. It continues with case studies—real life organizing stories—experienced and written by renowned professional organizers. We then move on to mini interviews conducted by Maria Gracia and answered by professional organizers around the world. Finally, it concludes with Industry Polls and Words of Wisdom to motivate and inspire you.

This bonus section, included with your purchase, is an essential addition to the *Ultimate Guide for Professional Organizers*. Let's start this journey together.

Challenge #1: General Clutter

1. **Put them at ease.** First and foremost, you'll want to put your client at ease. The second they suspect you believe they live or work in a disaster zone, they're going to lose confidence. Give them hope. Obviously, with a little bit of know-how and energy, any organizing job can be tackled and accomplished.

2. **Follow the "Bare Naked" principle.** To begin, empty out as many items as possible into boxes, bags or piles in the corners of the rooms. What you want to start seeing are surfaces, like the wood surface of a desk or the walls of a closet.

3. **Use the "Keep, Don't Keep" System.** Make two distinct sections in each room you tackle. One section will be "Keep" and the other section will be "Don't Keep." You can use boxes, bags or the corners of a room. You'll want a fairly even distribution (50/50) in each section. Better yet, go for a higher percentage in the "Don't Keep" section. Pick up each item. Have your client make the decision (you may have to assist). If you find your client is always choosing the "Keep" section, start over again explaining that you need to end up with at least a 50/50 split between the Keeps and Don't Keeps.

4. **Eliminate all the "Don't Keep" Items.** Every item in the "Don't Keep" section should immediately be placed in boxes or bags and a) driven over to the nearest charity organization (or scheduled for a pick up), b) put out for the trash collectors or c) given to someone else who doesn't live in that particular house.

5. **Sort through the "Keep" Items.** Once all the "Don't Keep" items are removed from the room, it's time to tackle the "Keep" items. Make two Keep piles: a) The items that belong in this room and b) the items that do not belong.

6. **Remove the intruders.** Now that you have two Keep piles, remove the "intruders"—the items that don't belong in this room. Move them where they belong or, if they are homeless, into a different room in another box for another organizing session.

7. **Clean up.** Since this room is now fairly empty, it should be easy to clean up. Have your client dust, vacuum, scrub—whatever it takes to get this room looking good. This is also an excellent time to suggest painting the room if needed, but only if the client is in agreement. Should you help them clean? That's a decision you will have to make. Many professional organizers will do light cleaning to assist the client. If it's very dirty, you might suggest hiring a cleaning team to get it spruced up.

8. **Secure needed storage.** Looking at the "Keep" items, now is a good time to determine if the room needs extra storage units, such as shelves, cabinets, containers and baskets. Keep the client's taste and style in mind so he or she will want to use the organizing systems you set up. You'll want the customer in the store with you or sitting next to you if you're purchasing online. You may even find storage containers and baskets in the client's house—many people have storage possibilities they're not even using!

9. **Give everything a home.** Be sure you give every item in the "Keep" pile a permanent home in the room you're organizing. Take photos and/or notes so the client will remember where an item should go when it's not being used.

10. **Add finishing touches.** The room should look very organized by now. Add a few finishing touches to really make this room special. Perhaps add new artwork or family photographs to the walls. Maybe add some greenery—real or artificial. A new lamp could add excellent lighting. You get the idea.

Challenge #2: Paper Clutter

1. **Find an empty table to work on.** When sorting papers, it's best to have an empty table to help you lay out and sort. If the table in the room is filled with papers, just stack those papers in a pile and put them on the floor. If there is no table available, bring in a portable one.

2. **Have a shredder and recycle container nearby.** As you go through each sheet of your client's papers one by one, shred and/or recycle whatever you can. This includes anything that is outdated, not financially or legally required to possess, or otherwise not needed anymore.

3. **Start making "piles."** Using the empty table, begin making piles. Categorize each pile with a sticky note stuck on the table in front of each pile. Once you see one of these piles getting large, put those papers in a manila file folder and place the sticky note on top of the file folder. You'll probably be making a permanent file for this category, or you may discover later that you need to split this category up into two or more categories.

4. **Stick with large categories first.** When making categories for your piles, be sure to use large categories first, such as Financial, Personal, Family, Travel, etc.

5. **Break the large categories into mini-categories.** Once all the papers are sorted into your main categories, work with one main category at a time breaking it up into smaller categories. For example, in the main category entitled Financial, you may have mini-categories entitled a) Assets, b) Debts, and c) Stocks and Bonds.

6. **Consider a pre-categorized filing system.** Rather than doing all the categorizing from scratch, consider a pre-categorized filing system such as the Get Organized Now! *My Oh-So-Organized Filing System*, available from the www.getorganizednow.com web site. Why reinvent the wheel every time you have to begin a new filing system?

7. **Insert hanging file folders into the filing cabinet.** These will act as "holders" for all of the manila file folders. We suggest either one color or a maximum of five colors for 5 large categories. You should end up with no more than 5 large categories.

8. **Insert the manila folders into the hanging folders.** Insert all the categorized manila file folders into the hanging file folders in alphabetical order.

9. **Put "Action" papers into a Tickler System.** Papers that require Action, such as those that need to be read or acted upon on a specific date, should be filed into a 31-Day Tickler System. There is one included with the *My Oh-So-Organized Filing System;* or you can read about how to set one up in my book *Finally Organized, Finally Free for the Home.*

10. **Cross reference.** Intricate filing systems usually require a cross reference. Type all the large and mini-categories into an Excel spreadsheet or Word document, with descriptions if necessary, so your client can find what he or she needs later when you're gone. When they need to find a sheet of paper, your customer can simply use the "find" feature to locate that paper quickly.

Challenge #3: Virtual Clutter (Email)

1. **Delete all the junk.** Eliminating all the junk in the typical email inbox will help you eliminate at least 50% of the email messages there. Get rid of spam, advertising, forwards from friends (jokes, etc.) and anything else that can otherwise be classified as junk.

2. **Make a To Do folder.** Any email requiring an action should immediately be dragged into a virtual To Do folder in the client's email program.

3. **Make a Reference folder.** After deleting the junk and moving the To Do's, determine what is left over in the email inbox. It should only be email that needs to be kept for reference later. A main "Reference" folder should be created. If necessary, further categorize the Reference folder into smaller mini-folders, such as "Friends", "Family", "Shopping" and "Travel."

4. **Handle the To Do's.** Next, your client will need to begin handling the To Do's one by one. I recommend they handle anything that requires a quick and easy response first. This way, those email messages can be dealt with and then deleted. It may be necessary to schedule time each day to handle the To Do's if there are many, but these definitely need to be addressed on a daily basis for a minimum of 30 minutes to keep them under control.

5. **Set up filters.** Set up email filters for your client. Be sure he or she knows how to do so in the future. By doing this, incoming email messages can be automatically sent into either the Delete folder or into the categorized folders you've set up.

6. **Instill the "Empty Each Day" Mentality.** The goal is to have an empty email inbox every single night before the computer is turned off. The junk should be deleted, the To Do's should be attended to, and the reference email messages should be moved to their appropriate virtual folders.

7. **Unsubscribe from lists.** Help your client contact any companies or organizations sending email that your client is not interested in. Examples would be newsletters that aren't being read, advertisements from stores your client doesn't shop at, and the like.

8. **Check out all the options.** Teach your client how to easily sort through incoming email, such as sorting by name or subject, flagging email messages of specific importance and identifying email with attachments.

9. **Make canned messages.** Show your client how to make and save canned responses to typical questions in his or her word processing program or directly in their email program. When a basic question comes in, that response can then be copied and pasted into the email response and customized further, if needed. This can be a huge timesaver.

10. **Schedule time for email handling.**
    Establish a schedule for your client to attend to his or her email on a daily basis. Perhaps an hour each morning, or 30 minutes in the morning and 30 minutes in the afternoon, can be assigned specifically for deleting, sorting and responding to email.

Challenge #4: Virtual Clutter (Computer)

1. **Tackle one "folder" at a time.** Sitting with your client, choose one folder at a time, opening each document or spreadsheet if necessary. Delete anything your client created that is no longer needed.

2. **Logical names.** Rename files that have non-descript names like file001.doc. A file name that is more descriptive, such as letter-emily-abcaccount.doc, will help your client locate files in a snap.

3. **Start clean.** Begin making logical folders and sub-folders based on what your client needs on his or her computer. Start with main folders, such as Personal, Financial and Family for a residential client, or Marketing, Human Resources and Vendors for a business client. Begin dragging and dropping files into these sub-folders. As a main category starts to grow, begin making sub-folders and continue to drag and drop files.

4. **Archive.** Files that are not looked at very often or at all, but need to be kept, can be transferred to zip drives or external hard drives if additional space needs to be freed up on your client's computer. Note that photo files and video files take up lots of room. It is often worthwhile to move these files to external storage devices rather than allowing them to take up tons of room on your client's hard drive.

5. **Remember to back up.** Devise a regularly scheduled back-up system for your client. In the event of a computer failure, all won't be lost. Make it an easy system, so your client will actually do it—and build in a reminder system so your client remembers to do it.

6. **Clear out the cache.** Every time your client visits a web page, that page is stored on his or her computer. If your client uses Internet Explorer, this is a matter of clicking on Tools and Internet Options, and then deleting the temporary files from your client's computer. Use the Help menu in your client's browser to determine how to do this if they're not using Explorer.

7. **Organize favorites.** Most browsers allow you to save a list and description of favorite web sites for ease in returning to those web sites in the future. Just like your client's computer should have folders and sub-folders for their files, the same goes for their favorites. For instance, a main

folder for Favorites could be Personal, and the sub-folders could be "Shopping", "Restaurants" and "Health." For a business customer, a main folder for Favorites could be Employees, and the sub-folders could be "Articles and Tips", "Search Firms" and "Employee Related Forms."

8. **Organize the desktop.** Is your client's desktop swimming with icons? Get rid of the icons that are no longer necessary and organize them. One way to do this is to assign specific corners for specific icons, such as Online Programs: top left, Offline Programs: top right, Computer Maintenance Tools: bottom left, etc. Or, you can organize them alphabetically or in the order in which you use them (most used first, least used last.)

9. **Organize disks, zip drives and other external devices.** Be sure to organize your client's CD-ROMs into holders, their memory sticks into labeled boxes, and so on.

10. **Finalize.** Remove anything from the computer desk that isn't related to the computer. This area should be clear of clutter with ample workspace.

Challenge #5: Time Management

1. **Encourage them to use a Time Log.** Don't do anything until your client has filled out a time log—at least two weeks of data to see exactly where time is being spent. Then you will be able to assess the things that can be eliminated or streamlined. If this can't be done, you'll have to work hard to extract exactly what your client is doing from his or her memory and capture it all on paper for assessment.

2. **Begin eliminating.** The first thing that has to go is anything taking up tons of time but producing little or nothing at all. This may include volunteer efforts that are deriving little personal satisfaction, reports being done in a work environment that are rarely or never used or entertainment activity in excess, such as watching television for hours.

3. **Begin streamlining.** Some things may be necessary for your client to do but are taking up too much time. For example, your customer may be doing a report that is rarely used or duplicating information. This is where timesaving tips for your client can come in extra handy.

4. **Distribute to others.** You may find things your client is currently handling that can be shared by another person in the household or office. Keep teamwork in mind when possible to lessen the burden. Don't discount the fact that your client may be better off outsourcing, such as hiring a cleaning service for her home or a recruiting team for his business office.

5. **Teach to prioritize.** It's imperative that you teach your client how to distinguish between activities that are very important and those that are low on the totem pole. Devise an A-B-C Priority System, so they know what should get prime focus and what is not-so-important.

6. **Don't forget about goals.** In order for you to truly assist your client in determining how to prioritize, it's imperative for you to help him or her come up with basic goals. In doing so, they'll be able to pick and choose the activities that will move them closer to reaching those goals.

7. **Give them 2 Lists. 1) The Master List** is a holding place for every task that needs to be done, but in no particular order. It should include an area where a priority number or letter can be assigned. Each day, your client can

pull items off his or her Master List and move them onto the **2) Daily To Do List**, making sure there is at least one top priority item on the list. There should be no more than 5-6 items total. Nothing else goes on this list until the current items are completed.

8. **Determine what can be delegated.** Whether your client is looking for better time management at home or in the office, delegation is key. Determine what items can be assigned to other family members or co-workers.

9. **Don't forget to pad.** Teach your client to leave 15-30 minutes between specific activities for things that come up—phone calls that take longer than expected, traffic, necessary interruptions, etc. So when something does happen, they won't feel like they're totally off schedule. This, of course, doesn't mean if they finish an activity early, they can't start the next activity early. It just gives them padding to get through their day in a more stress-free and productive manner.

10. **Be sure there's room for fun.** While scheduling "work" type activities is necessary, scheduling time for relaxation and fun will help your client maintain his or her new schedule without feeling overwhelmed. It will also give them something to look forward to. Be sure there's an hour (a straight hour or 10 minute increments throughout the day) for fun activities like going for walks or reading for pleasure. In addition, schedule in another 30-45 minutes per meal for healthy eating and plenty of time for rest—at least 8 hours.

Case Study #1: Carmen Coker

I had officially been a professional organizer for one month when I decided to book an appointment at the local spa for a facial. I was slated to have head shots taken for my business portfolio and I naturally wanted to look my best for the shoot.

I was equally as new to the area, as my husband and I had just moved into town a few months earlier. Unsure of which spa to choose, I just picked the one with the neatest ad in the yellow pages and hoped for the best!

You just never know where or when you'll find your next client

On the big day, I made my way to the spa. Of course, I made no effort to get dressed up or anything. I just threw my hair up into a ponytail and didn't bother with make-up. I was paired with Katie* and as she started slabbing a thick, green, gooey mask on my face, she asked me what I did for a living. I explained that I was a professional organizer and that I just opened up my own business a few weeks earlier.

She listened patiently to me, not really saying much. I took it as the obligatory, polite reaction. You know the one…the "I have to listen to you because you are my client right now" treatment. But when she actually spoke, Katie's response surprised me: "Can you be at my house this Thursday?"

I accepted, naturally, and thought… "Note to self! When I go out in public, always have my game face on." I was shocked that Katie would even want to hire someone who looked as I did that morning—crazy hair, no make-up, casual clothes. I certainly didn't look professional. But as I would come to learn, Katie is as unpretentious and non-judgmental as anyone could be.

Just because it's neat, doesn't necessarily mean it's organized

That Thursday morning, I arrived as scheduled at Katie's farm house for her initial consultation. "My house is a total facade. It's really not as organized as it seems," Katie explained to me as I walked into her house for the first time. And she was right.

There was hardly an unkempt area to be seen, at least on the surface. That is, until she started to open doors and cabinets. Behind the tidy exterior, there was a mountain of clutter.

We sat down to start the formal part of the initial consultation. During this time, I like to administer a personality assessment because it helps me get to know the client in a short amount of time, plus it gives me a better idea of the client's likes/dislikes and daily habit patterns.

My assessment

Here are some of the questions that I reviewed with Katie and that I typically talk through with clients:

1. What compelled you to hire or look into hiring a professional organizer?

2. What is your biggest organizing problem?

   a. How long have you been struggling with it?

   b. How does it make you feel when you must deal with this problem?

3. Did you contact a professional organizer to help you with your biggest organizing problem or something else? If something else, then please explain.

4. Are you married? If so, for how long?

5. Would you say your spouse has the same feelings toward organization that you do? Or opposite?

6. Do you have children? If so, how many?

7. Are your children old enough to help you organize the house? If so, do they help you?

8. Do you run a home-based business?

9. Regarding the organizing problem for which you are seeking help…

   a. How does this play into your everyday routine?

   b. Have you tried organizing this on your own before without success? If so, when?

   c. If the project has already started in some way, what parts of the project do you think are going well and which ones aren't?

10. What is your goal with this project?

11. What is your time frame for this project?

12. What is your budget for consulting time?

13. What is your budget for organizing supplies?

14. Do you have any concerns or questions about hiring a professional organizer that you would like answered?

The hard truth is revealed

As I asked questions to break the ice with Katie, she became extremely open and frank with me. She shared how she had recently experienced an onslaught of personal challenges in the past 5 years—the death of a sibling, a bitter divorce, and her own battle with cancer.

Katie discussed that she was formerly a very organized person, but the emotional strain of the last few years had taken its toll. Little by little, she began to care less and less about keeping her life together and organized. It was as if she couldn't control it from happening to her. She couldn't stop the clutter from overpowering her life.

With the majority of my clients, an initial consult may last from 45–60 minutes. With Katie, we chatted for over 2 hours! It was obvious from our conversation that Katie had a lot weighing on her heart and mind. I found myself being an impromptu—yet uncertified—psychologist.

She was asking me questions like, "Is this normal behavior for a person to become disorganized after years of being organized?" and "How do you think I can change my habits?" I was convinced that Katie had the skills to be organized, but she clearly needed the motivation and guidance to bring those skills back to the surface.

Finding a focus

Katie mentioned that she wanted to organize her entire house right away. While understandable, it would have been both impossible and overwhelming to do so. We needed to decide upon one focus area and organize that focus area, then go on to rid the clutter from another focus area. But where should the starting point be?

I like the client to identify the first focus area, so I asked Katie if there was one part of her home that particularly frustrated her. She replied that her entire house was a frustration and so it really did not matter what room we started to organize.

However, in Katie's case, this was a crucial decision point. If a home-based business is part of the equation, I almost always suggest starting with the home office because its efficiency affects business processes and personal income. Katie physically worked at the spa, but she kept all her spa records at home.

Likewise, her farm was currently active, and so it was equally important for the farm documentation to be filed properly. Once I explained these points to her, Katie was totally onboard for de-cluttering the home office.

Estimating project time

Since we were now on the same page about the initial focus area, I wanted to personally check out the home office so that I could take notes and provide a project estimate. A month into my career as a professional organizer, I must admit that the cost estimate was my biggest fear. It was still very hard for me to judge how much time it would take to accomplish an organizing job. In order to counteract this problem from the very beginning, I provided myself a little wiggle room with customers.

I highlighted to Katie that I was new to the organizing profession and that I was still learning the ropes when it came to defining how long projects will last. Then I assured her that this would be of no consequence to her pocketbook and I demonstrated that assurance through my contract. I built two clauses into my contract that all my clients, including Katie, must agree to prior to hiring me:

Contract Clause #1

I understand that should the actual labor time exceed the anticipated labor time quoted in the estimate, there will be no extra charge to me. *(Exception: Factors beyond the organizer's control, such as excessive interruptions. This situation will be addressed when and if it arises.)*

Meaning for client: My estimate stands no matter what happens. If I underestimate project time, thus underestimating price, you will not incur any extra costs. There will be no surprises. And I will be here until the job is finished and finished properly.

Contract Clause #2

I understand that should the actual labor time be less than the amount quoted in the estimate, then I will only be responsible for the time completed. The fee will be rounded to the nearest half hour mark (top or bottom of the hour).

Meaning for client: If I make a mistake and overestimate the time for the project, thus overestimating price, you are not required to pay for those extra hours not needed.

My philosophy—no unhappy customers

I have used this philosophy with my patrons from the get-go, and I still use it to this day. Every now and then, I may end up working hours for no pay because I underestimate the time required for a project, but I have yet to have an unhappy customer—and that is the most important thing. Happy clients are more likely to be return customers and to refer you to family and friends.

For Katie specifically, she had mounds and mounds of paperwork and clutter in her office. Items that didn't belong in the study, such as cleaning supplies, were stuffed on the shelves. The file drawers were overflowing with documents. Random piles of papers were jammed in desk drawers. Who knows what we would uncover in each space and how long it would take us to weed through everything.

In addition to using my contract philosophy that I mentioned earlier, I decided I would double the time I initially thought it would take to accomplish a task. For example, if I thought it might take 1½ hours to comb through a file cabinet drawer, I then doubled that to 3 hours.

Katie's Home Office – Before Photos

Client Homework

I settled on 15 hours for total project time, reminding Katie that she may have some homework throughout the process. I think giving homework to a client is a very handy tactic:

1. It provides the organizer with insight into the client's progress with purging when there is no one to help or motivate him/her.

2. There are some things that slow up projects, such as going through heaps of paperwork. This is a task that the client can easily accomplish without the organizer being present, as long as there are guidelines set up beforehand.

In Katie's situation, I provided her with a standard form that I give to all my clients with paperwork issues.

Here is a short example of these guidelines:

Papers to Keep Long-Term	How Long?	Comments
Adoption and Custody Paperwork	Permanently	
Annual Retirement or Savings Plan Statements	Until you retire or close the account	For quarterly or monthly statements, keep until you receive your annual statement.
Auto Insurance and Registration	For the duration of ownership	Replace expired insurance cards and registration and shred the old.

Papers to Keep Short-Term	How Long?	Comments
Bank Records	1 year	Unless associated with taxes, business, home improvement, or mortgage. Store these bank records with the respective documents.
Bills for services and utilities	6 months	Most companies will not allow bill disputes after 3-6 months has passed.
Credit Card Receipts	45 days	Unless associated with taxes, then keep for 7 years.

Katie was able to use these guidelines and eliminate paperwork on her own time. By assigning simple jobs to the client for homework, one-on-one time between the organizer and client can be used for more important duties like establishing a proper, effective system of organization.

Once Katie narrowed down her piles of papers, she and I could talk through a suitable system of organizing those documents. Here is an example of a worksheet that I used to establish a filing system for Katie.

Main Category *Hanging Folder*	Sub-category *Manila File Folder*	Notes
1 Bills		Remember to keep personal, spa, and farm records completely separate from each other!
	A Insurance	
	B Cell Phone	
	C Credit Card	
	D Water/Sewer	
	E Electricity	
2 Taxes		
	A Employee Records	
	B W-2s	
	C Tax Regulations	
	D Records of Income	
	E Receipts	

A worksheet such as this can also be used later during homework sessions to label hanging files and manila file folders as well as to file the papers away under the appropriate heading.

Establish mini-sessions

Next, Katie and I decided to break down the 15 total project hours into 4 smaller sessions.

1. **First follow-up consultation**

   a. Took "before" photos with the client's permission.

   b. This session consisted of de-cluttering. Katie decided what to keep, toss, recycle, donate, return and repair/service.

      Keep, toss, recycle and donate are pretty self-explanatory actions. As for return and repair/service, here are my thoughts on these areas:

      Repair/Service: items that you would like to keep but must be fixed or updated in some way (add staples to the stapler or refill pens so they are in complete working order, upgrade message board with magnets, etc).

      Return: items that need to be returned to a certain person or to another room in the house.

   c. This session was the longest of all, lasting 6 hours.

      i. Once clients are on a roll with purging, it's best to keep things going.

      ii. When de-cluttering, I like to ensure that the biggest part of the purging is complete after the first session. You can assign the client homework to take care of the toss, recycle, donate, etc. Next time, you can both clearly focus on what items remain.

2. Second through fourth follow-up sessions

    a. During the 2nd and 3rd sessions, we focused on a second round of de-cluttering. The remaining items were examined more closely for "to keep" and "to go" features.

    b. At the 3rd session, the de-cluttering process was complete; what needed to be organized, how it needed to be organized, and where it could be organized became obvious. At this point, potential storage options were discussed.

To create a shopping list for a client, I normally use a spreadsheet similar to this:

Item	Quantity	Store	Comments
1) Business Card Organizer	56 Cards	Office Plus	Client wants notebook style organizer - Make sure there is room for expansion (adds 1-2 cards per month to collection - Client does not want to store electronically.

    c. During the 4th session, everything was put into its place. This is really where the client's likes/dislikes and habits come into play considerably.

    d. Each session was 3 hours long, scheduled as close together as possible.

i. Between the 3rd and 4th sessions, allow enough time for the client to shop online or in town for the necessary organizers.

ii. For online orders and shipping, I have found that a 10-day window between 3rd and 4th sessions works best. For in town shopping, I have found that a 2-day window works best.

e. Took "after" photos at the end of the 4th session.

Katie's Home Office – After Photos

On a roll

Throughout the entire project, Katie was sincere and enthusiastic. She really wanted her disorganized home to be transformed into an organized one.

Initially, Katie was hesitant to throw things away. Whenever we would stumble upon a hurdle such as this, Katie and I would talk about the object, along with its importance or sentimental value and how often she referenced it or used it.

By the end of the project, she was purging things left and right on her own, using the guidance that we defined at the start and reinforced throughout the entire project.

When Katie's office was complete, we had clocked 18 hours of project time, not including one homework assignment. So I underestimated the project by three hours, and those were three hours that I did not get paid for working.

However, what I learned from Katie was far more valuable than three hours of pay!

My venture with Katie illustrated that...

(1)   Getting organized is empowering.

(2)   Organizing is more than just clearing out physical clutter.

(3)   You don't have to have years of experience to be successful as a professional organizer.

(4)   Being an organizer really does make a difference and, as the organizer, that difference can make you feel very good because you improved someone's life.

While I had read about these results in magazines and books, working with Katie really brought the words to life for me.

2 months later

I received a call from Katie about two months after finishing her home office. She explained that she was putting effort into staying organized each day and she recently started organizing her basement all on her own.

Katie also expressed that she was so grateful to me for helping her to take control of her life again.

Her phone call to me really made my day!

It is so rewarding so see the fruits of my labor—to know that my work is positively affecting a person's quality of life. And the icing on the cake: Katie wants to do another organizing job with me in the spring, and she also recommended me to a friend who is building a $2 million home. Now that is what I call one satisfied customer and one heck of a recommendation!

* Name changed to protect privacy.

Carmen Coker honed her organizational skills during 7 years as an officer in the U.S. Air Force. She established Clutterbugs in May 2007 and currently provides professional organizing services to homes and businesses.

Carmen is a recognized expert in the organizing field. Her work has been highlighted in several popular publications including Scrapbooks, etc magazine, and she has been interviewed by multiple local and national media organizations such as FM 107.1 Minneapolis: Get Real Girls.

Her consultation and contact information are available on the Clutterbugs website: www.OrganizeClutterbugs.com

Case Study #2: Dianne Desroches

I have a sister that is very unorganized. For her entire life, she has been a clutter bug. I love her, but she's always late for everything and always seems to be rushing around trying to get things done. I have always been somewhat organized. I always hated clutter. I like that everything has a place.

Seeing is believing

One day, my sister made an attempt to go through some items in her home to have a garage sale and asked if I would come to her house to help. One of the items was a huge computer desk she had in her office—a corner unit that took up a lot of space and was always full of papers. After we brought it outside for the sale, I went back into her office and started cleaning, tidying and de-cluttering.

I brought out boxes upon boxes of stuff and made piles of books, papers, and more in her living room. I took everything off her bookshelves, put them in boxes and set them in the corner of the room. I rearranged her desk and bookshelves to be more efficient. Then she came in and saw what I was doing and got excited. It looked so much better!

We spent the rest of the afternoon sorting through papers, books and office items. I had her only keep items that applied to her businesses in that room. Other items were put into a box and set aside to find somewhere else in the house to store it. We had a huge recycling box, another box for garbage and then another box for garage sale/give away items. We categorized the bookshelves and began putting items back onto certain areas of the bookshelf that pertained to that specific business. It was kind of funny helping her as I would always ask the question, "do you really need to keep that?" and "why?" It seemed to be just enough of a push for her to finally give up the item.

What a feeling

When the day was done, she still had a pile of bags and boxes that she needed to sort through. She was so happy at what we had accomplished thus far and couldn't believe how great she felt. I felt really good too. I made a difference and it seemed that she was ready to make the commitment to stay organized in her office.

I joked about being a professional organizer, and then I found you!

It wasn't until we were enjoying dinner and a movie later that night when we were still chatting about what a great day it had been, and then I joked about being a professional organizer. When I got home that night I thought "you know, I'm just going to Google that phrase for a laugh," and there was your site—the Get Organized Now! web site. I was not aware that there was such a thing. I was amazed!

I was so excited that I ordered your *Ultimate Guide for Professional Organizers* immediately. I enjoyed it so much that I have already read it and have ordered more of your products.

The basement

Since the garage sale, I have gone back to my sister's home and helped her organize her basement for her boys. In the past their toys would be found everywhere throughout the house. It was hard for her to keep the house tidy. I helped her create a rule with the boys: no toys on the main floor. They absolutely love that they have their own "club house" so to speak. They have their own TV, play station, toys, and games down there and they love it when their friends come over. They even have a couch, a few extra folding chairs and a set of table and chairs. They have been seen doing their homework down there—it's truly an amazing transformation!

The rest of the house

I have gone back a few times and helped de-clutter her entry way, bedroom, sitting room, craft/sewing room and a spare bedroom. My sister is a new woman! I think I have repeated myself so much now that she gets it. And she is so thankful—so much so that she cried. I realized that I like the feeling of adding value to someone's life; to make a difference. I never dreamed that I could make this a business until now. I asked her what the space would be used for. What function would it serve? How often would it be used? Who would be using it?

The "Love Box"

My sister has two young boys that do great work at school. She is also a bus driver so she has many cards, hand drawn pictures, and other mementos.

We have made a "Love Box"—it's basically a cardboard box, but it is decorated and filled with these cards and papers that she loves.

She scrapbooks and will eventually put them into albums, but for now they're kept in one box—of course, only the ones that she really likes or those that mean something to her are included.

Frugal organizing

We never bought any special organizing supplies. I recommended she buy some totes when they are on sale, but for now we put items in boxes and simply labeled them. We did move an old dresser from upstairs into the boys "club room" to store smaller toys, games and the like. I tried to use existing pieces in different rooms to help organize other rooms.

Teamwork

My sister and I worked together mainly, although she sorted out most of her items alone. I helped her with the moving of larger pieces of furniture, boxes, bringing out garbage and other heavy work. I found the faster I could create the vision of the finished room, the more motivated she got. There were no major problems, except some heavy lifting. She didn't even answer her phone. Talk about focused!

The time it took to completion…

Office .... 6-8 hours
Entry Way and Sitting Room .... 2-3 hours
Basement .... 4-5 hours
Bedroom and Spare Bedroom .... 5-6 hours

Maintenance plan

I told her that, once a month, we would do a walk through of her rooms. I would help her if needed or give her suggestions on improving on her own. I'm over there often anyway, but if she were a customer I would start with monthly visits for maybe 6 months, then go down to quarterly.

Fate has given Dianne the opportunity to pursue her passion of organizing. She began her journey by establishing "Top To Bottom Organizing" in November of 2007 and immediately began focusing on families and small business organizing. Dianne received a warm welcome when she joined the Professional Organizers of Canada in December. She brings a non-judgmental, confidential and caring approach to all her consultations and loves the opportunity of working one-on-one with her clients to improve their lives

She is a very organized and vivacious person who shares the experience and talent she has acquired from various past positions with a warm enthusiasm for every project. She is enjoying enhancing her knowledge with on-going professional training, books and articles...actually anything she can get her hands on! Learn more about Dianne and her business by writing to: toptobottom@sympatico.ca or visiting her site: www.toptobottomorganizing.ca

Case Study #3: Elinor Warkentin

I am a Trained Professional Organizer with a full-time business, Goodbye Clutter! in Vancouver, Canada. I would like to introduce you to one of my favorite clients. I'll call her Mary.

Mary called me a few years ago at the end of February. She was stressed and overwhelmed about the clutter in her home. She described herself as tired and unclear about how to make some changes in her home, but wanting a change. Mary had retired several years earlier and spent time in her home, but her home was not the comfortable, nourishing home she desired.

System for new clients

When a client contacts me, I use my New Client template to ask questions and gather the information I will need. Each client gets asked some basic questions, like how they found me, what neighborhood they live in, what the size of their home or office is, etc. Then we discuss their "challenge." I avoid using the word "problem" with clients; I prefer a more empowering approach focusing on what they can do to help themselves, with my assistance.

I also take notes of what they say, so that we can look back later and measure what has changed for them. In this case especially, it has been valuable to look back on my notes so that I could quote accurately.

With Mary, my notes included that she wanted to "Reduce and eliminate clutter by getting stuff off floors, giving stuff away" and "Prepare for floor refinishing but more importantly, feel better about her home, increase her self-confidence and enjoy more peace of mind in her home." As our conversation continued, Mary was quite frank; she wanted "No trash on the floors and for her home not to look like a terrible mess."

The emotional effects of clutter

It appeared that Mary felt quite strongly about clutter and that she was really bothered by the state of her home. I could tell that Mary was somewhat aware of emotional effects of the clutter as she said she wanted to "feel more worthwhile, not so useless that I can't keep my home in order."

Mary seemed to have a lot of self-judgment, something many clients seem to experience. After recognizing this with clients, I have explained to them that I do my best to be non-judgmental about my clients as there is already the clutter of self-criticism and judgments in their experience and there is just not room or appropriateness to add any more. I explain that I am there to assess, share insights, reflect what I see, but that often clutter comes along with self-criticism, low self esteem about that area of their life, and negative self talk, so being judgmental about them would add more clutter to the clutter!

Compassion and caring go a long way in my work with clients. In the sea or C of clutter and chaos, why crash in a storm of criticism? Why not ride the soothing waves of compassion and caring instead?

Christmas in March?

After about 30 minutes on the phone, Mary was ready to meet me. She had been hesitant to begin, but after building rapport and trust, she wanted to take the next step. We booked an initial assessment appointment, which I offer at no cost.

When I arrived at Mary's home, one of the things that struck me was the Christmas wrapping, cards and decorations taking up most of her dining room table. It was March and although procrastination is often a part of being disorganized, I felt there was something symbolic about the leftover Christmas things.

I spoke with Mary and she began telling me about her only child and how the upcoming Christmas would be the first Christmas in about 35 years that her daughter would not be with her. The thought of spending a Christmas "alone" was upsetting, even though it was almost a year away.

This became an opportunity to talk about both the effects of clutter and the cause of clutter. As we talked and I learned what the Christmas things represented to Mary, I suggested a few other ways to look at things and possible options. Within a short time, Mary was considering the possibility of her own vacation to a sunny climate for the upcoming holiday. Even just the ideas helped Mary move forward and see how the reminders on her table were dragging her down. After her realizations, Mary was ready to pack up the Christmas wrap.

There is no relaxing among a sea of clutter

From the dining room, Mary took me to one of the most important rooms of her home, the place she relaxed, watched TV, read and did crossword puzzles—a room intended for relaxing and replenishing. My eyes took in a sea of clutter. Mary's floor was a mix of newspapers, flyers, junk mail, unopened important mail, grocery shopping bags containing paper, books, receipts, photos, and a whole mish-mash of assorted bits and bobs.

There was a six-foot stack of boxes against a wall, "hidden" by a blue blanket. Her couch was clear where she could sit, but not much else. Mary told me all the clutter was a 15+ year collection. When I asked Mary if she found it relaxing to watch TV, she replied "not really."

I suggested that there were thousands of small bits of visual distractions that her eyes were taking in, both consciously and unconsciously, as she sat on her couch. And most of it was on the floor or the lower three feet of the room. That meant her energy was being dragged down continuously.

I suggested that one immediate change would be to put something inspiring and uplifting on her empty walls at eye level or higher. It's much easier to feel depressed when we are looking down rather than up. I also suggested to Mary that this might be a case of what came first—the chicken or the egg, the depression or the clutter. Mary had shared with me that she was depressed about her daughter being away, and we talked about whether this had led to her dropping things in a helter-skelter way or did her disorganization get so chaotic that is was depressing to see and live with?

A lesson in marketing—clients can easily "lose you"

One of the humorous aspects of helping Mary de-clutter was the number of my ads I found amidst her paperwork. She had seen my articles and ads in a community paper and had several clippings dating back over a year. I laughed and told her that I had not expected to be throwing out my own ads in a de-cluttering process with clients.

I have since learned that it is not unusual to give a prospective client my business card, or to appear in a newspaper article, only to find out 6–18 months later that they lost the card or clipped the article, buried it in a paper pile and are finally following up.

Mary said she was thinking of getting organized for more than two years before we first met. Between desire and action were several moves, waiting for the "right time and place" and not feeling "ready." Then when she bought a home, felt it was a permanent move and settled in, she realized she needed to finally "get rid of stuff."

Mary also said her daughter was pressuring her to go through her things as her daughter did not want to do it after her Mom died. That is something I have heard from several of my clients' children, the "I'm so glad you are helping Mom and Dad because I don't want to do it later" compliment usually delivered with an air of relief and gratitude!

Finding the client's motivation

Wanting her floor refinished was a big motivation for Mary. She said, "I was overwhelmed at first and not sure where to start, but I felt I could do it because you were so supportive, you didn't force me, you gently and persistently nudged me when I balked, you sized it up, and gave me reasons about why to do it." From a hesitant and uncertain beginning, we booked several three-hour sessions and got started.

The process

We started on the floor, the couch and the surfaces. From there we moved to boxes that were often filled with more plastic bags stuffed with paper—the same as on the floor. As box after box was opened and dealt with, I began to look forward to opening each new box, curious to find out at first what year we were going to find and then what decade! Some paper clutter in the boxes was as old as the 1970's.

It was a sort and purge start. Facing a large volume of mixed paper, from the unimportant to important mail and documents, I would do a pre-sort, and then Mary would make the decisions. As we worked together, by asking Mary questions, we established parameters about what I could toss in the recycling, what needed to be shredded and what Mary wanted to handle personally.

Establishing trust

It took a while for trust to be established in the paper purging process. At first Mary would ask what I was throwing out if she didn't see the paper. Mary was quite apprehensive about identity theft, so each paper had to be looked at carefully. This was a very slow, time-consuming process and I wanted to move quicker. But I reminded myself that it was important for Mary to work at a speed she felt comfortable with.

After a while, we built an agreed-upon list, like old flyers and certain junk mail, that I could toss, and some things, like odd small papers with handwritten notes on them that she wanted to see. During the sessions, I would talk to Mary about the effects of the clutter, how her life would be without the clutter and sometimes about life in general. From time to time, I would check in with Mary, to see if the process was working for her and if we were accomplishing what was important to her. Over time, Mary began to see a light at the end of the tunnel of her overwhelming clutter.

Photo session

I took before, during and after photos with Mary, as I do with some clients, but not all. I use before and after photos in several ways. When I first started working with clients, I would ask them permission to take photos, explain they were for my before and after portfolio, and get their permission for use. Now I use my digital camera differently.

I sometimes take the photos during my initial assessment appointment. I feel more comfortable taking the photos and also have a better understanding of how they will help me, and I think that comes across to the client. If they ask, I explain that a) the digital record helps me plan how to help them get organized and b) that I often get ideas after I leave them and having a visual reminder helps. I explain confidentiality and get their permission.

I show the client the before photo at the end of a session to remind them of what it looked like to start. We have a mini *reveal* easily at hand. Confidentiality is important and not only have I agreed to a confidentiality standard when joining Professional Organizers of Canada, if I want to use the photos in any of my marketing material, I want to make sure I have the client's full understanding and agreement.

Mary has given me permission to use the photos at public trade shows and in my client binder, but does not want the photos shown on my web site.

A little project, expanded!

My work with Mary began in one room of her house and, over time, moved through almost her entire home. When we started, we worked together two to three times per week. Then after the first month, we worked once every week or two. Our sessions ranged from 4-6 hours, with one session of 8½ hours.

After about 3 months, we had made a lot of progress and Mary was quite happy. She decided to take a break and focus on several home renovations. Two years from the month we started, Mary called me again. She was ready to face her locker and off-site storage.

The vault...err, locker

When we had chatted at past de-cluttering sessions, Mary had told me about the locker. Her locker contained items she had not looked at for up to a decade. She had not opened her locker in over 5 years. She hadn't even wanted to "go there," physically or mentally. Now she was ready, though she stated firmly "I'm not going there without you."

I worked with Mary for five days, 5-6 hours per session, over a two-week period to clear out her 270 square foot locker (9' x 5' x 6'). Every day I estimated the pounds going to trash, recycling and charity. The five-day average was over 300 pounds per day. Time it took to sort, purge and clear it all out: 5 days. The estimated cost of the locker over the years was in excess of $7,000. Cost to the client for de-cluttering? Less than $1,500! Mary was so happy!

Her locker was cleared, empty and now part of the past. No longer was the locker haunting her, weighing her down. Over the years, in my work with clients, I have learned that the rewards of letting go of clutter are ongoing, with continued waves of relief and multiple moments of celebration.

Her thank you card arrived the day after our last session.

Future add-ons

Since that time, I have worked with Mary on two more occasions, de-cluttering and organizing some of the last corners of her home. While we work, we talk about life, sometimes laughing about the nuances of clutter, once using clutter as a metaphor to see if it was time to recycle the boyfriend based on the usual decision-making clutter questions, and becoming friends in the process.

While interviewing Mary for this article, she said she had first gone to a local workshop on clutter but decided the presenter was not a fit for her. She found my ad, called me and decided she didn't need to look any further. We worked well together because she "felt I could do it because you were so supportive, didn't force me, you gently and persistently nudged me" and "when I balked, you sized it up, gave me reasons about why to let go and I did." In my work with clients, I use questions, I listen, and I make sure to pack lots of compassion in my tool kit. Those are key aspects of how I work that clients consistently appreciate.

A party!

My most delightful visit to Mary's house was just before a recent Christmas holiday.

My visit was social, not business. Mary invited me for tea to show me her renovated floors, her redecorated room, a new door to a small patio where previously the six-foot stack of boxes had lived, a few furniture changes, and a home that was inviting and beautiful. I was so pleased.

The best part was that Mary was showing me her home just before hosting a party, which was going to be her opportunity to show off her home.

The difference in the home, and better yet, in Mary, was humbling. When we met, Mary had been depressed and avoiding visitors in many parts of her home. Now she was throwing a party!

Since then...

I have visited Mary since. Her home is not always completely neat, tidy and organized. She has her hotspots and challenges. But, she will never have the boxes of paperwork from the 90's, 80's and 70's to contend with. She'll never have a sea of paper and plastic bags covering an unfinished floor. She's not spending money needlessly on a locker. And she often reminds me of how I "changed her life" after which I always remind her that, "No Mary, I didn't change your life. I showed you the tools and helped you figure out how to change your own life!"

And that's why I do what I do: obvious, positive results for my clients, fun for me! I love my work.

Elinor Warkentin owns and operates Goodbye Clutter!, a one-woman business (that's one organized, hard-working, sincere, resourceful, Virgo, Mennonite woman!) Her career as a PO began while traveling in Wales in 2000 and officially launched her business in Vancouver in 2003.

She is a Silver Leaf member of Professional Organizers of Canada, was the Chair of their 2007 national conference and is one of 17 POC members with Trained Professional Organizer status. She combines her two passions, travel and organizing, as a Trustee of Women Welcome Women World Wide, an international women's travel and friendship organization.

Elinor has appeared on local TV and been featured by numerous local print media. For home or office organizing assistance, learn more about Elinor at www.goodbyeclutter.ca

Case Study #4: Ruth Cekola

I have always been a very organized person by nature and when I discovered that I could become a professional organizer and get paid for my talents, I was excited! I spread the word that I was starting my own business and a real estate agent acquaintance gave my name to her clients that she felt could use my services.

My very first client

My very first client was an elderly woman who was selling her house and moving out of state to live closer to her daughter due to health issues.

My initial meeting was to determine what her needs would be and how I could best assist her in getting her house ready to sell, which included sorting through everything in the house to determine what she wanted to take with her, and the rest was either donate, sell or pitch.

I asked her to show me each room, closet, cabinet, basement and garage. In each space, I tried to get a feel for what she was thinking of moving, I wrote that down and also included what was going to be left behind.

Her main concern was the basement because due to her health issues she was unable to spend much time in cold and damp surroundings. I quickly realized that I was going to be doing all of the heavy lifting and working on this project mainly with her guidance. It was going to be a big job and would take quite a bit of time.

After my complimentary initial consultation, I went home and studied my notes and re-read Maria Gracia's *Ultimate Guide for Professional Organizers*. The information in this guide is invaluable and has become a great resource for me.

My proposal: two phases

In my proposal, I divided the project into two phases a) to help get the house ready to sell and b) to help organize her belongings to move. I outlined how I would accomplish these phases and also included that I could help her select a mover and pack her belongings if that service wasn't included with the movers.

I decided to price it by the project and gave detailed payment instructions in the proposal. Later, I realized that pricing by the project was not a smart idea and I was basically giving away my services—experience really is the best teacher.

The next step was to meet with my prospective client and present my proposal. I was nervous. Did I price it too high? Would she accept? To my relief, she was agreeable to the terms and signed it right then. I was excited, my first client! But of course, I didn't tell her that!

We decided on a timetable, discussed when we were both available to get started and we chose to take the weekend off and start the project on Monday.

A shocking phone call

On Sunday, I received a call from her daughter that her mom had been taken to the hospital the day after I met with her and had passed away. I was in shock. It hit me that I was probably the last person to see her alive.

After the shock wore off, I wondered if this was a sign that I shouldn't become a professional organizer!

Her daughter assured me that they still wanted my services and that she would contact me in a few months. I gave her my condolences and told her that I would wait to hear from her.

For me, the project was the same, but less complicated. The family would now choose what they wanted to keep and everything else would be sold, donated or pitched.

A new proposal

Since I would be starting this project with a new client, I decided that I should have a new proposal signed. At this point, I chose to change the terms. I stated that the original proposal price was valued at a certain number of hours but worth a few more (giving free hours and added value) and then any additional time would be billed at an hourly rate.

My client willingly signed the new proposal but after talking to her brother, they decided only to use my services for the initial proposed time. However, as those hours were used, it was evident to them that they still needed my services and I continued working with them until the project was complete.

My (new) client came into town with her children, dog and niece and I became her right hand. I spent two to four hours a day for approximately three weeks helping to sort, pack or pitch everything in the house.

While I was working side by side with my client, she would frequently say "Mom, why did you keep this? What were you saving this for?" It was hard for them to go through it all, but with my help and gentle persuasion, we were able to get it done.

I came to the conclusion that leaving it for your family to handle after you're gone is really tough. I am glad I was there to help.

A difficult situation, but we persevered

I know my client felt overwhelmed at first because she was away from her home, her business and her husband, she was in a town that she was unfamiliar with, and was emotionally drained every day. She appeared to me to be strong, though, and knew what needed to be done and had specific ways she wanted to accomplish it.

I was able to provide basic information for them, like places to eat, how to get to the grocery store and where the nearest movie theater was. With each passing day, the progress became more and more evident, but for at least a week it seemed like pure chaos.

The needs of this project were many. I found a local organization of student haulers that came periodically to remove the many garbage bags full of stuff and bigger items that we wanted to pitch. I asked a piano tuner to evaluate the two pianos in the basement, assess their value, and actually found a family that wanted one of them and they only had to pay to have it removed—what a deal for them!

I helped sort and organize for a three-day yard sale, identified organizations that would pick up donations, took clothing to a local consignment shop, arranged for a resale/consignment shop to sell some of the furniture, picked up packing materials and packed over 60 boxes to be shipped to various locations throughout the U.S.

After my clients had left town, I found buyers for the remaining furniture by placing ads in the local newspapers, helped clean and even stripped wallpaper and painted interior walls to increase the value of the home. Some of the things were "above and beyond" the call of an organizer but I wanted to help the family as much as I could. I had become personally invested in this project.

When the project was complete, I gave my client a thank you gift of china storage items from an organizational container store. I also asked her for a letter of recommendation because I wanted to compile a binder to show prospective clients who had not been personally referred to me. This client gave me a glowing recommendation and upon reading it, I realized how beneficial my services are and that keeping a positive attitude during a project is very important.

I enjoy being a professional organizer because it is a rewarding occupation that is as diverse as each clients needs—and I meet some wonderful people.

Ruth Cekola is an organized person by nature and felt she could help so many people, so she started "Organize It!" in 2005.

She currently provides organizational assistance to people who are downsizing and moving from their current homes and also has helped many clients that just needed to get out from under their clutter and didn't know where to begin.

Ruth can be contacted at r_cekola@yahoo.com for further information.

Case Study #5: Christine Rice

As a professional organizer, I have spent the past several years helping people become better organized in both their homes and offices. Many of my clients also run businesses from their homes. These circumstances present many unique challenges for those attempting to become or stay better organized.

Oftentimes, business owners who combine their livelihood with their living space discover that the boundaries easily become blurred resulting in cluttered surroundings. It becomes necessary to incorporate dual-function storage solutions, while being very selective about what items you actually need to keep, in order to function efficiently in your business. It also takes a fair amount of discipline to maintain a clear division between home and office while, at the same time, creating a space where the two function successfully and happily commingle.

Keeping tabs on business and home records

As one of my former clients found, files and paperwork in particular can quickly grow out of hand if you do not keep close tabs on your business and home records. This situation can be very overwhelming for many people, whether you own a business or not. I had been working with this particular client at various times throughout the early stages of her business and during its continued growth period, both in a coaching capacity and with hands-on organizing assistance. Prior to starting her home-based business, my client had been in a private-type practice, which operated from a traditional office setting.

When she decided to leave her previous line of work, my client brought all of her old files and paperwork with her. Coupled with her personal household files, and now paperwork entailing her new role as a business owner, there was an overload of printed material to contend with.

Need for visual reminders

My client, as with many people who suffer from chronic disorganization, happened to be what I would call a visually stimulated person. For the most part, she felt she needed to have daily, visual reminders of things she needed to do. As a result, there was a conglomeration of books that needed to be returned, things that needed to be mailed out and other various items that reminded her of tasks that needed to be completed.

She was also very information driven. She frequently made notes on everything from scrap pieces of paper to restaurant napkins and those also got added to the mix. Nearly every horizontal surface was covered in paperwork or items that needed attention.

The office was the family dining area

Combine all of this with the fact that her office also served as the family dining area situated in an open floor-plan home, and you can imagine that even when the business sign said "closed" it was not an easy task to put the office out of sight or out of mind. This finally proved too much one day when I received a call for help.

My client had set out upon the daunting task of sorting through a backlog of papers and files so as to bring some order to the area. The trouble being that nearly every stack of paperwork and file box housed numerous reminders of things that "needed" to be done. At various times during the course of her business, each of these tasks seemed extremely important to accomplish. In actuality, some things probably could have now been crossed off her list. But when you are staring at each one of these things at that exact instant, it is difficult, if not impossible, to discern between extremely important, secondary and unnecessary tasks. They are all shouting at you for your immediate attention.

What prompted my client to call me

This was the position my client found herself in that particular day and what prompted her call to me. In her current state, my client was quickly becoming agitated with herself and distracted by the lingering reminders of everything that, in her opinion, she had failed to complete. In her mind, she was berating herself for all the things that remained undone and that were holding her back in furthering her business. This was taking her away from the more pertinent task at hand, which was to sort and purge paperwork.

As a professional organizer, it is your job to defuse the situation and bring calm to not only the surroundings, but also to your client. You often have to think outside the box to accomplish this. I first reassured my client that the process of sorting and purging was a necessary tool in helping to weed out the unneeded paperwork and would eventually pave the way for a more organized, efficient way of running a successful business.

I went on to point out all of the things she had already achieved in her business and life that, at this particular moment, she was unable to see. Putting things in perspective often helps give additional enthusiasm for an organizing project that would have otherwise been on the verge of going awry. You have to be in the right frame of mind to muster the emotional and physical energy necessary to tackle a project of this magnitude and it's sometimes up to you, the organizer, to provide this.

The Box

Finally, I showed up at her house with a box in hand. On the side I had written in large permanent marker "To Be Forgiven." Instead of seeing all of the things she needed "to do," I gave my client a place to temporarily put those things that would need her attention at a future point in time. Right now it was time to get her organized.

There would be time to deal with the other tasks at a later date. After all, they had waited this long. It would not serve her well at this point to criticize herself for not getting them completed. By doing this I gave her permission to let go of all of the tasks that remained undone and to forgive herself for things that may not have gotten accomplished in the past. This would help give her the inspiration to continue sorting, purging and organizing paperwork until the area was in a more manageable state. Then, and only then, would my client be able to fully begin to address and prioritize those issues still needing her attention. It's okay to set aside some portions of a project in order to realize the long-term goal.

It has been over a year since that day, and my client still mentions how that one box changed her outlook on organizing as well as her business. When faced with an organizing project, she is now more easily able to assess the situation and tackle it head on, breaking it down into more manageable pieces and working with one aspect at a time instead of focusing on an overwhelming number of things at once.

Christine Rice is a professional organizer, author and speaker, but she'll be the first to admit she wasn't always a very organized person. The story of her own personal journey to organization is included in the inspiring pages of her latest book, A Life Less Cluttered: Expert Secrets to Your Own Organizing Epiphany.

Christine's own experiences with disorganization and chaos have helped countless others reach their own "organizational enlightenment" by offering hope that you, too, can become better organized, even if you weren't born with it. She offers step-by-step methods for incorporating the characteristics of organized people into your daily life. Christine's contact information and products can be found through her website at www.organizeittoday.com

Case Study #6: Suzanne Kuhn

Nancy* became my first customer when she won a gift certificate for organizing services that I had donated to a fund-raising auction at the high school both our daughters attended.

She elected to use my services to organize half her basement in preparation for a construction project to finish it.

A sense of belonging

Quickly I learned that Nancy had a huge collection of Christmas wraps and decorations, along with every toy her only child, then age 17, had ever owned.

As we worked and chatted, a portrait emerged of an isolated woman who, although American, had been raised in Asia by military parents and had only come to America after marrying.

Even after fifteen years here, Nancy still did not feel at home in the United States.

She tried to create a sense of belonging by surrounding herself with objects that had emotional triggers—her child's toys, voluminous photos, correspondence and other memorabilia, and quantities of household furnishings reminiscent of the ornate Asian style of her childhood.

Did not want to toss…anything!

Nancy emphasized early in the first session that she was completely closed to the idea of disposing of any of her many possessions. She described how she had walked out of a local organizing talk when the instructor announced that the first step to getting organized was purging your home of 50% of your belongings.

Although I had been thinking how desperately Nancy needed to purge her home, I made the decision at that moment that I was not going to tell her to get rid of anything.

Instead, I would focus my efforts on creating order in the possessions that she had. I must confess that there was a dual motivation here—although I did empathize with Nancy, I also didn't want to lose my first customer!

The organizing work in that first session was not too challenging—categorizing, consolidating and packing things away in preparation for the impending construction. What impressed Nancy about me, she later shared, was my work ethic—the way I rolled up my sleeves and got to work without any concern about getting dirty. She also liked my organizational creativity. For example, I suggested having her construction workers create a gift-wrap closet with two entrances, one on either side of the basement.

We discovered storage bins in the process

Six months later, the renovations were complete and Nancy called me back to organize the newly built gift-wrap closet and her Christmas decorations. During the first session, we pulled out all the gift wraps from the chaos in the unfinished storage area on the other side of the basement—even more chaotic now because the workmen had hurled things there pell-mell—and organized them on the shelves she had had installed in the closet.

This took one full four-hour session. In the process, I also discovered that Nancy had a vast collection of storage bins in various sizes. This would be quite a resource for the projects that followed, and we put some to use right away.

Prioritize, Organize, Place

From there, we moved on to create the storage area for the Christmas decorations. Characteristically, Nancy had already purchased four sets of Ikea shelves and three stainless baker's racks on wheels for the project. We set them up in one-third of the unfinished half of the basement. This in itself was a challenge, as the area was already jammed with possessions.

We designated the renovated section as sorting space, and I established a Prioritize-Organize-Place procedure that would serve us repeatedly over the ensuing months:

1. Clear a space in the storage area.

2. Decide what should go there, prioritizing placement in ABCDE order based on ease of access and frequency of use.

3. Pull out items by category into the sorting area and consolidate and containerize them there.

4. Place on shelves according to plan.

5. Repeat.

We repeated this process six times before the job was done. Consistent with my initial decision, I made little attempt to get Nancy to purge. After we had prioritized and placed the entire collection using the ABCDE system, I asked if she would feel comfortable letting some "E"s go, and remained impassive when she reluctantly pulled out two minor items. At this point, I was consciously building trust.

More organizing

Nancy and I finished the Christmas storage area in three four-hour work sessions, and I was feeling pretty pleased with myself. "I really can do this!" I thought.

I felt affirmed in my perception when Nancy announced that she wanted to start the next project immediately—the rest of the basement storage area.

Working with the physical layout of the space, we established two areas, one for unused home décor and one for her daughter's outgrown toys and memorabilia. We continued to use Nancy's inexhaustible collection of storage containers, along with the Prioritize-Organize-Place procedure I had established previously.

Although I was floored by the large quantity of unused home decorations and toys, I stuck with my resolve not to pressure Nancy to let go. Whenever she came up with a small article she could part with, I praised her lavishly and got it out of the house that very day, dropping it at Goodwill on my way home. I privately considered it a great victory when she turned over a large plastic trash bag filled with every Happy Meal toy her daughter had ever gotten, and I assured Nancy that they would have a good home at an orphanage to which I contribute.

Comfort in a time of loneliness

The deciding moment in my relationship with Nancy came midway through this second phase, when one of her beloved purebred Persian cats died unexpectedly. I had lost a child suddenly to cancer six years before and, strange as it may seem, the experience equipped me to comfort this lonely woman, whose pets substituted for her far-away family.

I spent one entire session listening to her talk, sharing personal insights, letting her cry and hugging her. I continued to do so on and off over the next two months. Without announcement, our relationship entered a new phase where it was clear that Nancy would be my weekly client for the foreseeable future. We finished the basement and set to work organizing the remainder of Nancy's home.

Nancy and I have now been meeting for over a year, and we have organized two bedrooms, two home offices (hers and her husband's), the dining room, the pantry and the garage. Throughout this year, we have drawn on her collection of containers (it's still not used up!) and my Prioritize-Organize-Place procedure.

In the interim, her daughter has gone off to college. This was another emotional event for which my own life experience equipped me to offer support.

The new college tuition payment has made money tighter for Nancy and her husband, so our meeting frequency has diminished from weekly to semi-monthly.

Most sessions now involve maintenance of the systems we established together.

The struggle continues, but baby steps help

As Nancy has come to trust me more, she has become a little more relaxed about letting things go, but it is still a struggle for her.

As she has seen the effort we must exert to find homes for things in her overcrowded spaces, she has become more judicious about impulse shopping.

I still itch to purge her overabundance of belongings, but I continue to keep my thoughts to myself, and I praise every baby step.

What did my first customer teach me?

❖ Organizing is most effective when there is a dialogue between partners, rather than the imposition of preconceived ideas by an "authority" on a "subject."

❖ Good organizing often has a therapeutic dimension to it. With Nancy, I find the talking we do to be just as important as the sorting, categorizing and containerizing, a way of contributing to Nancy's internal order. This has been borne out since by other clients.

❖ In light of this, it is important for an organizer to establish emotional boundaries with a client. I respect Nancy because she never violates my personal boundaries, even though we speak about intimate subjects.

❖ I bring my whole life experience to my profession as an organizer. My experiences with death, motherhood, marriage and even my religious faith contribute just as much to my ability to serve Nancy and other clients as my skills categorizing and arranging objects.

❖ I bring my heart as well as my head to organizing. My heart-based decision to build trust by not forcing Nancy to purge her possessions has been key to our ongoing work together.

❖ I can trust my instincts, even when they're not "by the book."

❖ I am resourcefully capable of meeting new challenges.

❖ I feel blessed to have had Nancy as my first customer. This initial positive experience has launched me with confidence into a new and deeply satisfying career. These lessons I have learned with Nancy are available to other would-be organizers with their clients, too.

My best wishes and encouragement go to all who read this.

*Nancy's name and biographical details have been changed to protect her privacy.

Suzanne Kuhn, B.S., M.A. has loved to organize all her life, refining her skills in such varied occupations as Fortune 500 manager, college instructor, accounting professional, volunteer, wife, mother of four, and caregiver to an ageing parent.

Since January 2006, she has been a professional organizer, speaker and writer in the Philadelphia area, specializing in time and paper management for individuals, small business owners and students age 11+.

Reach Suzanne at AceOrganizing@verizon.net

Case Study #7: Audrey Cupo

I have been a professional organizer since 2004, specializing in residential organizing. One organizing project that I am particularly proud of is a home office wherein I organized the space for a very busy woman who not only has four children but runs three businesses out of her home office. There was so much paperwork that needed to be organized. It required a very detailed filing system in order for it to function.

Normally, I would schedule an initial consultation wherein I would meet with a new client so that I could evaluate the space in question, discuss with the client what they expected to achieve and take photographs of the space so that I could use them to work out the space planning.

I cannot stress enough how important it is to listen closely to what the client has to say.

When asked, they should be able to tell you how they envision the space to function and look. Everyone has their own style of functioning and everyone has different taste as far as style, whether contemporary or Victorian, etc. If you listen closely to what they are telling you, you will be able to provide your client with a room that not only functions well but reflects their personality.

Consultation and project-start in one

However, in this instance, we combined the initial consultation with a four-hour session due to the fact that she was so desperate to get the paper clutter under control as quickly as possible. She was completely unable to function in the space as it was.

We began by discussing her particular situation—namely keeping track of paperwork for all of her family members, the youngest being 15 years old and the three businesses which include managing property rentals on the family farm, being a property manager for rehabilitated homes throughout the county which she not only purchased but supervised the improvements to be made in them so she could rent them out, as well as developing a day lily farm business.

Needless to say, there was a considerable amount of paperwork involved in running these businesses, as well as her own general household management. Besides the day-to day paperwork, there was also five years of historical paperwork involving her divorce from her first husband and current support and custody issues still pending in the courts for her own two children. Lastly, I noted that the arrangement of the furniture and filing cabinets needed to be redesigned to better accommodate my client's ability to function in this space.

The initial sort

After taking photographs to assist me with space planning, I immediately began sorting through the mountains of paperwork on the counter tops in the office space to determine with my client what categories needed to be created. I created categories temporarily in empty file folder boxes…one box for each of the family members, one for the farm, one for bills, one for bank statements, one for investments, one for farm plans, and one for copies of tenant cancelled checks.

This covered most of the general categories which had been scattered on the counter tops. Other pieces of paper were immediately filed in the currently existing filing system in a four drawer filing cabinet located in this room until the new system was implemented.

Color coding

I determined that the best way to manage the various categories was to use a color-coding system for the various categories throughout the entire filing system. For example, **the first category** we discussed was the farm which was both used for commercial and personal purposes. Therefore, dark green was chosen for any commercial documentation related to the farm and light green for any personal documentation relating to living on the farm.

The color green reminded my client of the outdoors and the farm. This is an example of using color association and it's a great way to identify where something gets filed. The dark green files contained sub-files for the various rentals on the property. The sub-files were identified by coordinating colored labels.

The second major category of files included the six (6) rental properties located throughout the County. Each property was color coded, so that anything relating to that particular property was easily identified not only by name but by the color of the folder. Some properties had more than one unit so I created a sub-file for each unit.

Aside from the color coding system, I also created manila file folders for various types of forms that would be used for all of the properties; basically anything related to running this particular business. They included, for example, Bids &

Contracts, Utility Companies, Banking File, Insurance, Credit Cards, Trash Removals and contracts for each building. Files were also created for Monthly Visa Receipts, Monthly Bank Statements and Receipts and Monthly Miscellaneous Receipts, just to name a few.

The third major category of files related to the day lily farm. Since this particular business was up and coming and the business was not expected to be truly active for at least another three years, it did not require a large or detailed filing system. However, there was planning documentation being collected. This system was color coded pink.

Lastly, each family member was color coded with pastel colors to differentiate from primary colors used for business files. Each family member's folders held documentation relating to school, medical and so on. Once these categories were determined, we then talked about the current lay-out of the furniture and how I could create a better functioning space for her wherein she would have a nice counter space to spread out on when working.

We would consolidate the four filing cabinets down to two. They would be moved next to each other against the back wall. We would utilize the glass front cabinets with a counter top over them to use as additional space to work. We also discussed hanging a bulletin board and some of her favorite artwork on the wall where the large counter space would be located so she could enjoy it while working.

At the end of the first session, by creating the basic categories, the table top was cleared enough for my client to keep sorting through the paperwork and address some of the outstanding bills and other important issues which needed to be addressed immediately.

Upon my return . . .

I would be working with my client to relocate the furniture as we discussed in the room. I would then begin to work with her on putting together the filing system for the rental properties, which was the most complicated one to create.

My plan, thereafter, was to address the farm, day lily farm and family filing systems. Finally, we would create a hanging filing system for my client to maintain the monthly Visa receipts, bank statements with coordinating receipts, and monthly miscellaneous receipts.

We discussed having an expandable file system that contains 1 through 31 wherein she could file per personal bills to be paid on the appropriate day and then grab a week or so of bills at a time to get them paid promptly.

It was important that we kept the business related documents separate from personal documents when developing these systems for paying bills as well.

Feeling better

After **our very first session**, my client commented that she felt better already just by having a clearer counter top. I told her it would only get better! I believe it is important to show the client the progress that's been made, even in the first session.

I like to reiterate what was accomplished so far and how much better it will be as we keep working at it. I always make sure I let the client know that I recognize how hard they are working and that they are doing a great job.

Positive reinforcement keeps the client motivated to move forward. Also, I am always prepared to let my client know at the end of each session what we will be doing at our next session. It shows that I have a good feel for the project and they feel comfortable knowing what to expect.

At **our second session**, we ended up spending the entire time working on the layout of the room. We ended up bringing in two book cases from the family room and put them on the wall to the right as you walk in.

Then we put the two beige floor cabinets next to each other with a black wood counter top on it and placed them slightly away from the right wall.

Since the counter top is much larger than the cabinets, this allowed room behind the cabinets to store some of my client's portfolios of her art work in a location that was accessible yet hidden from view. The large surface of the counter top provided my client with plenty of space to spread out and work as we discussed.

Due to the fact that she had a bad back, she preferred to stand when working. Therefore, we did not incorporate any seating for her.

We took the green 4-drawer filing cabinet that was in the right front corner of the room and put it on the right back corner. We placed the beige 4-drawer filing cabinet next to it.

Getting creative

We then became creative and alternated the green drawers with the beige drawers in both cabinets so that they looked more cohesive. It had a "checker board" effect.

This idea avoided our having to paint the cabinets the same color; it made them look like they went together. It worked well with the color of the carpeting in the room as well. It also showed my client's artistic side.

Two old brown filing cabinets, two white book cases and a shelving unit which was no longer needed were removed from this room altogether. By eliminating the extra pieces, it freed up more space in which to move around the room.

To the left of the two 4-drawer filing cabinets we placed three glass-front cabinets on the floor with another piece of laminate wood on top of them to serve as another flat surface for my client to use. These were centered under the window in the back of the room.

With the new arrangement, I was able to create a much larger space in the center of the room for my client to navigate more easily. She was no longer bumping into cabinetry.

At **our third session**, I showed my client the plan I had created for using the filing cabinet drawers for specific categories. I named the drawers in the left cabinet L-1, L-2, L-3 and L-4. The drawers in the right cabinet were named R-1, R-2, R-3 and R-4.

The left cabinet was basically used for business and the right cabinet was for personal documentation. We then began creating the hanging folders for each of the six rental properties and using the color coded file folders previously selected and created a sub-file for each of the property units.

We then created another set of hanging file folders and color coded sub-files for each property, namely: original loan documents, agreement of sale, deed, appraisals, letters of satisfaction, use and occupancy documents and certifications.

We created additional hanging files for a third drawer for other forms. Basically, the first three drawers of the left filing cabinet were strictly being dedicated to my client's rental property paperwork.

At **our fourth session**, we would be creating the filing system for the farm: commercial - dark green; personal - light green.

At our fourth session, we were able to complete the detailed rental property filing system, the commercial and personal filing systems for the farm, the day lily business filing system and the family filing systems.

My client began to organize some of her art supplies on the top of the two book cases we had recently relocated into this room and she put her business related books on the book case shelves while I created the files mentioned above.

At **our fifth session**, we filled the file folders I created and eliminated those documents which were no longer needed. There were at least five old filing cabinet drawers from the two cabinets we had removed from the room previously which were full of old documents that needed to be sorted through, so it took quite a bit of time.

I also assisted my client by helping her go through her piles of unopened mail and paperwork and filing it in the correct place. I created the table top monthly filing system for the rental property business and the farm. We used a hanging folder system which included a folder for each month of the year for her various property rentals and another hanging folder system for the farm expenses, banking information and loan payment documentation. All of this documentation needed to be easily accessible to my client so she could grab it and bring it to her accountant on a regular basis.

At our **sixth and final session**, we continued to fill the file folders with paperwork for the two current businesses. We were able to sort through the rest of the paperwork and organize the bills to be paid and taxes owed. My client would work to get these up to date. We finished the project by hanging some art work and reviewing how the paper management system should be maintained.

Because this detailed filing system was put into place and the furniture was rearranged, my client was able to focus and work in a more productive environment. She now had a system for paying bills and taxes on time. She had wide open spaces in which to work more efficiently. She had a bulletin board on which to put important information and some art work on the walls for her to enjoy while spending time in this space.

Success without breaking the bank

All in all, I was able to create the home office my client had envisioned and she was very pleased. This was achieved with only having to purchase some file folders and labels. I was able to make use of the furniture already in the space and eliminate those pieces that were no longer necessary.

Because I was able to break down the project into manageable parts, I made sure that my client never felt overwhelmed. By taking the time to plan out the project, I also felt confident about how the project progressed at each session.

At our last session, I took the "after pictures." It was fun for my client and me to view the "befores" taken at our first session prior to beginning the project and to look around the room to take in the final outcome. By taking the time to do this, I was able to show my client the complete transformation of her home office. I love to end my projects with my clients by sharing these "before" and "after" photos. Believe it or not, sometimes they had forgotten what the room looked like before we started. It has quite an impact.

I spoke with my client several weeks after completing the project. Although I thought that my client might need a maintenance program in order to keep her paperwork under control, she advised that she was able to maintain the system I had implemented on her own without my assistance. I always tell my clients that they are free to give me a call any time after we have completed the project if they have any questions or concerns.

Audrey Cupo is a professional organizer who specializes in residential organizing. Audrey started her own business, A BETTER SPACE, based in Bucks County, PA, in 2004 to assist others with the sometimes overwhelming prospect of getting organized. Prior to starting this business, Audrey worked in the legal profession for over 23 years as a legal secretary and paralegal. In the fast-paced and detail-oriented world of litigation, she was given the opportunity to sharpen her paper management, scheduling and problem-solving skills.

Today, Audrey offers a full range of residential services, including household organization, space planning, storage solutions, paper management systems, interior redesign and home staging. Audrey has been seen on Action News, written articles on the subject and is a regular contributor to the A Better Space Blog which provides Quick Tips for A Better Space. To contact Audrey at A BETTER SPACE, visit her website at www.4abetterspace.com

Case Study #8: Kathy Braud

My client had approximately 48 photo albums and she wanted them copied onto some type of long-term storage, in case of fire.

Coming up with a price

I didn't know how in the world to charge for this service, since I had never done it, so I began calling places like Kinko's and other professional scanning services in order to place a bid. I knew that the client was going to hire me because she did not want the albums to leave her home, and there aren't any companies willing to do that. I submitted a very conservative bid because she was also willing to pay my travel expenses. I ended up charging $1.50 per page.

Research prior to tackling the job

Almost all of the albums were 12" x 12", so I had to research scanners, most of which were made for standard 8-1/2" x 11" or 8-1/2" x 14" paper size.

After purchasing the scanner and having it delivered to her home, I installed the hardware and software on her computer and had just one day to learn how to use it! I also researched storage devices and discovered that "flash" drives or "jump" drives were the best route to take. I originally purchased a couple of 2-gigabyte (GB) flash drives because I had no idea how much data (photos) would fit on one.

My photo organizing system

I flipped through the first album in order to name it and save it. If it didn't already have a title, I would assign one, depending on the content (i.e., "Africa", "Family", "Childhood", etc.). I then wrote the name that I had given the album on a sticky note and put it on the inside cover of the album.

I also created a running spreadsheet of the project, which included the name of each album and how many pages they each contained. This came in tremendously handy when preparing my invoice, since I charged per page.

I also realized that approximately 1/3 of the albums involved the client's travels, so I created a folder called "[Client's] Travels" and named each "travel" album under the Travel directory, naming it by either the travel destination and/or the year (i.e., North Pole/40th Birthday). I will explain later how I learned the hard way about what type of document to save it as!

After scanning the first album to determine the size (in megabytes, or MB), which ranged from 1000 to 5000 MB per page, I added up the total number of MBs for the entire album, divided it by the number of pages in the album, and then converted it from MB to GB. This was also a learning experience, as I have always had a "mental block" when it came to MB, KB, GB, etc. I simply Googled "convert mb to gb" and printed the chart. Believe me, if I can do it being as mathematically impaired as I am, anyone can!

Working through some obstacles

Working almost 7 days a week for two weeks, I was only halfway through.

Big Mistake #1: I asked the client's personal assistant if she wanted me to take all of the pages out of the plastic sleeves, because if she did it would take much longer than anticipated. So, I scanned a few pages with the plastic on and then without the plastic, and they looked exactly the same—that is, on the computer screen.

Once we printed them to compare the two versions, however, you could actually SEE the plastic on the first set. Fortunately, she hired someone else to remove all of the plastic sleeves from every page.

Big Mistake #2: I had saved all of the albums as .PDF files because they took up much less disk space than saving them as a .JPEG file, which I thought was pretty frugal of me! However, after printing a few sample pages (again, which I should have done after one album; not 24), we soon realized that the quality was terrible, and my client, being the perfectionist that she is, was not happy!

So, I had to RE-scan the first 24 books, not only because of the plastic showing through, but also to save all the photo pages as .JPEG files. There were a few pages that contained text only, so I didn't re-scan those, because the PDF file format worked fine.

In addition, since the .JPEG files are at least three times the size of a .PDF file, I soon realized that these 2GB flash drives were NOT going to work. After more research, I learned that these flash drives go up to 8GB, so I bought three of them, because the client wanted backups stored in three locations.

Beginning to think this project would never end, I began what I called "Round 3" – which was scanning the second half of the 48 albums and making sure that each was, in fact, saved as a .JPEG file. Having printed a couple of samples, I finally completed the job after 6 weeks of trial and error.

The moral of the story

I didn't charge nearly enough money for this. I sure hope this saves someone from nearly pulling their hair out!

Kathy Braud, owner of KayBee Design, LLC, is a professional organizer who specializes in small business/home office organization. After 18 years in the legal field (in LA, TX and CO) and a total of 25+ years in Corporate America, Kathy began a consulting business in 1995. Being self-employed offered many opportunities to assist organizations and individuals in improving their productivity by applying her organizational skills, attention to detail and creativity. After moving back to her hometown of Baton Rouge, LA in 2004, she worked as Office Manager for a CPA firm, Operations Manager for a nonprofit organization immediately following the hurricanes, and formed KayBee Design LLC in 2007.

In addition to her organizational skills, Kathy loves creating personalized, one-of-a-kind gift baskets (for any occasion) and custom, high-quality scrapbooks. She is passionate about the long-term recovery efforts in the hurricane-stricken area and hopes to assist many evacuees returning to their homes.

Today, Kathy offers a full range of services, including household organization, space planning, storage solutions, paper management systems, office relocation, project management and photo archiving. For more information, contact Kathy at KayBee Design LLC at 225-772-5610 or kaybeedesign@yahoo.com.

Case Study #9: Monique Ellis

In the world of the US Military, cleanliness, attention to detail and being organized to defend our country is the average service person's main focus—until they get home. When I walked into my first assignment, it literally looked like a battlefield. Like a true soldier, I scanned the area quickly with my eyes, assessing the situation quickly and coming up with a strategy. I was in charge of this mission as I gave the orders. With that in mind the soldier was asked, "If this was an on base barrack, would this pass inspection?"

Separating and Sorting Clothes

Everything from the floor needed to be picked up and sorted:

A. Dirty clothes

   a. Military apparel

   b. Civilian apparel

B. Clean clothes

   a. Military apparel

   b. Civilian apparel

Using a large hamper, in went the dirty clothes. Clean clothes were folded and put in areas designated as military wear and civilian wear. This made it so easy for the soldier to dress for duty without being stressed out before he got there. On days off, he went to the civilian side of the closet. Hampers for dirty clothes were put on each side as uniforms take more detail than everyday clothes.

Paper, paper and more paper

A. We disposed of all the junk mail into the trash can.

B. We shredded documents that needed to be shredded because they contained personal information.

C. We put all the current bills in one place.

Once we followed the above A, B, C steps, we found instant countertops, end tables and even a kitchen table!

The military is very systematic and punctual. They get paid on the first of the month at exactly 12:01 A.M. without fail. Many mothers have asked me to please help them get their sons (and daughters) to be more responsible and pay their bills on time. Very simple. Their pay is direct deposited and they have auto pay in their accounts.

A. We made a list of monthly bills, including the name of the creditor, address, telephone number and account number.

B. We entered the creditors into the banking system.

C. We authorized payments to be taken out on the first of each month (at 12:01 A.M.). After all, you can't spend what you don't have and it all happens when you are asleep. Most banks will give you a printed statement of your deposit and the payments for a particular pay. No need for printing as it's on your bank statement, creditors are happy AND you're building good credit.

I carry a portable printer, copier and scanner with me. I encourage my customers to get one of these all-in-one Professional Organizer's dream tools.

Year books, proms and other school stuff

We took all the things from high school year books, senior prom photos and more and consolidated them into one box. We then sent them home to Mom for safe keeping. Things are lost when they are being shifted around during the chaos of deploying. I recommended that life be made simple.

I scanned some photos into his computer, so he has a few to look at when he wishes. I also advised him that I could upload any scanned photos to the local drugstore and print out a few for .19 a copy if a few printed copies were needed. Now we have found the TV, stereo, remotes—plus, leftover pizza and snacks! Window cleaner and a little furniture polish made a big difference.

The Kitchen

We grabbed a trash bag for anything expired, not going to be eaten or half eaten. We removed racks and sprayed the inside. While doing that, we retrieved a bowl of water and warmed it in the microwave. We set a small box of baking soda in the refrigerator and a lemon slice to absorb the odors quickly. For the "burned smell" i.e.: popcorn, some salt did the trick. It felt good to open the windows and let in some fresh air. When we returned from taking out the garbage, the inside and outside of the refrigerator were wiped down. The microwave, because of the warm water system, was easily cleaned.

His living space was small, so it was quick to put the dishes, glasses and silverware in the right places. The toaster and coffee pot were put away, being that he used it less than two times a week. Making breakfast and meals was not a major priority so when it came to gift giving, military gift cards to be used toward food was a great bet for family members.

With that said, in about three hours we had a very relaxed soldier and very clean and organized surroundings. The look of pride on his face, and the faces of so many other military personnel I've helped, is more than worth the simple effort I have just done to make a chaotic life more simplified and a place to want to come home to. I've gotten so many thank you hugs, calls from elated parents and even calls from military superiors telling me the difference they see in each person. This by far is the most rewarding organizing work I have ever done.

Just another small project regarding upkeep on military bases

Upkeep on ground maintenance in Southern California is a high priority. One thing I have had success with is getting management companies to put trash bins by the mail box centers. I actually started this trend after waiting for two days to get my refrigerator fixed as my husband was deployed. I called the office and they were backed up with work orders.

On my morning walk, I noticed all the workers making the grounds look so beautiful. I stopped to chat and a man came up to me and apologized that he had my work order but had to pick up discarded paper each day that were dropped at the mailboxes and blew into the landscaping. I trotted into the management companies' office and gave them the suggestion of trash bins (of course designer type bins) by each mailbox center. It had to be cheaper than having the maintenance men do it and they could do what they were hired to do.

Monique Ellis has been a Professional Organizer for nearly 10 years in San Diego, California. After the war began, the nine military bases in the area could not house everyone and they began to buy entire apartment complexes near the bases to house the troops. She started with organizing both of her brothers, and she learned from them how to make sure what you started stays that way.

With the military it's all about simplicity. Their lives and days are complicated enough. Then when their friends saw the results, they wanted their places done.

Giving her services away wasn't helping her, nor the person she organized. Making an investment makes people take ownership of what you have done. She started an incentive program that, for each place she did, she wanted three paying referrals. Then the troop gets an additional two hours free for any consulting they need.

She has so much work to do, that she doesn't have a website, nor does she advertise. She has since trained spouses of deployed military the art of professional organizing. It's a win/win situation.

Monique is the proud wife of a United State Marine, a sister of a Naval Intelligence Officer and an US Army Military Police Staff Sgt. Her heart is her beautiful daughter, Jeanine. Being the daughter of an Army father and the wife of a Marine, she has been blessed to have seen a lot of the world.

Her job as a Professional Organizer for the military is her way of giving back to those who make such big sacrifices so that we are free. Every job she finishes makes her as happy as the first one she did.

Additionally, Monique is a mystery/fiction writer. She has written since she was a junior in high school through her graduation from Ohio State University. Additionally, she is a jewelry designer. Her latest project was to design bracelets for the American Cancer Society Breast Cancer run.

Monique Ellis
3792 San Ramon Dr. #71
Oceanside, CA 92057-7222
(760) 721-2656
pacificcoastgirl@yahoo.com

Case Study #10: Jena Webber

You just never know

I have always enjoyed organizing, but I had never done it for pay until this opportunity came along. I was having a conversation (at a cocktail party) with one of my husband's co-workers about how much I enjoyed organizing. The next week, that man became my husband's boss. The week after that, he called Will and asked me if I could help him organize the training center/shop for the company.

Up until this point, I had not worked outside the home the entire time I'd been married. I have five children and homeschool, so this was not an easy decision to make. Because we felt it would be a good experience and the pay beneficial, we decided to take the job.

Not the typical situation

It was not a typical situation because the company has a high security clearance and works in the aerospace industry. I had to have a background check as well as work through a contractor. I had a time constraint as well as an hour requirement.

I took the job in October and was required to be completed with it by the end of December. I had to log my own hours on a sheet and submit them to a contracting firm. I could work from home as well as on site and fulfill my 200 hours.

Getting started

When I saw how expansive the training center was, I was a little overwhelmed at first. There were cabinets full of drawers and drawers full of little teeny tiny pieces. All of these pieces had a serial number, a name and an aircraft/program that they went with. Unearthing that information was half of the "fun."

Every little piece had to be entered into the computer with the Cabinet/Drawer/Section of drawer on a spreadsheet. Actually, no one was there to tell me what to do or supervise me, so I had to figure most things out as I went. After a cabinet was completed, I took a picture of it and laminated it. I hung it up inside the cabinet where the pieces/ parts were.

Obstacles

Working in a center that many people use/supervise was part of the complication. I knew we had an inspection coming, but people still wanted to use the center to train/teach classes in. I also learned which engineers would be willing to answer my questions. I learned all sorts of neat vocabulary like "spilt bushing" and "internal retaining ring pliers." Incidentally, these were all new thoughts to me.

Safety

Part of the goals of the team that hired me was to have proper safety signs up everywhere. I had to get clever and find out exactly what are the hazards of chemical XYZ. There were a lot of exit, safety and caution/warning signs everywhere.

Completion

The last week I worked there, I was working 30 hours a week, just to get it done. It was a huge undertaking. When they hired a manager for the training center a few months later, I'm sure he was happy it was organized.

The company passed its inspection, and they were happy with my work! It was a great feeling.

Jena completed this organizing job with the intention of taking up a real job in organizing down the road, but not right now. It took a toll on her family. So, for now, she writes about organizing on her blog:

http://organizedeveryday.blogspot.com/

She would like to be a public speaker someday and talk about organizing. Probably the only thing she likes better than actually organizing is talking about it!

Jena has training in public speaking and writing. If you have an event coming up that requires a speaker, contact Jena at: organizingmommy@sbcglobal.net

Case Study #11: Lisa Luisi

Excited about my new photo organizing project

I was called upon by a regular client of mine to help her family with a photo organizing project. Being an avid photographer myself, this is one of my favorite organizing services. I'm always looking for new ways to keep all my photos in order.

It is very important to have a reliable system on hand if you are a frequent picture taker. This project was not for organizing digital photos, but for the now considered "old fashioned" photos we would wait to have developed and get back in an envelope a few hours or in some cases, even days later. Remember those?

Many of us have quite a few of these photo envelopes we haven't seen in years, stored in boxes, drawers or cabinets. My mission with this family was to organize and bring back life to the photos that have been put aside somewhere and forgotten.

30 years of photos to sort!

During my first visit to the house I found six large moving boxes containing more than 30 years of photos all in need of sorting and organization. There was no rhyme or reason as to how they were stored in these boxes; not by event or date, or any kind of category or order. No one knew where anything was.

Basically it was "one day I am going to put them into albums, but for now I'll throw them in these boxes." Not the best idea. I believe many of us are guilty of this at one point or another. The boxes had all the photos that never made it into albums: the family vacations, birthday parties, kids sporting events. It was always going to be done "later." Well, later was now, and I wanted them to start enjoying all the photos they had taken over the years as soon as possible.

Questions

This would be a two day job. The first day was for consultation and preparation, and the second day we would actually sort through the boxes. There were certain questions I needed to address as I did the walk through. How can this be done to best benefit the family? Where did they want to store hundreds of pictures? A better question is: where did they have the space to store these pictures? A bedroom, a basement, maybe a cabinet?

I do leave that up to the client to decide, but I also suggest where I think they should store them according to available space within their home. It is essential to consider storage space when handling a large job like this. Luckily, we both agreed the basement had the best storage area for the project.

We had the where; now we needed the how

Sometimes if you create too many files, even though everything is neatly labeled and packaged, it creates just as big a mess as keeping everything in one big unorganized box. The plan I devised required the client to purchase some inexpensive organizing supplies we would need for the project.

One of my favorite items is the shoebox size plastic storage case. Inexpensive and easy to find at most houseware stores, these cases are great for a project of this size that requires lots of sorting and storing.

In addition to the cases, a plastic shelving unit was purchased. This unit has five shelves on it and it fits right into the basement closet where the pictures were going to be kept. I liked the idea of using the shelving unit for this particular project. It is perfect when working in someone's basement. I believe it is important to store your valuables off the basement floor. In case of flooding in the basement, you know your keepsakes are stored safely on the shelves.

Last, but certainly not least, we needed my trusty digital label maker. There is no job I do without it. This is a tool every organizer and household should have. Make this machine your best friend. It is a lifesaver when it comes to home or office organization!

My client was overwhelmed

At first, my client was a bit overwhelmed at how we were going to get these boxes with hundreds of pictures in order. It was understandable. Anyone looking at this project would be. I told her it would take time and a bit of patience, but to work with me and we would have a great system for her family to enjoy by the end of the day. Most clients are a bit nervous when starting an organizing endeavor. After all, this is the reason they call you in the first place. Most of the time they feel they cannot do it alone. They need the assistance and guidance. I was confident I could help them achieve what they were looking to do.

Sorting into categories

Time to get those boxes. We needed a sizable area to sort and categorize the photos. The table was too small, so onto the floor we went! Often there are jobs where I am crawling around on a floor or climbing into dusty areas. Never be afraid to get a little dirty. It's part of being a Professional Organizer.

This was a time consuming project and an "as you go along" type job. We tackled it one box at a time, each taking a small pile of photos to sort through. We created categories as we went through the boxes. You won't know how to sort until you see what you have. I decided the best way to do this was to devote one of the shoebox cases to each family member (it was a family of five: mom, dad and three children). They all had a labeled case for their own photos. Our other categories were different family events: recitals, travel, birthdays, softball and basketball games, and holidays. We also had cases for extended family and wedding pictures.

Sorting into chronological order

Once the photos were sorted into the cases, we put the pictures in chronological order. This really helps a family when they are trying to locate the 1989 Puerto Rico vacation photos or the 7th grade softball game shots.

Making it fun

In this instance I knew the family well, so I was able to identify some of the people in the photos. Most times you will not know the client and/or family you are working with, therefore, it is important for the client to work alongside of you throughout the project to identify the photos. Otherwise, there is no way for you to know who "Uncle Mike" is, and in which case he belongs.

Throughout the day I also worked with her children, and they helped guide me as to which pictures should go where. As you can imagine, when a family participates in a project such as this, most look at it as a boring chore. That's the reason it wasn't done in the first place. No one really wants to sit and go through the pictures.

When you have an organizer there to assist you, I think it is much easier for the client to complete the task at hand. With this project it actually turned out to be a fun time for the client and her family. Each photo we pulled out of a box seemed to trigger a story about a person or a vacation. It was a great trip down memory lane. Smiles appeared on their faces as they found old pictures from as far back as mom and dad dating, or grandma and grandpa in their younger years. There were laughs all around! Most importantly, they were beginning to see the light at the end of the tunnel, or should I say at the bottom of the pile.

A lifetime of memories

Now the family enjoys their photos any time they want and for one simple reason: they know where everything is! It is easy to locate pictures of a certain event or person. They are no longer collecting dust in a box far back in a closet or forgotten because they are not accessible. All the cases are on the shelves with clearly marked labels.

I've been told there are still some more photos in a few drawers throughout the house, but now whenever they find one of those old photo envelopes, the pictures are filed properly and put in a place where they can be found again in just a few moments.

Why have the photos if you cannot enjoy them and cherish the times and special occasions you have captured with your family and friends? Treasure your pictures…that's why you took them in the first place!

Lisa Luisi graduated Seton Hall University with a Bachelor's degree in Communications. She began her professional career as an assistant in the human resources department in one of New York's top law firms where she later became a recruiting coordinator. Soon after, she worked in the entertainment industry in the Sales & Marketing department of a major cable network. Experience has taught her to master time management, namely how to help over-extended executives manage deadlines, calendars, meetings, projects and files.

Lisa met theses challenges head on and became the most organized person in the office. She created a method to the madness and realized she had a passion for organization. A business was born: It's All In Order. Lisa has the skills and experience to change your cluttered home or office into an area where you can live and work comfortably and achieve the highest potential for your space.

Lisa Luisi
It's All In Order
917-363-7938
lisa@itsallinorder.com
www.itsallinorder.com
New York City & New Jersey

Case Study #12: Melanie Eggleston

Not enough time in the day

The first thing my client said to me was something like, "There is not enough time in a day to do everything I need to do." I simply replied "I can help you with that."

Our initial interaction was a quick over-the-phone consultation. He said that he didn't feel a sense of accomplishment after a day was complete. Since he had so many things going on in his life, he wanted to figure out a way to balance them all. I told him that once we meet and go over his goals he would feel that sense of accomplishment.

It was pretty easy to determine that my client needed help with time management. All the key signs were there. He didn't feel as if there was enough time in a day and he didn't feel a sense of accomplishment.

He even told me that he barely had enough time to meet with me. I told him that we could do two small sessions, which would be about an hour each. We ended the call by agreeing to meet the following week at a local coffee shop.

What would you like to accomplish?

During our first session a lot was accomplished. I began by asking my client to tell me a list of what he would like to accomplish in a day. Asking him this question gave me an idea of if what he wanted to accomplish in a day was realistic. He said that he wanted to be able to go to work and come home to do the following activities:

- Work on his business plan

- Work on his graduate studies

- Check his email

- Surf the web for a new job

- Cook

- Watch television

- Wash clothes

- Work out

- Spend time with his girlfriend

- Spend time with his dog

I then asked him to tell me what he usually did in a day. He told me the following activities:

- Work out

- Check his emails

- Surf the net

- Watch television

- Spend time with his girlfriend

- Spend time with his dog

I asked him specific questions such as did he sometimes go out during the week and did his daily habits change often. He said yes. This was not unusual to me because most people have schedules that fluctuate.

My client then went on about how it was so hard to get organized. I let him vent for a while and calmed his fears by telling him that it wasn't. With him, I had to take it one step at a time.

We then ended our session and agreed to meet the following week. I asked him, as a homework assignment, to track what he does every day until the next time we meet. He agreed and we parted ways.

I thought that our first session went really well. I felt like we were at a confessional and he was confessing to me his organizing sins. After the session I was sure that the next session would be very promising. Although my client seemed very unorganized, I knew my ideas would ease his mind.

Getting started

I was very excited to get started. Since I'm fairly new at organizing, I'm always excited and nervous at the same time. The Wednesday before meeting my client I sent him a quick email just to see how writing down his schedule every day was going. He said he was still trying to get the hang of it, but it was going fairly well.

Before meeting my client I purchased him a daily organizer that had enough space to write down his daily activities and had a section for a Things-To-Do list. My client seemed to always make plans but quickly forget them when something else came up. Since he can never remember his plans, I thought that this item would work best. My client constantly overextended himself and didn't keep track of his after work activities. It caused problems for him and others that he broke plans with. My client's issue wasn't too complicated; he just needed a little push.

When I met with my client for our last visit he seemed to feel better about organizing his daily activities. He said that writing down his daily activities worked well, but he still would change his plans and end up forgetting that some stuff he wrote down was important.

Bag of Treats

I then presented him with his "bag of treats." Inside were a black leather planner and 3 highlighters (orange, yellow and blue). I told him that once he writes down his daily activities he should then review them and highlight according to importance.

One color could be for primary activities. These activities are extremely important and must be completed today. Another color could be for secondary activities that came up and were semi-important but should only be completed after primary activities were completed. The last color was for something that wasn't very important at all and could be shifted to the weekly to do list. The weekly to do list were things that he needed to do but could be done on any given day that he had time.

Like I said before, my client's issue wasn't too complicated. He just wanted someone to show him what to do. The concepts I shared with him were things that he had heard of but simply never tried. By showing him how easy it was and leading him in the right direction he was able to successfully grab a hold of his after-work activities.

Follow up

I followed up with him over the next month and he said that writing down his daily activities and color-coding them in order of importance helped him a lot. Now he didn't have to try to remember that important thing that he needed to do after work it was clearly highlighted in his planner. However, he also said that he would occasionally forget to look at his planner and his daily activities would have to get pushed to other days in the week. Although his job was pretty monotonous, he even started to write a To Do list at work as well.

I was proud of this experience because it demonstrated to me that sometimes everyone needs assistance no matter how easy or simple it may appear to someone else.

After earning her bachelors degree in Broadcasting, Telecommunications and Mass Media from Temple University, Melanie Eggleston entered the corporate work environment.

She currently works full time for a major telecommunications company. Melanie also attends graduate school where she is pursuing a dual major in Marketing Management and Business Administration.

After a few years of working, Melanie became more conscious of the fact that those around her were in need of some organizing assistance. She then decided to hone in on her organizing skills and start a business.

Melanie Eggleston
Organized Stylez
www.organizedstylez.com

Mini-Interviews

What is your best tip for people interested in becoming professional organizers?

Barry Izsak, Arranging It All, Austin, TX

Don't expect to "hang out your shingle" and have people immediately flocking to you for your expertise. As in any business, it takes time, commitment and perseverance. If becoming a professional organizer is really what you want and you work hard to make it happen, then it will happen!

Elizabeth Hanley, Coyote Professional Organizing, Hagersville, Ontario, Canada

If you love it, go for it. Learn everything you can from people who know. And most of all, don't let anything stop you.

Blanca Robinson, A Calming Effect, Houma, LA

Do your homework. Do ample research so that you can have knowledge and establish credibility. Offer to do a few freebies for some very close friends. Share your ideas and enthusiasm for your new business with those who are close to you and who will be supportive of your efforts. Avoid those who can't wait to say, "I told you it wouldn't work." And be prepared to give it your all. From my own perspective, I do believe the field of Professional Organizing is still a relatively young one. I for one have definitely found an untapped market.

Beth Larence, Tidy Up! Organizing, Washington, DC

Once you get a client or two, things will really start to develop. Stick with it and be confident about your skills. You are helping someone get a new lease on life. That's important.

Mandie Sohn, My Method to Your Madness, Inc., Denver, CO

Don't quit your day job if you don't have to. A steady paycheck takes some of the stress out of starting a new business.

Patricia John, Room 2 Room Organizing, Oshawa, Ontario, Canada

Join the POC (Canada) or NAPO (United States). The people you meet from these organizations can teach you so much. I have met some great ladies and have made some wonderful friends. That's the best part!

What type of organizing do you specialize in?

Janis Nylund, Orderly Concepts and Solutions, Vancouver (Surrey) B.C. Canada

Residential and small business. I am also working with people who are building new homes, giving them ideas for organizational systems that can be built in to suit their lifestyles and family needs.

Phyllis Paster, It's About Time, Wellesley, MA

I specialize in organizing homes, home offices, small businesses, physician offices and medical groups. Special organizing services I offer include paper and file management and compiling memorabilia as well as form and brochure design.

Elaine Shannon. Organization Plus!, Rothesay, NB Canada

I specialize in working with entrepreneurs.

Mandie Sohn, My Method to Your Madness, Inc., Denver, CO

I specialize in Residential Organizing, Offices: Home, Small Business and Legal - Document/Paper Management, Time Management and Goal Setting, Wedding: Small Event Planning and Household Consolidation.

Patricia John, Room 2 Room Organizing, Oshawa, Ontario, Canada

I organize homes, small offices and schools.

Gina Miles, Here To Help Organize, St. Clair Shores, Michigan

I specialize in homes with families... I have found that I really enjoy creating special places for children to grow and learn.

Gina Goldenberg, Mess Management, Toronto, Ontario, Canada

I specialize in both home and office organization including: financial and paper management (including filing systems), chronically disorganized, ADD/ADHD, LD, and automobile purchasing consulting.

Elinor Warkentin, Goodbye Clutter! Consulting and Organizing Services, Vancouver, BC, Canada

I am best at helping people let go of clutter, whether that is at home, in a home office, or at work.

Describe your typical workday.

Ina Hopkins, Organizational Concepts, Broomfield, CO

My workdays are not typical...thank goodness! Sometimes I see only one client a day if it's an all day appointment, sometimes two, as I work anywhere from two to six hours with each client.

I may have shorter appointments and fill in with hour-long consultations for prospective clients or coaching/teaching appointments, either in the client's space or over the telephone.

If I'm giving a workshop, which lasts four hours including a break, I usually only do consultations or coaching on those days.

In order to accommodate my clients in order that our work together doesn't interfere with their business day or their families, I will often begin work at 6:00 A.M., or work in the evenings or even on a weekend.

I do limit my weekends to only one client per weekend, and I adjust my regular work week accordingly.

I love what I do, but I'm definitely not a work-a-holic!

Figen Genco Haigh, Genco Organizes, Langhorne, PA

Depending on Chamber committee meetings, my day might start at the Chamber or at my home office. I do my administrative office work in the mornings, organize, file, do expenses, read and reply to e-mail, write articles, check out some Web sites for my professional growth, prepare literature to send out, work on my Web site, read/write literature and brochures and make phone calls.

If I have an appointment in the morning, the order changes, office work is done in the afternoon.

I also have networking meetings and percolator meetings—through the Chamber mostly in the morning and business card exchange events in the evenings. Client appointment hours differ according to the client's available hours, so I don't have a fixed schedule.

Hisca Weggeman, Professional Organizer, Rotterdam, the Netherlands

On the day(s) I work for my business, early in the morning I prepare the organizing session with the client, I travel and work with a client for 2-4 hours. I return home, make notes about the session, answer emails, and sometimes do some writing (announcements about my workshop, short articles) and reading.

In the afternoon I prepare my evening workshop. I always try to be specific for every person in my group with questions, advice, etc. I pack my car with books, overhead projector and all my other things and after a quick dinner I drive to the place where the workshop will be held.

Elinor Warkentin, Goodbye Clutter! Consulting and Organizing Services, Vancouver, BC, Canada

My sessions with clients are usually 3-6 hours. We choose an area that is challenging to them and work through the room, purging the clutter and organizing what is left. Sometimes there is a lot of talking and occasionally some tears.

By the end of the session, I am usually physically exhausted but mentally primed, aware of just how much the energy in the space and person has changed. Common phrases I hear when I am leaving are "I feel so much lighter" and "I feel so much better."

Mandie Sohn, My Method to Your Madness, Inc., Denver, CO

I work full-time for a law firm, so I spend part of my weekends on my organizing business. If I don't have a job set up, I try to market as much as I can.

Patricia John, Room 2 Room Organizing, Oshawa, Ontario, Canada

It depends on the day. Monday, Wednesday and every other Friday, after dropping the kids off and if I don't have a project to do, I then get on the computer and check e-mail and do business related work. In the afternoon I do errands if needed. Tuesdays, Thursdays and every other Friday, I do business related stuff and then spend time with my daughter. Weekends are for my family.

Elaine Shannon, Organization Plus!, Rothesay, NB, Canada

I meet with a client in the morning. In the afternoon I do business development.

Why did you become a professional organizer?

K.J. McCorry, Officiency, Inc., Boulder, CO

I have always had a skill for organizing throughout my life. I used to be general manager for a small natural products company back in the mid 90's. I began helping other small companies with set up of their office systems and protocol and received terrific response. Two professional mentors encouraged me to start a professional organizing business. At that time, I had not heard of NAPO nor others doing this sort of work so I was thrilled to learn that it was actually an industry!

Karen Denton-Betts, Space Makers, Dearborn, MI

Even though I always wanted to be a highly organized person, I did not become one until about 3½ years ago when I became pregnant with our first child, Joshua. There were always aspects of my life that were very organized—anything work and school related—and areas that were not—my bedroom and closet. During my pregnancy, I vowed to get it all together. It took time, but I made it!

Then, when I was offered a consulting position with General Motors to train all levels of employees and leadership on "organizing the organization," I jumped at it. Along with my training partner, I was able to develop and teach a 3-day workshop on "Workplace Organization and Visual Controls."

However while I loved my job, I hated being away from my son. I knew I needed to make a change and I kept thinking about many workshop participants who would tell me things like, "I was so inspired with everything I learned that I went home and organized my garage, or basement." Also, during that time, I would get requests to do one-on-one organizing sessions on weekends at GM employee homes. I had to turn down most of them because I devoted that time to my husband and son.

So after researching the professional organizing industry and home-based businesses, I took the risk and quit my corporate job and opened my own firm, Space Makers. It has been one of the best decisions I've ever made! I firmly believe the combination of being able to relate so well to clients, my corporate organizing and training experience, and especially being able to be the Mother that Joshua deserves, has made this first year in business well worth everything I left behind.

Judy Marcelliano, Perfectly Organized, Clinton Township, NJ

I became an organizer simply because I love to organize. It gives me great pleasure in seeing things orderly and in their place. I have an eye for it and after being home with my kids for a few years, doing another part-time home-based business, I felt that it would be a great opportunity for me to be able to continue with a flexible schedule.

Jennifer Towns, Order Restored, Covington, GA

I "officially retired" from teaching after one year because I found that I really didn't enjoy it like I thought I would. After I had my first child in 2000, I became a stay-at-home mom. It didn't take long for me to get cabin fever and realize that I had too many ideas running through my head to stay at home. So, I began to think about what jobs I could have without having to go back to school or put my kids in daycare. After falling in love with the organizing shows on TLC and HGTV I knew what I was meant to do. ORGANIZE! It was a light bulb moment for me. I thought, "you know, I have always done that for myself and friends and family—so why not get paid!"

Amelia Herrera, Amelia R. Herrera, Professional Organizer, Nevada, CA

I have always loved to organize people's things and rooms. Growing up, I would always spend time organizing my friends' rooms, rather than hanging out with them. I really feel that I can take this knack and turn it into success for disorganized people.

Gina Miles, Here To Help Organize, St. Clair Shores, Michigan

I became a Professional Organizer because I thrive on neatness and order, but also because I have a passion for helping others. For me, being a PO is very rewarding.

Gina Goldenberg, Mess Management, Toronto, Ontario, Canada

I believe that being organized plays a vital role in truly being able to live a more relaxed and fulfilling life. I have always been an organized person in every aspect of my life, and many times I've been asked by friends and family to help them get back on top of tasks they've fallen behind on or to declutter their space. Helping them get organized so they could have more time to enjoy things in life gave me a sense of personal accomplishment. It's a win-win situation.

Describe your greatest success in this field.

Janet Hall, Overhall Consulting, Port Republic, MD

I had a client that was so determined to get her WHOLE home organized that she rented a dumpster and parked it in the driveway. We went through the whole house, including the attic, basement, garage, and backyard, and filled it up!

Audrey Thomas, Organized Audrey, LLC, Bloomington, MN

I was working with an individual at her place of employment. She was considering leaving the field because of her disorganization. After working together, she not only decided to stay in her field, but to get her Masters degree and pursue her career even further.

She felt the skills and habits she learned enabled her to quit running from other areas of her life. I felt as if I really made a difference in this woman's life. It was a proud moment for me.

Heather Levin, Simply Organized Home, Asheville, NC

Well, it's a little too soon for me to have won awards or be featured on HGTV, but for me, so far, I'd say my greatest success has just been having the courage to start my business. It's like taking a leap of faith. You don't know if you're going to fly or fall, but that's what makes it so worthwhile. You jump, and flail your arms and gasp and try so hard, and if you don't give up, if you flap hard enough, eventually you soar.

Teine Kenney, organizethis™, Newberry Park, CA

I was called to assist an elderly woman who just had a tiny stroke. Her family actually found me for her while she was still in the hospital. I knew enough about hoarding, shopping, and chronic disorganization to take on the enormous job of emptying 9 years of stuff (that had never been put away) from her apartment. It was my largest job to date.

I bid the job accurately and used a 5 person crew. It was most satisfying because I figured out or knew how to handle the special needs of this wonderful lady. (My daughter had a stroke so I knew what she was recovering from.)

I organized and labeled everything from her medical files to her underwear! When I returned to give her the complimentary photo album of the project, she was just opening her mail, I watched as she effortlessly filed a tax document. She was able to put paper in its proper place for the first time in her whole life. We celebrated with a pear cider!

Frank Murphy, Inventory Management Services Inc., Greenville, SC
Our client list is our success story. One of the most memorable was consolidating 27 satellite storage areas embracing 65,000 square feet into 3 storage areas totaling less that 30,000 sq. ft.

Tammy Costa, The Organized Consultant, Plainville, MA
I feel that my greatest success in this field is the reality that I am doing what I love to do. How many people can say that? I love the whole idea of organizing as a profession. The ability to relieve stress in someone's life. There's no better feeling.

Mary Beth Peterson, The Organizing Experts, Mokina, IL
Honestly, my greatest success is the organizing of my clients and their ability to function at a higher level of life because I was there.

Mandie Sohn, My Method to Your Madness, Inc., Denver, CO
When clients express or at least admit that they feel lighter and less stressed/overwhelmed due to our work.

Kathryn Jones, Simplified Living Systems, Louisville, KY
Creating an organizational system for a client's 4000 square foot home, and teaching them to develop and maintain organization in their home and life. I redid their kitchen, closet, and office developing unique systems for each.

Rebecca Schmidt, Streamline Organizing, Raleigh, NC
Making people cry. It's a good thing! Whether it's helping their home transitioning, teaching their kids good time management skills or creating a system for an ADD client that they get and can use! When they cry at the end of a project, it's my reason for living.

Stacy Walker, Gettin' Around To It Professional Organizing, Edmonton, Alberta, Canada
I would have to say that my greatest success so far is simply that EVERY client that I have worked with has been tremendously happy with the result. It has reinforced my confidence in my career choice and gives me great personal satisfaction!

What do you find to be the most exciting part of your business?

Janette Gomez, Artistic Archiving Solutions, South Florida
Finishing. Not because I don't like it, but because it is exciting to see the results of a project. The bigger the better. It is very rewarding. Especially when the clients can't contain themselves and they give me a big hug.

Jessica Duquette, In Perfect Order, Woodland Hills, CA
I love seeing and sensing the feeling of relief that my clients experience after we have finished a job that has kept them unsettled for months or years. They have a renewed sense of purpose and they are so excited and grateful, and I love feeling a part of that. Also, I am a very visual person, and seeing a desk or file cabinet or closet go from chaos to order feels very rewarding to me in my soul.

Linda DePaz, Be Clutter-Free, Western NY
Seeing the joy on people's faces or the excited tone in their voice when they are actually seeing progress—it's a sense of satisfaction. I love receiving "thank-you's" in my email inbox!

Patricia Coughlan, Clutter-Free Professional Organizing, Edmonton, Alberta, Canada
Speaking and offering seminars is definitely the most exciting part for me. I love having the opportunity to share how to have an "organized lifestyle" with others. I love interacting with a group of individuals who want to learn. It's the teacher in me, I guess. Second to this, I love organizing spaces—making a room function more efficiently and look beautiful, too.

Janette Gomez, Artistic Archiving Solutions, South Florida
Finishing. Not because I don't like it, but because it is exciting to see the results of a project. The bigger the better. It is very rewarding. Especially when the clients can't contain themselves and they give me a big hug.

Mary Beth Peterson, The Organizing Experts, Mokina, IL
The most exciting part of my business is having a satisfied customer. I never leave a job with a dissatisfied customer. I communicate my desire to make sure they are satisfied. I repeat to them the words they use to describe how they feel and how they have benefited. Remember, if a customer is happy, they will tell 10 people, if they aren't they will tell 100.

What do you find to be the most frustrating part of your business?

Shari Beck, Sandcastles, Ajax, Canada
Having never been a pack rat or a clutter bug, I find that I often have to bite my tongue!

Laura Bishop, Eliminate Chaos, LLC, Mill Creek, WA
The most frustrating part of business is when clients cancel at the last minute with no notice or only a couple of hours notice. This is not enough time to schedule another client, so the time is wasted, not to mention we lose that income for the time we weren't able to bill.

Crystal Sabalaske, Cluttershrink, Philadelphia, PA
The most frustrating part of my business is dealing with clients who are indecisive. It is often difficult for them to commit to the process of getting organized, so there are multiple cancellations, reschedulings, and back and forth e-mails regarding when a project is going to begin.

Mandie Sohn, My Method to Your Madness, Inc., Denver, CO
Convincing clients that they need a lot less than they think they do.

Kathryn Jones, Simplified Living Systems, Louisville, KY
The only thing I really find frustrating are clients who know they need your help, hire you, but then do not change their habits. While they make wonderful repeat customers, their lives can be so much fuller if they understood the reason behind their disorganization.

Rose Zappa-Jehnert, Get It 2gether Organizational Services, Forest Hill, MD
I think, if not frustrating, the most time consuming part of my business is educating the public about the pros of a Professional Organizer. I have to admit, though, that the new television shows, *Mission Organization* and *Clean Sweep*, have helped somewhat.

Frank Murphy, Inventory Management Services Inc., Greenville, SC
A lack of consistent application of organizing principles implemented during the setup and reorganization.

Describe a successful, creative marketing technique that you use, or that you've used in the past.

Patty Kreamer, TimeFinders, Inc., Pittsburgh, PA

I send a postcard to a client 4 weeks after I am done organizing their office. This postcard is hand written asking if they have any questions. It gives me an opening to call back and see if they have received it.

At that time we get around to referrals. I then follow up 4 weeks later with another postcard offering a 25% discount off of a "tune-up" hour to make sure that they are still on the right track. And again, another opportunity to call them for referrals and a check-up.

Hellen Buttigieg, We Organize U, Oakville, Ontario, Canada

I am a member of Toastmasters International and when I enter speech contests, I get the chair-person to ask me about my business during the get-to-know you interview. Afterwards, I have several people approaching me to ask for more information.

Diane L. Campion, Organize This!, Albany, NY

Free and reasonably priced workshops have been the most successful form of marketing for me. Additionally, I have forged relationships with a couple of reporters that have gotten me some business after articles have been printed about my services.

Cynth'ya Lewis Reed, Accord Unlimited, Muncie, IN

Coupons! My goodness how people just LUUUUV coupons, especially if they have a quick expiration date. Also free rewards for consistent service, little unexpected "thank you notes" with an offer for some special sale item or information that might be offered at the time. Rocket scientists need not apply. By far the simpler the plan, the better the chances for success.

Andrea Croley, Professionally Organized by Andrea, NC

Free presentations. I really enjoy doing these and I usually get a few clients too. I love to talk, so that's no problem and I love computers, so using PowerPoint or other programs to design a presentation is fun for me. I usually give free handouts to the class with a tri-fold brochure and business card too. I also put 2-3 $20 gift certificates under chairs so that there will be some prizes. Occasionally I do some type of raffle as well.

Which one marketing technique have you found works the best for you? Please describe.

Sue DeRoos, Organize U!, Macomb, IL

My work is guaranteed! If a client is not 100 percent satisfied with the services I have provided they don't have to pay. It takes the "risk out of the fear of the unknown!"

Christine Rice, Organize It Today, Columbus, Indiana

I have magnetic vehicle signs that I get quite a few comments on. People call and say they saw me driving around and need my services. I also rely heavily on word of mouth advertising.

Lauriann Davies, Leave It To Lauri, Atlanta, GA

Word-of-mouth referrals from happy clients are my most powerful marketing techniques. I find that when my clients are excited about my work, they tell all their friends, who then call me for a consultation as well.

Greg Payette, Gregory Home Services, Inc., Massachusetts and Rhode Island

Direct mail is still one of the best ways to get your message into the hands of your target prospect. Although I use postcards, a sales letter where you can "sell the sizzle" is typically more successful.

Kelly Dawicki, Organize Now, Mattapoisett, MA

I have found that most of my clients have picked up my card at local coffee shops.

Blanca Robinson, A Calming Effect, Houma, LA

I have recently joined a networking group that is in essence a referral group. It's one of those where there is only one representative from a given industry or field, so I am the only Professional Organizer in the group. I had attended a couple of meetings as a visitor and was very impressed at the caliber of members, their professionalism, etc. At my very first meeting as a member, I got one strong referral (which will become a definite job) and two other leads. I knew several people in the group, one of whom is a client, and another who has seen "proof" of my work. Both gave me very strong testimonials, which further upped my credibility.

Who is your primary target audience?

Donna Turner, Simply Organised, Northern Beaches of Sydney Australia
The "organizationally challenged" corporate employee.

Lorraine Pirihi, The Office Organiser, Melbourne, Australia
Businesses with 50-250 employees. Although that is my target, I have many clients in small business.

Joan Huguenard, ClutterFly Corner, Business located in a motor home
The general public, as there are needful everywhere (as you well know.) However, I have specialized somewhat on mothers of preschoolers (having brought eight of my own through that stage) and on senior citizens (having entered their ranks many years ago.)

Beth Randall, Joe Organizer, Plainfield, IL
Most of my presentations have been to mothers' groups that are associated with churches.

Barbara Myers, The Time Manager, Newark, OH
My primary audience is women between the ages of 30 and 65.

Elizabeth Hanley, Coyote Professional Organizing, Hagersville, Ontario, Canada
Usually females, either busy moms or seniors.

Christine Rice, Organize It Today, Columbus, Indiana
My primary target audience is busy, working mothers, and dual income families.

Crystal Sabalaske, Cluttershrink, Philadelphia, PA
My target audience . . . it's hard to say. There is potential for people to be disorganized regardless of where they live or work. I tend to focus on marketing to people who own small businesses or stay at home moms.

Sue DeRoos, Organize U!, Macomb, IL
People—Grandma's, teenagers, stay-at-home moms, working moms, business owners, new home builders...it has no boundaries as to who. I guess I'd just say that it's anyone who wants a better quality of life!

Every person interested in entering the professional organizing field is wondering, "Can I make enough money doing this?" What is your outlook on this question?

Frances C. Walker, Organization Sensation, Signal Mountain, TN
How much is enough? There are so many variables. Size of your community, areas of focus, willingness to do what it takes to get the job done, choices of advertising, etc. I can tell you that this business has supported me for over 4 years and I don't have any needs that have not been met by this profession. I do suggest keeping prices low enough to encourage repeat business.

Jeannie Triezenberg, Hire Order, Inc., Naperville, IL
If you are willing to make the commitment, you can make a living at it. It takes a lot of time and hard work. You cannot quit a full-time paying position today and make the same salary organizing tomorrow; you have to build your client base. There is a lot more to being a professional organizer than just organizing. If you want your own business, you can plan on spending as much time on the behind the scenes work as you do on organizing. If all you want to do is organize, then I recommend you find another organizer to work for.

Mary Wallace, Homemaker's Idea Company, Kalispell, Montana
I have been making a very respectable income for working only about 5-8 hours per week, and I was able to begin making money from the very first clutter control workshop I did! I think there are many families out there who are in the same boat as I have been and who want to simplify their lives.

Barry Izsak, Arranging It All, Austin, TX
Yes, you most definitely can! It's not going to happen overnight, but with perseverance and commitment, it will happen. It all depends on you!

Joan Huguenard, ClutterFly Corner (works out of her motorhome!)
Oh, I think without question if you have good organizing sense, have done plenty of homework and legwork and love to work hard, there is plenty of money to be made in the organizing field.

Mandie Sohn, My Method to Your Madness, Inc., Denver, CO
I think how much you make is directly proportionate to how much time you spend on your business-following up with current clients, marketing to new clients, etc.

As an organizer, what professional organizing information or tools are you always on the lookout for?

Katherine Trezise, Absolutely Organized, Monkton, MD
Containers. I look forward to checking the mail for new catalogs with the latest containers for everything imaginable.

Jennifer Towns, Order Restored, Covington, GA
Any ideas, tips or solutions that I haven't thought of yet…and I'm sure that's a lot! I also like to check out new systems for organizing things. So, surfing the web is the easiest way I've found to "shop."

Beth Randall, Joe Organizer, Plainfield, Illinois
I love to read all the new organizing books to get ideas to share with my students and clients.

Teine Kenney, organizethis, Newbury Park, CA
Ingenious solutions for helping a chronically disorganized person who suffers from ADD and/or depression.

Lea Schneider, Organize & More, Jackson, TN
I am always on the lookout for concrete tips or steps for projects that I can use as an educational tool. I like to teach people how to maintain their environment. In addition, I use this material in my public speaking.

Cinthanie Crenshaw, Get It All Together, St. George, Utah
I read a lot and I frequently get on the Internet to see what other PO's are doing. I would like some information on calendar events that pertain to PO's. I also wouldn't mind some free help with some affiliates and how that works.

Phyllis Paster, It's About Time, Wellesley, MA
I am always looking for easy to use tools and tips for clients. As an example, I provide my clients with guidelines for preserving important documents which includes a check off list so they know which documents are stored on site and which are in the safe deposit box.

Looking ahead, what do you see as your greatest challenge?

Teine Kenney, organizethis™, Newbury Park, CA
I want to be able to make money while I am not actually working. This means I need to create a product that will sell after I have created it the first time. I'd like to write a book. That is a challenge and a life long goal.

Lea Schneider, Organize & More, Jackson, TN
My greatest challenge will be to stay fresh and continually challenge myself to work constantly at marketing.

Christine Rice, Organize It Today, Columbus, IN
I think my biggest challenge is managing business growth during the transition of making this my sole source of income.

Barbara Myers, The Time Manager, Newark, OH
Staying organized is my greatest challenge. Isn't that funny?! My business is growing so quickly, however, I find it difficult to keep up some days.

Mary Wallace, Homemaker's Idea Company, Kalispell, Montana
Reasonably priced storage containers that are versatile, moveable, and attractive. The Homemaker's Idea Company products are all that, and they are made to work together, and to pull a "look" together, according to the customer's likes and lifestyle. I also advocate the "use what you have" philosophy, encouraging my customers to look inside their own homes before going out to buy organizing products.

Melissa Wiese, Professional Organizers Unlimited, Parker, CO
Finding good newsletters with lots of information, such as the Get Organized Now!™ Organizers Newsletter.

Figen Genco Haigh, Genco Organizes, Langhorne, PA
Filing tools, drawers, closet and shelf dividers, folder and plate holders. Practical, functioning, inexpensive products which can make my clients' lives easier.
To tell the truth I am not finding many functional tools out there that are worth the price. So, sometimes I end up using a tool or something else, other than it was originally aimed for.

As a professional organizer, do you have a funny story to share?

Beckie Bordenaro, Perfectly Put Away, McHenry, IL

I had one client call and say that she wanted help in her sewing room. She said it had gotten so bad that she actually had to remove her sewing machine from the room to sew!

Stacey Agin Murray, Organized Artistry, LLC, Fairlawn, NJ

I once helped a woman organize the closets in her bedroom. We worked for about two hours when she told me she was tired and asked if I would mind if she were to lie down for a few minutes.

Ten minutes later she was sound asleep and didn't wake up for an hour—even though I was organizing ten feet away from her the whole time!

Frank Murphy, Inventory Management Services Inc., Greenville, SC

In the early stages of organizing a parts storeroom in a power plant, I had to move a wooden box that was on the top shelf of an 84 inch high shelving unit. Instead of doing the smart thing by getting a ladder and removing it properly, I stood on my tippy-toes and tilted the box toward me to slide it off.

As the top of the box became visible, my brief and inglorious life flashed before me as I watched a hand grenade roll down the box toward my face. I ducked and it hit me squarely on the head (I was wearing a hard hat). It was a WW2 "pineapple," a dummy practice grenade and no one knew how it got there. I have it displayed on the bookcase in my office.

Gina Goldenberg, Mess Management, Toronto, Ontario, Canada

I was helping a newlywed couple organize their apartment and while I was pulling out the overflowing, overstuffed drawers to their dresser I came across a plastic Ziploc bag that had fallen behind the drawers.

Inside the bag was the woman's wedding ring. The couple became hysterical! It turns out that they had been looking for the ring for over a month and had just ordered a duplicate ring from the jewelers the previous day. The client could not remember when or why she put her ring in the drawers or the bag!

Industry Polls

Here are the results of polls we've posted on the Get Organized Now! Web site for Professional Organizers. The responses are exclusively from professional organizers who have visited our web site. Hope you find it interesting to know what your colleagues are doing, thinking, etc.

Do you wear all the hats in your company, or do you hire outside help?

62% I wear every hat! I'm the organizer, marketer, administrator and financial person!

4% I have one or more partners, and we share the responsibilities.

7% I have one employee who assists me with at least one aspect of my business.

9% I have several employees that assist me with various aspects of my business.

11% I don't have employees, but I outsource some of my organizing projects, administrative work, marketing, etc.

7% I actually work for someone else who has an organizing business.

Total Votes: 45

How many other professional organizers do you know that live within a 30 mile radius of your location?

36% Just me—I'm the only one I know of in my area.

9% Just one other that's nearby.

17% There are at least two or three.

17% Somewhere in between three and ten.

21% Over 10. My area is overflowing with professional organizers!

Total Votes: 47

When it comes to organizing jobs you've done, have you had any negative experiences?

29% Thankfully no. Every job I've done has been a positive experience.

64% For the most part, no, but there have been one or two experiences I'd rather not repeat.

2% Yes, I've had many negative experiences.

5% Unfortunately, nearly all of the jobs I've taken on have been negative experiences.

Total Votes: 42

Do you have regular business hours you try to keep to?

5% I have definite "open and close" hours for my business.

52% I try to keep consistent business hours, but you'll sometimes catch me working off schedule too.

43% I have no set schedule. I work on my business on random dates and at random times.

Total Votes: 89

As part of your organizing services, do you also "clean"?

18% No way! I leave that job up to the Cleaning Experts. I only help organize.

47% I will do some minimum cleaning if necessary.

33% Yes, that's absolutely part of my services.

2% This doesn't apply to me, because I either consult, speak or write. I don't do physical organizing.

Total Votes: 105

How would you best describe your business goals and your goal results?

8%   I well exceeded all my goals!

19% I'm pretty much right on target.

17% I did OK, but it's less than I planned for.

15% I way overestimated. My results were much lower than my original goals.

23% I just got started in the business.

18% What goals?

Total Votes: 52

If you had to choose the one room you enjoy organizing the most, which would it be?

15% Kitchen

5%   Adult Bedroom

3%   Child Bedroom

2%   Living Room or Den

0%   Dining Room

2%   Bathroom

23% Home Office

1%   Attic

0%   Basement

0%   Foyer or Mudroom

3%   Garage

40% All of the above. I love organizing, no matter what room it's in.

6%   None of the above. I don't really enjoy organizing. I just do it for a living.

Total Votes: 124

You organize for a living, but do you consider yourself organized?

17% Yes, I'm super organized in all aspects of my life!

68% I'm pretty organized, but can always improve a bit.

15% Don't tell anyone, but I'm not very organized at all. My clients would not pay me if they saw my home!

Total Votes: 118

Do you write a blog?

7% Yes, I have several for both business and pleasure!

10% I write a business blog.

10% I write a personal blog.

25% I'm interested in writing a blog, but have not started one yet.

33% I'm not interested in writing a blog.

15% What the heck is a blog?

Total Votes: 48

When it comes to paid organizing projects (or workshops) I secure . . .

10% They're mostly one-time-only projects.

14% They're mostly continuing projects.

25% They're a combination of one-time-only and continuing projects.

1% I don't do organizing projects. I sell tangible items like books, planners and organizing gear.

50% I haven't secured a paid organizing project yet.

Total Votes: 73

Have you ever submitted your organizing articles to newspapers?

2%   Yes, all the time. I have a regular column.

9%   Yes, and many of them have been printed.

3%   Yes, a lot, but only a few have been printed.

0%   Yes, but I have yet to have one printed.

55% No, I've never done so, but will give it a try soon.

31% No, I've never done so, and likely never will.

Total Votes: 65

How did you create your web site?

20% I did it myself from scratch.

17% I did it myself using an online template service.

8%   I did it myself using purchased computer software.

9%   I had a web site creation company do it.

1%   I had my web host do it.

10% I had a family member, friend or associate do it.

26% I don't currently have a web site, but will soon.

9%   I don't currently have a web site, and likely never will.

Total Votes: 100

Are MOST of your customers . . .?

45% Home Consumers

14% Small-Medium Businesses

1%   Large Businesses

1%   Schools and/or Government Organizations

0%   None of the above, but something else.

1%   It's an even mix of the first 4 answers.

38% I haven't had a "customer" yet.

Total Votes: 86

133 Organizing Words of Wisdom to Inspire You and Your Clients

It's how we spend our time here and now, that really matters. If you are fed up with the way you have come to interact with time, change it.
—Marcia Wieder

Today, be aware of how you are spending your 1,440 beautiful moments, and spend them wisely.
—Unknown Author

People become really quite remarkable when they start thinking that they can do things. When they believe in themselves they have the first secret of success.
— Norman Vincent Peale

Today is a smooth white seashell. Hold it close and listen to the beauty of the hours.
—Unknown Author

Realize that now, in this moment of time you are creating, you are creating your next moment. That is what's real.
—Sara Paddison

You're writing the story of your life one moment at a time.
—Doc Childre and Howard Martin

Your greatest resource is your time.
—Brian Tracy

Either I will find a way, or I will make one.
— Sir Philip Sidney

Hard work spotlights the character of people: some turn up their sleeves, some turn up their noses, and some don't turn up at all.
—Sam Ewing

When the time is right, you just got to do it.
—Jack Simplot

You can't turn back the clock. But you can wind it up again.
—Bonnie Prudden

Never believe there is something you cannot do until proven otherwise.
— Joshua Hill

Time is the most valuable thing a man can spend.
—Laertius Diogenes

Time is the substance from which I am made. Time is a river which carries me along, but I am the river; it is a tiger that devours me, but I am the tiger; it is a fire that consumes me, but I am the fire.
—Jorge Luis Borges

Life consists not in holding good cards but in playing those you hold well.
—Josh Billings

I am definitely going to take a course on time management…just as soon as I can work it into my schedule.
—Louis E. Boone

When you make a mistake, don't look back at it long. Take the reason of the thing into your mind and then look forward. Mistakes are lessons of wisdom. The past cannot be changed. The future is yet in your power.
—Hugh White

Time is at once the most valuable and the most perishable of all our possessions.
—John Randolph

Time flies. It's up to you to be the navigator.
—Robert Orben

When we are doing what we love, we don't care about time. For at least at that moment, time doesn't exist and we are truly free.
—Marcia Wieder

In truth, people can generally make time for what they choose to do; it is not really the time but the will that is lacking.
—Sir John Lubbock

Time = life; therefore, waste your time and waste your life, or master your time and master your life.
—Alan Lakein

To change and to change for the better are two different things.
—German Proverb

Time is the most valuable coin in your life. You and you alone will determine how that coin will be spent. Be careful that you don't let other people spend it for you.
—John Dryden

Self-confidence is the first requisite to great undertakings.
—Samuel Johnson

Take care in your minutes, and the hours will take care of themselves.
—Lord Chesterfield

You will never find time for anything. If you want time, you must make it.
—Charles Bixton

Visualize this thing you want. See it, feel it, believe in it. Make your mental blueprint and begin.
— Robert Collier

Nothing is a waste of time if you use the experience wisely.
—Auguste Rodin

The average American worker has fifty interruptions a day, of which seventy percent have nothing to do with work.
—W. Edwards Deming

Until you value yourself you will not value your time. Until you value your time, you will not do anything with it.
—M. Scott Peck

Time is the most precious element of human existence. The successful person knows how to put energy into time and how to draw success from time.
—Denis Waitley

You cannot kill time without injuring eternity.
—Henry David Thoreau

Lost wealth may be replaced by industry, lost knowledge by study, lost health by temperance or medicine, but lost time is gone forever.
—Samuel Smiles

Once you have mastered time, you will understand how true it is that most people overestimate what they can accomplish in a year, and underestimate what they can achieve in a decade!
—Anthony Robbins

Don't be fooled by the calendar. There are only as many days in the year as you make use of. One man gets only a week's value out of a year while another man gets a full year's value out of a week.
—Charles Richards

Lost time is never found again.
—Proverb

Neither can the wave that has passed by be recalled, nor the hour which has passed return again.
—Ovid

If you haven't got the time to do it right, when will you find the time to do it over?
—Jeffery J. Mayer

Lost, yesterday, somewhere between sunrise and sunset, two golden hours, each set with sixty diamond minutes. No reward is offered for they are gone forever.
—Horace Mann

If you want to make good use of your time, you've got to know what's most important and then give it all you've got.
—Lee Iacocca

Anything that is wasted effort represents wasted time. The best management of our time thus becomes linked inseparably with the best utilization of our efforts.
—Ted W. Engstrom

Until we can manage TIME, we can manage nothing else.
—Peter F. Drucker

The most important work you and I will ever do will be within the wall of our own homes.
—Harold B. Lee

Time is like money, the less we have of it to spare the further we make it go.
—Josh Billings

To choose time is to save time.
—Francis Bacon

To think too long about doing a thing often becomes its undoing.
—Eva Young

Never let yesterday use up today.
—Richard H. Nelson

A wise person does at once, what a fool does at last. Both do the same thing; only at different times.
—Baltasar Gracian

The bad news is time flies. The good news is you're the pilot.
—Michael Althsuler

Don't say you don't have enough time. You have exactly the same number of hours per day that were given to Helen Keller, Pasteur, Michaelangelo, Mother Teresa, Leonardo da Vinci, Thomas Jefferson and Albert Einstein.
—H. Jackson Brown

The environment you fashion out of your thoughts, your beliefs, your ideals, your philosophy is the only climate you will ever live in. The key is in not spending time, but in investing it.
—Stephen R. Covey

Ordinary people think merely of spending time. Great people think of using it.
—Unknown Author

It's not so much how busy you are, but why you are busy. The bee is praised. The mosquito is swatted.
—Mary O'Connor

Determine never to be idle. No person will have occasion to complain of the want of time who never loses any. It is wonderful how much can be done if we are always doing.
—Thomas Jefferson

I'm working to improve my methods. Every hour I save is one added to my life.
—Ayn Rand

Time is our most valuable asset, yet we tend to waste it, kill it and spend it rather than invest it.
—Jim Rohn

Those who make the worse use of their time are the first to complain of its shortness.
—Jean De La Bruyere

Time is the coin of your life. It is the only coin you have, and only you can determine how it will be spent. Be careful lest you let other people spend it for you.
—Carl Sandburg

The butterfly counts not months but moments, and has time enough.
—Rabindranath Tagore

Better three hours too soon, than one minute too late.
—William Shakespeare

A man who dares to waste one hour of life has not discovered the value of life.
—Charles Darwin

All great achievements require time.
—David Schwartz

I think the world today is upside-down. It is suffering so much because there is so little love in the home and in family life. We have no time for our children. We have no time for each other. There is no time to enjoy each other, and the lack of love causes so much suffering and unhappiness in the world.
—Mother Teresa

Time stays long enough for anyone who will use it.
—Unknown Author

I would rather be ashes than dust! I would rather that my spark should burn out in a brilliant blaze than it should be stifled by dry rot. I would rather be a superb meteor, every atom of me in magnificent glow, than a sleepy and permanent planet. The proper function of man is to live, not to exist. I shall not waste my days in trying to prolong them. I shall use my time.
—Jack London

It's not enough to be busy. So are the ants. The question is, what are we busy about?
—Henry David Thoreau

Don't spend time beating on a wall, hoping to transform it into a door.
—Dr. Laura Schlessinger

Time is a circus, always packing up and moving away.
—Ben Hecht

The time you enjoy wasting is not wasted time.
—Bertrand Russell

The great dividing line between success and failure can be expressed in five words; "I did not have time."
—Franklin Field

The surest way to be late is to have plenty of time.
—Leo Kennedy

We are too busy mopping the floor to turn off the faucet.
—Unknown Author

There is nothing so useless as doing efficiently that which should not be done at all.
—Peter Drucker

What would be the use of immortality to a person who cannot use well a half an hour.
—Ralph Waldo Emerson

Nobody sees a flower, really. It is so small. It takes time. We haven't time and to see takes time, like to have a friend takes time.
—Georgia O'Keefe

Time will explain it all. He is a talker and needs no questioning before he speaks.
—Euripides

Sooner and later are not days of the week.
—Greg Hickman

Time is free, but it's priceless. You can't own it, but you can use it. You can't keep it, but you can spend it. Once you've lost it, you can never get it back.
—Harvey Mackay

We always have time enough if we will but use it right.
—Goethe

Whether it's the best of times or the worst of times, it's the only time we've got.
—Art Buchwald

So much of our time is preparation, so much is routine, and so much retrospect, that the path of each man's genius contracts itself to a very few hours.
—Ralph Waldo Emerson

Dost thou love life? Then do not squander time, for that is the stuff life is made of.
—Benjamin Franklin

The difference between a mountain and a molehill is your perspective.
— Al Neuharth

This time like all times is a very good one if we but know what to do with it.
—Ralph Waldo Emerson

To fill the hour-that is happiness.
—Ralph Waldo Emerson

Everything comes to him that hustles while he waits.
—Thomas Edison

Waste no more time arguing what a good man should be. Be one.
—Marcus Aurelius

Time you enjoyed wasting is not wasted time.
—T. S. Elliot

The "how" thinker gets problems solved effectively because he wastes no time with futile "ifs."
—Norman Vincent Peale

It is an undoubted truth that the less one has to do, the less time one finds to do it in.
—Earl of Chesterfield

It's a mere moment in a man's life between an All Star Game and an Old Timer's Game.
—Vin Scully

You may delay, but time will not.
—Benjamin Franklin

Never leave 'till tomorrow which you can do today.
—Benjamin Franklin

Even if you're on the right track, you'll get run over if you just sit there.
—Will Rogers

Just do it.
—Nike advertisement

Clutter drains your energy and you don't realize it till it's gone. Every item in your home has an energy to it. When items go a long time unused, unloved and uncared for, they become stuck, stagnant energy that actually physically drains you of your energy.
—Ariane Benefit

Three Rules of Work: Out of clutter find simplicity; From discord find harmony; In the middle of difficulty lies opportunity.
—Albert Einstein

Amidst all the clutter, beyond all the obstacles, aside from all the static, are the goals set. Put your head down, do the best job possible, let the flak pass, and work towards those goals.
—Donald Rumsfeld

We believe it's time to be simple and compelling. It is important to break through the clutter.
—Paul Ballew

Simplicity in character, in manners, in style; in all things the supreme excellence is simplicity.
—Henry Wadsworth Longfellow

People's homes are a reflection of their lives. It is no accident that people have a huge weight problem in this country, and clutter is the same thing. Homes are an orgy of consumption.
—Peter Walsh

Clutter is a problem buyers have trouble looking past. Everything should be crisp, clean and very minimal. Walk through a model home and use that as your model.
—Vicki Fazzini

I'm really a counselor and clutter therapist. I am not looking at something and thinking it's a mess, I'm looking at the potential and what can be done to make the client happier in their surroundings.
—Janine Godwin

Order marches with weighty and measured strides. Disorder is always in a hurry.
—Napoleon I

Chaos often breeds life, when order breeds habit.
—Henry Brooks Adams

Order is a great person's need and their true well being.
—Henri Frédéric Amiel

Good order is the foundation of all great things.
—Edmund Burke

If you don't know where you are going, any road will get you there.
—Lewis Carroll

Simplicity is the seal of truth.
—Proverb

Never do anything standing that you can do sitting, or anything sitting that you can do lying down.
—Chinese Proverb

It is far more difficult to be simple than to be complicated; far more difficult to sacrifice skill and easy execution in the proper place, than to expand both indiscriminately.
—John Ruskin

Everything is simpler than you think and yet more complex than you imagine.
—Unknown Source

The art of art, the glory of expression and the sunshine of the light of letters, is simplicity.
—Walt Whitman

I adore simple pleasures. They are the last refuge of the complex.
—Oscar Wilde

Outward simplicity befits ordinary men, like a garment made to measure for them; but it serves as an adornment to those who have filled their lives with great deeds: they might be compared to some beauty carelessly dressed and thereby all the more attractive.
—Jean de la Bruyère

There is one quality which one must possess to win, and that is definiteness of purpose, the knowledge of what one wants, and a burning desire to possess it.
—Napoleon Hill

Our plans miscarry because they have no aim. When a man does not know what harbor he is making for, no wind is the right wind.
—Lucius Annaeus Seneca

Begin, be bold and venture to be wise.
—Horace

The mind's direction is more important than its progress.
—Joseph Joubert

From a certain point onward there is no longer any turning back. That is the point that must be reached.
—Franz Kafka

One day Alice came to a fork in the road and saw a Cheshire cat in a tree. "Which road do I take?" she asked. "Where do you want to go?" was his response. "I don't know", Alice answered. "Then," said the cat, "it doesn't matter."
—Lewis Carroll

I catnap now and then, but I think while I nap, so it's not a waste of time.
—Martha Stewart

No wind serves him who addresses his voyage to no certain port.
—Michel Eyquem de Montaigne

He is not only idle who does nothing, but he is idle who might be better employed.
—Socrates

Do not then stand idly waiting, for some greater work to do. Fortune is a lazy goddess; she will never come to you.
— Ellen M. H. Gates

If you think about disaster, you will get it. Brood about death and you hasten your demise. Think positively and masterfully, with confidence and faith, and life becomes more secure, more fraught with action, richer in achievement and experience.
— Edward Rickenbacker

Success! It's found in the soul of you, and not in the realm of luck! The world will furnish the work to do, But you must provide the pluck.
— Edgar A. Guest

In short, the way to wealth, if you desire it, is as plain as the way to market. It depends chiefly on two words, industry and frugality. That is, waste neither time nor money, but make the best use of both.
— Benjamin Franklin

Your friend is a person who knows all about you, and still likes you.
— Elbert Hubbard

I see something that has to be done and I organize it.
— Elinor Guggenheimer

Sometimes your joy is the source of your smile, but sometimes your smile can be the source of your joy.
— Thich Nhat Hanh

The happiest people in the world are those who feel absolutely terrific about themselves, and this is the natural outgrowth of accepting total responsibility for every part of their life.
— Brian Tracy

68 Words of Wisdom to Inspire Your Personal and Business Growth

Take the attitude of a student, never be too big to ask questions, never know too much to learn something new.
—Og Mandino

Anyone who lives within their means suffers from a lack of imagination.
—Oscar Wilde

There was never any fear for me, no fear of failure. If I miss a shot, so what?
—Michael Jordan

Winning is not a sometime thing; it's an all time thing. You don't win once in a while, you don't do things right once in a while, you do them right all the time. Winning is habit. Unfortunately, so is losing.
—Vince Lombardi

Don't limit yourself. Many people limit themselves to what they think they can do. You can go as far as your mind lets you. What you believe, remember, you can achieve.
—Mary Kay Ash

I suppose I could have stayed home and baked cookies and had teas, but what I decided to do was to fulfill my profession which I entered before my husband was in public life.
— Hillary Rodham Clinton

What I know is, is that if you do work that you love, and the work fulfills you, the rest will come.
—Oprah Winfrey

In all realms of life it takes courage to stretch your limits, express your power, and fulfill your potential. It's no different in the financial realm.
—Suzie Orman

Everyone experiences tough times, it is a measure of your determination and dedication how you deal with them and how you can come through them.
—Lakshmi Mittal

Obviously everyone wants to be successful, but I want to be looked back on as being very innovative, very trusted and ethical and ultimately making a big difference in the world.
—Sergey Brin

I'm a big believer in growth. Life is not about achievement, it's about learning and growth, and developing qualities like compassion, patience, perseverance, love, and joy, and so forth. And so if that is the case, then I think our goals should include something which stretches us.
—Jack Canfield

Without an open-minded mind, you can never be a great success.
—Martha Stewart

I feel sorry for the person who can't get genuinely excited about his work. Not only will he never be satisfied, but he will never achieve anything worthwhile.
—Walter Chrysler

The three great essentials to achieve anything worth while are, first, hard work; second, stick-to-itiveness; third, common sense.
—Thomas Edison

A customer is the most important visitor on our premises. He is not dependent on us. We are dependent on him. He is not an interruption in our work. He is the purpose of it. He is not an outsider in our business. He is part of it. We are not doing him a favor by serving him. He is doing us a favor by giving us an opportunity to do so.
—Mahatma Gandhi

A leader has the vision and conviction that a dream can be achieved. He inspires the power and energy to get it done.
—Ralph Lauren

You have to put in many, many, many tiny efforts that nobody sees or appreciates before you achieve anything worthwhile.
— Brian Tracy

I don't care how much power, brilliance or energy you have, if you don't harness it and focus it on a specific target, and hold it there you're never going to accomplish as much as your ability warrants.
—Zig Ziglar

If you do build a great experience, customers tell each other about that. Word of mouth is very powerful.
—Jeff Bezos

Your most unhappy customers are your greatest source of learning.
—Bill Gates

This may seem simple, but you need to give customers what they want, not what you think they want. And, if you do this, people will keep coming back.
—John Ilhan

I feel I'm able to serve my customer by knowing what she or he wants. One of the ways I'm able to do this is through my website, and email: people give me great ideas, tell me what they want, what they don't want. It's really instrumental, and helps me stay in touch with people.
—Kathy Ireland

We intend to conduct our business in a way that not only meets but exceeds the expectations of our customers, business partners, shareholders, and creditors, as well as the communities in which we operate and society at large.
—Akira Mori

The most important adage and the only adage is, the customer comes first. Whatever the business, the customer comes first.
— Kerry Stokes

Your needs will be met once you can find a way of projecting energy and fulfilling someone else's need.
—Stuart Wilde

The fact is, everyone is in sales. Whatever area you work in, you do have clients and you do need to sell.
—Jay Abraham

No matter what your product is, you are ultimately in the education business. Your customers need to be constantly educated about the many advantages of doing business with you, trained to use your products more effectively, and taught how to make never-ending improvement in their lives.
—Robert G. Allen

A market is never saturated with a good product, but it is very quickly saturated with a bad one.
—Henry Ford

I think that our fundamental belief is that for us growth is a way of life and we have to grow at all times.
—Mukesh Ambani

Don't quack like a duck. Soar like an eagle.
—Ken Blanchard

I'm probably never going to be satisfied with anything we do. I think there's always the possibility of doing better. And I'd say we're doing better than we were a year ago, in terms of delivery and quality of service, but nowhere near what we should be doing.
—Steve Case

To succeed in life in today's world, you must have the will and tenacity to finish the job.
— Chin-Ning Chu

What great changes have not been ambitious?
—Melinda Gates

In the realm of ideas everything depends on enthusiasm. In the real world all rests on perseverance.
—Johann Wolfgang von Goethe

If you want more, you have to require more from yourself.
—Dr. Phil

Like most business people, I want every aspect of my business to be perfect. I know that this goal is unachievable, but it is nevertheless what I strive to achieve.
—Bob Parsons

For me life is continuously being hungry. The meaning of life is not simply to exist, to survive, but to move ahead, to go up, to achieve, to conquer.
—Arnold Schwarzenegger

High expectations are the key to everything.
—Sam Walton

The turning point, I think, was when I really realized that you can do it yourself. That you have to believe in you because sometimes that's the only person that does believe in your success.
—Tim Blixseth

Self-esteem is a huge piece of my work. You have to believe it's possible and believe in yourself.
— Jack Canfield

The way you think, the way you behave, the way you eat, can influence your life by 30 to 50 years. Most people believe that aging is universal but there are biological organisms that never age.
—Deepak Chopra

There are many qualities that make a great leader. But having strong beliefs, being able to stick with them through popular and unpopular times, is the most important characteristic of a great leader.
—Rudy Giuliani

I believe in giving everything my best shot. I do not believe in holding back. I am very driven by the fact that we are destined with these opportunities.
—Shailendra Singh

I believe through learning and application of what you learn, you can solve any problem, overcome any obstacle and achieve any goal that you can set for yourself.
— Brian Tracy

Believe in yourself, in all you can do. And for you, the deals will start to work in your favor. You need to be open to such deals, and they will come, I assure you.
—Ivana Trump

I believe that being successful means having a balance of success stories across the many areas of your life. You can't truly be considered successful in your business life if your home life is in shambles.
—Zig Ziglar

It doesn't matter how many times you fail. It doesn't matter how many times you almost get it right. No one is going to know or care about your failures, and neither should you. All you have to do is learn from them and those around you

because all that matters in business is that you get it right once. Then everyone can tell you how lucky you are.
—Mark Cuban

Failure is the opportunity to begin again, more intelligently.
—Henry Ford

You have to pretend you're 100 percent sure. You have to take action; you can't hesitate or hedge your bets. Anything less will condemn your efforts to failure.
—Andrew Grove

Failure is a word I don't accept.
—John H. Johnson

Obstacles are necessary for success because in selling, as in all careers of importance, victory comes only after many struggles and countless defeats.
—Og Mandino

For a while after "The Jerk" (movie) I had a feeling of failure. I was a little scared. First people discover you and they love you. You get big and then you fail. And people are glad that you fail. But I've always come back and I've started to trust myself.
— Steve Martin

Success is not built on success. It's built on failure. It's built on frustration. Sometimes its built on catastrophe.
— Sumner Redstone

Sometimes when a person is too successful too rapidly, he goes off in all directions, and doesn't know how to cope with it. We say do not be ruined by your first failure, or spoiled by your first success.
—Jose Silva

I have no Napoleonic dream. I'm just hard-working and pragmatic.
—Roman Abramovich

Someone once told me: "Luck is when opportunity meets preparation." And that's what I really feel with my music. I've worked really, really hard on it. It was like, "this is really what I want to do. What do I have to do to make it work?"
—Erica Baxter

I've always worked very, very hard, and the harder I worked, the luckier I got.
—Alan Bond

Genius is 1% inspiration and 99% perspiration. Accordingly a genius is often merely a talented person who has done all of his or her homework.
—Thomas Edison

Think not of yourself as the architect of your career but as the sculptor. Expect to have to do a lot of hard hammering and chiseling and scraping and polishing.
— BC Forbes

If money is your hope for independence you will never have it. The only real security that a man will have in this world is a reserve of knowledge, experience, and ability.
— Henry Ford

To me, money is a means to do good.
— Eli Broad

To attract money, you must focus on wealth. It is impossible to bring more money into your life when you are noticing you do not have enough, because that means you are thinking thoughts that you do not have enough.
— Rhonda Byrne

It is impossible for a man to learn what he thinks he already knows.
— Epictetus

The secret of joy in work is contained in one word--excellence. To know how to do something well is to enjoy it.
— Pearl S. Buck

Become the change you want to see. Those are words I live by.
— Oprah Winfrey

You can't wait for inspiration. You have to go after it with a club.
— Jack London

Twenty years and $40 billion. They seem like good round numbers.
— Michael Dell

Never, never, never give up.
— Winston Churchill

Special Thanks

Sandy Drifka, Senior Editor

Sandy Drifka is a lifelong resident of Wisconsin and lives in Oshkosh. She enjoys the daily challenges of working in litigation as a legal assistant in a large law firm.

Sandy likes to be involved and is currently a member of the Wellness Committee at work and President of FVALP (Fox Valley Association for Legal Professionals).

When not working, Sandy is a moderator on the Get Organized Now! Discussion Forum. Her interests include organizing, Jazzercise, orchids, shopping and collecting penguins.

Joe Gracia, Senior/Contributing Editor, Husband, Best Friend and Inspiration for this Guide

Joe Gracia is the founder of Effective Business Systems, a small business consulting firm specializing in helping small business owners maximize their business growth and profits through proven-effective marketing strategies.

Throughout his 30 year marketing career Joe has made his clients literally millions of dollars in increased sales and profits with his unique approach to small business marketing and management techniques.

Joe is also the creator of the Give to Get Marketing web site, co-creator of the Get Organized Now! web site and is the author of the small business marketing guide, The Give to Get Marketing Solution and other marketing publications and products.

When he's not working, Joe enjoys spending quality time with his wife and daughter, playing guitar and reading—especially anything with historical significance.

About the Author

Maria Gracia, founder of Get Organized Now!, specializes in helping people get better organized to live the kind of stress-free life they've always dreamed of.

During her ten years with Dun and Bradstreet's Nielsen Media Research in New York, Maria worked as a marketing, organizing and management specialist. Throughout her tenure, she managed the data analysis department, worked with hundreds of TV stations and ad agencies and developed effective, productive systems for her clients and staff.

Today, Maria, her husband, Joe, and their beautiful daughter Amanda Grace, live in Watertown, Wisconsin. Joe and Maria own and operate their company, Effective Business Systems. Maria founded Get Organized Now! as a division of the company in 1996.

The Get Organized Now! Web site is currently visited by over a million people per year. Maria has hundreds of thousands of people on her Get Organized Now! newsletter list.

Specializing in peak time and space management, Maria has over 20 years of organizational experience. Her broad range of skills covers clutter control, planning, scheduling, peak productivity, records management, space planning, time and paper management, filing systems, computer oriented-organizational systems and more.

Maria Gracia has appeared at, wrote for, or has been interviewed by hundreds of international, national and local media and organizations such as Woman's Day Magazine, Country Living Magazine and USA Today.

Maria is the author of the Finally Organized, Finally Free series. Her books have been read by thousands of people all over the world. In addition, she has created a variety of other helpful organizing products, sold worldwide, which can be found on her web site: www.getorganizednow.com

Maria is a proponent of family time and enjoys as much time as possible with her husband, Joe, and daughter, Amanda. She has served on the board of the Watertown Newcomers Club in a number of positions including President, is an avid scrapbooker, attends monthly book chats and enjoys cooking, working out, traveling and entertaining.

Other Products Available from Get Organized Now!

Finally Organized, Finally Free – For the Home
You'll discover tons of tips and ideas to help you get your home and your life organized, including how to banish clutter, better manage your time, get more done and so much more!

Finally Organized, Finally Free – For the Office
You'll discover tons of tips and ideas to help you get your office and your life organized, including how to banish office clutter, better manage your time, be more productive and more!

The Easy Organizer
It's not just a planner. It's much, much more! Loaded with easy-to-use forms to help you eliminate those notorious scraps of paper and consolidate all of your home-related data into one place so you can find your info when you need it.

The Easy Bill Paying System
Pay your home-related bills on time, easily organize your statements and conveniently keep track of your expenses with this simple, but powerful, system.

Give to Get Marketing Solution
Have a small to medium-sized business or thinking of starting one? Kick start your marketing program into overdrive with this all-encompassing guide that will help you develop a solid strategy for attracting customers to your business.

The Christmas Holiday Planner
A must-have planner to help you get and stay organized for a stress-free, enjoyable holiday season.

My Oh-So-Organized Filing System
This is the new, revolutionary, easy and time-saving way to file, organize and find all your documents and files within seconds! This pre-categorized filing system makes the job of setting up either your home or business filing systems a breeze.

For more information about any of these products, please visit: www.getorganizednow.com and click on the STORE link.

Your Tips, Ideas and Comments

Write to us
Do you have an organizing tip, success story or comment you'd like to share? We'd love to hear from you. Feel free to write to us at:

Get Organized Now!
611 Arlington Way
Watertown WI 53094

Please include your name and full mailing address on all correspondence. If you send an organizing tip or a success story, we may publish it, along with your name, city and state as the contributor, on our Web site, in our newsletter, in a media press release or in one of our future products.

Spelling or link corrections
While careful care has gone into the writing and editing of this book, there's always the possibility that we may have missed something. In light of this, if you happen to notice a spelling error or a Web site link that no longer works, please feel free to write to us at the above address. We'll then have the opportunity to correct it in future printings. Please be sure to include the page number where you located the error.

Grammatical corrections
As far as grammatical errors, Maria Gracia has always said, "I write the way I speak. If I followed every grammatical rule there was, my writing would be awfully stiff and stuffy. My main concern is that I get my point across." But feel free to write to us about any grammatical error that truly bothers you and we'll bring it to Maria's attention for consideration.

Correspondence
Although we do respond personally to some of our mail, due to the thousands of email messages we receive each week, we regret that we can't respond personally to every single one we receive. However, please be assured that we do read and consider all correspondence.

Notes

Notes

Notes